Louis Bourdaloue

Eight sermons for holy week and easter

Louis Bourdaloue

Eight sermons for holy week and easter

ISBN/EAN: 9783741110986

Manufactured in Europe, USA, Canada, Australia, Japa

Cover: Foto ©Lupo / pixelio.de

Manufactured and distributed by brebook publishing software (www.brebook.com)

Louis Bourdaloue

Eight sermons for holy week and easter

EIGHT SERMONS

FOR

Holy Week and Easter.

Eight Sermons

FOR

Holy Week and Easter

Translated from the French of the
Rev. Father Louis Bourdaloue

by the

Rev. G. F. Crowther, M.A.
OF S. JOHN'S COLLEGE, OXFORD.

LONDON
WELLS GARDNER, DARTON & CO.
2, PATERNOSTER BUILDINGS

PREFACE.

In presenting to the public this selection from the sermons of Bourdaloue, the translator has found it no easy task to express in clear and idiomatic English the well-balanced periods of the original. He hopes, however, that he has not entirely failed to convey to his readers some idea of the author's style, and, what is of more consequence, that the translation, such as it is, is not an unfaithful rendering of the author's impressive words.

The little that is known of the life of Bourdaloue is so familiar to all who are interested in such matters, that it is not necessary to repeat it here. As an orator, Bourdaloue was clear, antithetical, harmonious; his learning was wide, and he always handled his subject in a masterly way. In his references to the Fathers, it is not so much their very words, as their teaching and their arguments, which he reproduces in a modern form. But we do him an injustice if we regard him merely as an able reasoner. It has been well said that he was "one who valued a victory over the heart of the humble listener, more than over the judgment of the man of taste."

There is one point which must strike those who read these sermons on the Passion; the preacher never permits us to lose sight of the great truth, that the sufferer is God. Keeping in view the impersonality of the Saviour's Manhood, Bourdaloue does not shrink from saying, that it is a God who suffers, a God who is being tortured and crucified, a God who is dying. These eight sermons, most of which were preached before the French Court, will be found to be remarkable alike for their originality and completeness. The translator hopes they may be an aid to the better understanding and the deeper realization of the august mysteries of which they treat. I may add that in this translation the texts of Holy Scripture have generally been quoted from the A.V., except when the rendering of the Vulgate materially differs from it, in which case attention is called to the fact in a footnote.

G. F. C.

St. Luke's, Soho.
1884.

CONTENTS.

SERMON I.

"All this was done, that it might be fulfilled which was spoken by the prophet, saying, Tell ye the daughter of Zion, Behold, thy King cometh unto thee, meek."—S. MATTHEW, xxi, 4, 5.

pp. 1–31

SERMON II.

"The Jews require a sign, and the Greeks seek after wisdom: but we preach Christ crucified, unto the Jews a stumbling block, and unto the Greeks foolishness; but unto them which are called, both Jews and Greeks, Christ, the power of God, and the wisdom of God.—1 CORINTHIANS, i. 22–24.

pp. 33–72

SERMON III.

"There followed Him a great company of people, and of women, which also bewailed and lamented Him. But Jesus turning unto them said, Daughters of Jerusalem, weep not for Me, but weep for yourselves, and for your children."—S. LUKE, xxiii. 27, 28.

pp. 73–115

SERMON IV.

"Now is the judgment of this world: now shall the prince of this world be cast out. And I, if I be lifted up from the earth, will draw all men unto Me. This He said, signifying what death He should die."—S. JOHN, xii. 31–33.

pp. 116–154

SERMON V.

"Who His own self bare our sins in His own body on the tree, that we, being dead to sins, should live unto righteousness."—
1 S. PETER, ii. 24.   pp. 155–203

SERMON VI.

"Who was delivered for our offences, and was raised again for our justification."—ROMANS, iv. 25.   pp. 204–239

SERMON VII.

"He saith unto them, Be not affrighted: ye seek Jesus of Nazareth, which was crucified: He is risen: He is not here: Behold the place where they laid Him."—S. MARK, xvi. 6.   pp. 240–279

SERMON VIII.

"And it came to pass, that, while they communed together and reasoned, Jesus Himself drew near, and went with them. But their eyes were holden that they should not know Him."—S. LUKE, xxiv. 15, 16.   pp. 280–293

I.

SERMON FOR PALM SUNDAY.

EASTER COMMUNION.

S. Matthew xxi. 4, 5.—"All this was done, that it might be fulfilled which was spoken by the prophet, saying, Tell ye the daughter of Zion, Behold, thy king cometh unto thee, meek."

Sire,—The prophet had foretold that the Saviour of the world should enter into Jerusalem in glory and triumph; and it is in the mystery of this day that this utterance of the prophet ought to be fulfilled, as, indeed, it is fulfilled. But, why do the Jews receive the Son of God with so much pomp and solemnity to-day, and whence that zeal which they show in rendering Him honours that they had never bestowed before? They had seen Him amongst them a hundred times, without scarcely thinking of Him; but now, by an unlooked-for change, the Gospel represents Him to us in a kind of triumph, entering the city amidst public acclamations, escorted by a crowd of people, and solemnly recognized as Son of David and the sent of God. "Hosanna to the Son of David, blessed is He that cometh in the name of the Lord." Let us not be surprised at it, Christians, since the Evangelists teach us the reason. This adorable Saviour had just worked a miracle, the fame of which had spread throughout all Judea. All the inhabitants of Jerusalem had been witnesses of the resurrection of Lazarus, a man who had been four days dead and shut in the tomb. They had all admired this miracle, the circumstances of which rendered it indisputable; it was a miracle, as S. Augustine tells us, which appealed to people even in his day, and which the most obstinate incredulity could not disavow. This miracle was what had raised Jesus Christ so high in the estimation of the people of Jerusalem. It was, in consideration of this miracle, and as a public recognition of the Author, that they ran to meet Him, carrying palms in their hands, intending thereby, S. Chrysostom remarks, to honour the victory which that God-Man had gained over death. Such, my dear listeners, is the sum of our Gospel in its historic and literal sense; now listen to its mystical sense and its application. The time draws near, Christians—we are close upon it—the time when Jesus Christ, by a spiritual and internal, but yet more powerful and effectual, action, renews this great mystery of the resurrection of Lazarus, reviving, by the grace of penitence, souls which are dead in sin and buried in the habitual practice of it. After the manner of this miracle, the Church, which all the prophets have spoken of under the figure of Jerusalem, prepares for this divine Saviour a holy and honourable entrance into the hearts of the faithful by the Easter Communion; and, in accordance with her plan, it is my duty to speak to you to-day about this Communion.

Two sorts of people to-day, receive, as it were, the Son of God in Jerusalem. On the one hand,

His disciples who made profession of following Him, and who were in a special manner attached to His side; and on the other hand, the Pharisees, the priests, the doctors of the synagogue, who, by an extreme blindness, had rejected His teaching, and were secretly banded together against Him. His disciples regarded Him with respect, with warmth, with joy; and that is why He came to them, as it were, in triumph, and, according to the prophecy, in the character of a King, "Behold, thy King cometh unto thee, meek." The Pharisees, on the contrary, regarded Him with feelings of bitterness, and with a determination to take instant counsel against Him, and destroy Him: that is why He came to them like an enemy, and shed over these blind folk tears of compassion, "When He beheld the city, He wept over it." Two very natural types of what passes each year in the Easter Communion: in the reception of the one I see the type of a worthy, and, in the manner in which this same God was received by the other, I see the type of an unworthy and sacrilegious communion. To the just who are the true faithful, the Saviour comes like a gentle and gracious King; but, to the wicked who obstinately persist in their sin, He comes as a terrible and an awful enemy. These are the points to which I would direct your attention.

I. Would you know, Christians, what is really meant by a communion made in a state of grace? Listen to S. Chrysostom, he will teach you. It is, saith this Father, a solemn reception by us of Jesus Christ into ourselves, and a triumphant entry of Jesus Christ into us. Could he explain the fact in a more noble way, and am I not right in adopting his theory, and speaking to you now of the triumph and entry of the Saviour of the world into Jerusalem as an expressive type of a good communion?

But, that we may understand this better, let us examine in detail the circumstances mentioned in the Gospel; it may even seem God's purpose to set clearly before us by means of them the most perfect model of the holiest action in Christianity, that is, of communion. For, firstly, that God-Man is honourably received in Jerusalem; but by whom? By His friends, by the votaries of His teaching, by those who were pointed out in Judea as belonging to Him; in a word, by His disciples, who, notwithstanding the envy of some, yet made a considerable party, since S. Luke states that they came forth in a crowd: "The whole multitude of the disciples began to rejoice." Secondly, these warm-hearted disciples, full of zeal for the Person of their Master, did not wait until He reached the gates of their town before they got ready to receive Him. At the first rumour of His coming, they came out of their houses, and, to show Him respect, went to meet Him: "When they heard that Jesus was coming to Jerusalem, they went forth to meet Him." Moreover, they presented themselves before Him, some carrying branches of palm trees, and others branches of olive trees, which they had plucked on the mountain. But the palm is the sign of victory, and the olive the sign of peace, and this has a mystic signification, as I am going to show you. Lastly, they stripped off their garments, and put them under the feet of Jesus, spreading them along the road, over which He was about to pass. An excellent figure of the communion of the just, and of the holy feelings which a Christian ought to bring to the participation of the Body of Jesus Christ, and of His adorable Sacrament. But it is not enough for us to have this idea; God wishes us to apply it to ourselves in practice, and that we should convert this figure into a truth. Try then, my dear listeners, to enter thoroughly into these holy lessons which I am going to unfold.

We must, then, be disciples of Jesus Christ so as to deserve to receive Him in His Sacrament; that is the first disposition. But in our character of Christians are we not all His disciples? It is true, my brethren, and I know it; but I say that, to participate in this divine mystery, it is not enough to be disciples of Christ by an outward profession, which often only increases our unworthiness, as when it is not proved true by our conduct. Hence I add that we must be disciples in spirit and religious feeling, since without this, far from acknowledging us as His disciples, Jesus Christ regards us as His enemies. It is urged, indeed, that He Himself declared that He would not celebrate the Passover but with His disciples. Then, however, He was only speaking of the Jewish Passover which He was going to celebrate according to the law. Ah! I admit it, replies S. Chrysostom; but if He spake thus of the ancient Passover, what did He think of the new Passover which was to be the gift of gifts, and the most excellent of all graces?

And if they had to be His disciples, who ate with Him a passover which was only a type of His body, what must not he be who eateth that which is verily and indeed His body? In short, doth not faith teach us that all which took place in the Jews' Passover was a lesson for us, even an exact and precise lesson, of what ought to take place in the Christian Passover?

Let not any one be rash enough, concludes S. Chrysostom, to presume to present himself at that Passover and receive the true Lamb which is sacrificed, without having this special title that he is the disciple of Jesus Christ. Let no Judas, no Pharisee, that is to say, no traitor, no hypocrite, no one who is guilty of simony or profanity, present himself there: these are the words of that holy Father,* "Let no one approach except he be a friend, no covetous person, no usurer, no unchaste person. For I warn you," adds that holy doctor, "that this divine table is not for them. If there be a faithful and sincere disciple, let him come," because it is he who, by the choice of Jesus Christ Himself, ought to be admitted there. As for the worldlings, the easy livers, the impious, they are excluded from it; and if they dared to show themselves there, we, who are priests of the Lord and dispensers of His mysteries, we are not afraid of making use of the power, which the living God hath placed in our hand, to ward off such from His altar. Even though he were the greatest conqueror, or the

---

* "Nemo accedat nisi amicus: nullus avarus, nullus fœnerator, nullus impudicus; nam et tales haec mensa non suscipit. Si quis est discipulus, adsit."

chief monarch in the world, we would make known to him the prohibitions and threats of the Sovereign Master, whose heavenly banquet he was about to profane. It was thus that man of God, acquitting himself of the same ministry as mine, prepared the people of Antioch for the most important Christian act; and such is the import of those brief words addressed by the great Apostle to the whole Church, those words, which, according to the Council of Trent, nevertheless contain a summary of all the feelings requisite for a participation of the Sacrament of the Son of God, "Let a man examine himself." That is to say, let a man consult himself, let him question his own heart; and without blindfolding himself, without flattering himself, let him examine, before God, if in reality he be of those who belong to Jesus Christ, and whom Jesus Christ acknowledges for His true disciples. For, if our consciences do not render us a favourable testimony on this point, and we cannot humbly apply to ourselves this name, we may not partake of the Passover, and we ought not to think of it. I am wrong here, Christians: let us speak more correctly, and say that we ought to think of it, and to think of it for the honour of Jesus Christ Himself; and if, from not having thought of it, we fail to receive Him in that solemn Passover, we are committing a new crime, and we are disobeying His orders. What then? Is it Jesus Christ's command that we should receive Him without being of the number of His disciples? God forbid, Christian brethren; so far from that being the case, He expressly requires us to profess ourselves to be His disciples, and if we be not yet of that number, He wishes us to join it, so as to satisfy the indispensable obligation which binds us to take our place amongst the guests whom He invites. That is not only the precept of the Church, but the order of God, which is made known to you to-day by the shepherds of your souls: yes, the Saviour of men, whatever your state may be, wishes to celebrate the Passover with you. You are unworthy of that grace, but He wishes that you should render yourselves worthy of it; you are sinners, but He wishes that you should become just; you have sinful and worldly ties, but He wishes that you should break them off, and that you should prepare yourselves to approach Him. There can be no excuse, no delay; you must obey Him. At other seasons of the year, perhaps you might act deliberately, and set yourself a time in which to make your resolution; but to-day it is no longer a question of resolving, it is time to execute and carry out God's purpose. The time is come, and the Master of masters sends to you to say that it is with you that the Passover is to be celebrated, "The Master saith, my time is at hand; I will keep the Passover at thy house." To that end your heart, which is, as it were, the abode and sanctuary which He hath chosen, must be purified by penitence; and the same commandment which binds you to receive Him, obliges you also to prepare for Him. Hence you must break your bonds, and by noble efforts free yourselves once more from the creature and from yourselves. And therein the precept of the Son of God is admirable, I mean, in that it compels you to this. For otherwise nothing is left but for you to choose between being either sacrilegious or excommunicated: sacrilegious, if you receive this holy God without being prepared for Him by a sincere contrition; excommunicated, if by your impenitence you be in an unfit state to receive Him.

But, to be disciples of the Saviour it is not sufficient for us to deserve that He should come to us; we must run to meet Him and forestall Him. You know how those crowds which went out of Jerusalem proceeded as far as the Mount of Olives, and did not wait until Jesus Christ had arrived before they began to greet Him with their homage. "When they heard that Jesus was coming to Jerusalem, they went forth to meet Him." Thus did they with active zeal anticipate the coming of that God-Man; and this is a second disposition necessary for receiving Him according to the rules and the spirit of true piety. Let me explain what I mean; for the custom now-a-days—a custom which the indifference of the age hath rendered but too common—is to wait until the day of communion to think about it; to put off until the festival of Easter the preparation which religion demands; to believe that we have acquitted ourselves of our duty if we have snatched a few moments beforehand for silent meditation in God's presence; coming in a hurry with a crowd of other people to accuse ourselves of our misdoings, and straightway presenting ourselves at the Holy Table; mixing penitential exercises with the Communion, and often communicating without having performed any penitential exercise. Ah, Christians! that is dishonouring God; and whoever acts in this way draws down upon himself S. Paul's anathema, in which the Apostle reproaches him for not discerning the Lord's body, and warns him that the participation of that heavenly food will add to his condemnation. I speak to you, my dear listeners, who, living a worldly and dissipated life, but rarely approach these sacred mysteries; you who content yourselves with eating perhaps once a year of that bread which Jesus Christ hath appointed to be our daily food; this concerns you. For, as for those innocent souls who make it their regular nourishment, although they have reason to fear, they have more reason to hope. One communion is a preparation for the next; the regulated life which these people lead, the good works which they practise, their frequent attendance at the altar; all that, according to the teaching of the Fathers, serves them as a continual preparation for this divine Sacrament.

But as for you who maintain a directly opposite line of conduct; you who hold it a duty not only to belong to the world, but to live according to the maxims of the world; you whose engagements, habits, amusements and occupations are nothing but a train of sins incessantly added one to another; you who make no use of the things of God, and who let whole years slip by without perhaps one serious thought concerning your salvation; you whose last care is to watch over your heart, and who, having made your conscience free, nay, rather, having made it indulgent, find it very convenient never to look into it, and to remain in ignorance of all that goes on there; you, in short, who only communicate when propriety requires you, and the rule of the Church obliges you, for you to put off your preparation until the very day on which you must fulfil that obligation, that, let me tell you, is an insult to God and an outrage to His Sacrament; in fact, it is to make His coming of none effect, and thus expose yourselves to an almost inevitable offence. For, indeed, my brother, suppose you were to apply to me during the days of this solemn season, and I do not find you fit to receive the grace of reconciliation, without which you cannot communicate (but among such men as you, what is more common than that state?), what, think you, should I do then? Should I grant you the grace of absolution which you ask from me? I should then betray my ministry. Should I refuse it to you? Then you cannot partake of the Lamb with the rest of the faithful, and must be absent from the table of Jesus Christ. If I admit you to it, I am unfaithful to my trust, and condemn myself with you; if I exclude you from it, you will shock the Church. Do you not see to what an extremity you force matters, because you have not taken the steps which God's law and Christian prudence suggest to you? It is not likely that, out of consideration for your person, I should ever compromise the honour of the Sacrament which hath been entrusted to me. I know too well what are the limits of my power; and the splendour of your fortune and of your dignity will never dazzle me. What will happen then? Just what I say, that you will have neither Easter nor Sacrament, nor religious worship, and so you will be a marked person; he who is entrusted, as shepherd, with the care of your soul, will be anxious and troubled about it; your bad example will begin to spread to others, and recklessness will begin to get the upper hand, and you will be responsible for the abuse which will result from your conduct: why? because you have never used the diligence to prepare yourself. If, convinced as you were by your conscience of your unfitness, you had, from the commencement of this holy season, had recourse to the remedy which the Church offered you, and if with Christian forethought you had then come to submit yourself to her tribunal, all would have been well. You were not then fit to partake of the body of Jesus Christ, but you might have been made fit; you were too weak to eat of that Bread of Life, but you would have been strengthened, you would have been healed of your wounds, you would have been aroused to break off your evil habits, you would have had to pass through the trials of penitence; and, after these trials, clothed in the marriage garment, you would at last have been received into the festal room. Besides, Christians, Lent was appointed for that purpose, and we learn from the ancient councils that, during the first days of this solemn fast, the faithful were obliged to sanctify themselves, that is to say, as the Scripture expresses it, to purify themselves by confession, and in this way they prepared themselves for a worthy celebration of the Passover. If there were also any open sinners, they were made to appear on Ash Wednesday clothed in hair shirts, so as to be formally admitted, so to speak, among the penitents. Such was the custom; and there are still some churches where traces of this religious and praiseworthy discipline may be found. Moreover, as the angelic doctor, S. Thomas, remarks, these sinners were not more guilty than many of us; and the body of Jesus Christ, which they should receive, was not more holy, nor more worthy of adoration, from them than from us. But in the present day people have found out a way of cutting matters short, and, if I may make use of the expression, of getting acquitted much more cheaply.

I do not say this in support of any private opinion, and I have no need to justify myself on that point; but, in truth, my dear listeners, let us admit it to our confusion, we have much degenerated, and we are degenerating still more every day from the holiness of our faith. Of all those leading lives of sin whom I am now addressing, and who in all probability make up the majority of my audience, there are perhaps scarcely any who have made the least effort to get ready for their Easter Communion. Do I go too far, and can I be so fortunate as to be mistaken? On that festival, which is close at hand, we shall, I doubt not, see men corrupt with vice, and still buried in iniquity, men who have been dead, not four days as Lazarus was, but four months, four years, come forth in the face of the Church, full of a presumptuous confidence, and ask in the same breath to be unbound, and to be raised up, and to be admitted to the Lord's Table. Ah, my brethren! exclaims S. Bernard, it belongs to the Lord Himself alone to accomplish such marvels : our authority and our power do not extend so far, such a miracle is above us. What then must you do ? Just what those eager crowds did who went forth from Jerusalem, and who set out directly they heard of His approach, "When they heard, they went forth." You will learn it yourselves, Christians, and I now make it known to you from Him, "Behold, the Bridegroom cometh :" yes, my brethren, He is almost at the door of your heart, and in a very few days He ought to enter into it. Do not let yourselves be taken unawares. "Go forth ;" go forth, so to say, out of yourselves, out of the tumult of your passions, out of the entanglements of your wretched intrigues, out of the trouble and dissipation into which your temporal affairs drag you. Do not be like those foolish virgins who slept ; but keep yourselves ready, and go to meet the Master who comes to visit you : "Go forth to meet Him." If you have put off your preparation until to-day, after feeling shame in God's sight on that account, do your best to make up for the time you have lost. Think both of the holiness of the action you have to perform, and of the greatness of the God whom you have to receive. To make Him a suitable triumph and one which will satisfy His wishes, do not forget to send before you the poor loaded with your liberality and your alms. There are those who are forsaken in the prisons, languishing in the hospitals, overwhelmed with shame at home : seek for them, alleviate their sufferings, and they will unite their prayers to yours. But, above all, call to mind the great lesson of the prophet contained in these words,* " Let us come before His face with confession." Before this God of glory comes to you, anticipate Him and gain Him by an exact and sincere confession of all the misdoings of your life. Do not wait until the moment when you must give Him the kiss of peace; your mouth would then be polluted by the impurity of your crimes. This very day, if possible, cast aside the heavy burden which oppresses you, so that your soul, free and unencumbered, may advance with quickened steps towards this Lord who condescends for your sake to come down from the throne of His majesty. What, my brother, pleads S. Chrysostom, would not you be ready to do, if you were even now told that the greatest king of the earth is coming in person to stay with you; that he hath himself, by his own private choice, wished to bestow that honour on you, and that in so doing he hath no less an intention than to ennoble you for ever, to make your fortune sure and to load you with favours; what would not you do? What care, what eagerness, what activity you would display! What do not you even do every day for a friend? and how do you treat him? These illustrations are familiar and commonplace; but that is the very reason, saith S. Chrysostom, why preachers of the Gospel ought to make use of them, because they help to impress things on men's minds, and make the essential duties of Christianity more easy to be understood.

---

* Psalm xcv. (vulg. xciv.) 2.—" Praeoccupemus faciem ejus in confessione."

I say more. To receive Jesus Christ in communion, we must go before Him; but how? Like the disciples, with branches of palm and olive. From this circumstance I draw a third lesson. This is my thought. "They took," saith S. John, "branches of palm-trees" in their hands; "others cut down branches off the trees;" but those trees were olives, since it was to that very mountain, which took its name from these trees, that the disciples went to meet the Son of God, "When He was come nigh, even now at the descent of the Mount of Olives." What is the meaning of that? Nothing can be plainer, saith S. Augustine, than what the Holy Spirit teaches us by these two symbols: it is that neither you nor I ought to approach Jesus Christ, except we bear the palm in token of the victory that we have gained over sin, and the olive as a sign of the peace which we have concluded with God. Mark well, Christians, S. Augustine doth not say that to communicate well it is enough to have gained some advantage over the enemy, nor that we ought to be contented with having made a simple truce with him, and that it is enough if we have for a season escaped from his bondage, and have gained over him, or rather over ourselves, a reform of a few days. For that tempting spirit will not dispute with you for such a trifle, since he grants it to the most reckless; and it is a trick of his to bind them the more securely. There are few sinners so hardened but that during these holy days they curb and restrain themselves, and show the outward tokens of a Christian who is touched and converted. But that is nothing, my dear listener; that is not what Jesus Christ expects of you, nor the practical duty which is recommended to you. You have been told that to receive that God-Man, you must present yourself to Him with the palm, that is to say, after having truly, effectually, and perfectly overcome the sin which reigns in you. But you know that in this spiritual war, truces and suspensions of hostility have commonly no other effect than to strengthen your enemy more and more, to kindle your passion, and to stir up lust. You will give way then, by still more dangerous relapses, to new attacks. After an interval of liberty and false peace, you will find yourselves still more enslaved and more prone to sin than ever; and if that be the case, you are not of the number of those by whom Jesus Christ can be received in triumph. You must wear the palm, and be a conqueror: otherwise you have no right to join yourself to the band of His disciples. Why? Because you are still in fetters, and under the tyranny of the prince of this world. The fact is you must once get a fair start, and make the same effort which the Spouse of the Song of Songs made, when she said, "I will go up to the palm tree, I will take the fruit thereof." What are these fruits? The fruits of a healthful penitence. Up to the present time, you will say, I have gathered only the leaves: I have had only the appearance, the externals, fine words, ideas, useless and profitless desires: but to day I am determined to climb higher, and I wish to gather the fruit, "I will go up

C

to the palm tree, I will take the fruits thereof."
For a long time God hath been inviting me, and
I can no longer resist Him. These fruits will not
please the natural taste, but charity, whose taste is
much more exquisite, will make me find in them
delights which surpass all the pleasures of the senses.
It is thus, I say, Christians, that you ought to act,
and that you will make Jesus Christ triumph.

Lastly, the disciples stripped themselves of their
garments and spread them on the path along which
the Son of God was about to pass, " A very great
multitude spread their garments in the way." This
is a ceremony the mystery whereof it is needless
for me to explain, since you are already acquainted
with it ; a ceremony, which by itself teaches you,
much better than I can, this great truth, that to
receive the Saviour of men worthily in the sacrament of the altar, you must give up all that is called
worldly superfluity, especially superfluity of dress,
of attire, of ornaments, which, according to the
thought of Tertullian, is a kind of idolatry and
worship which you pay to the body : this, I say, you
ought to give up, not for worldly reasons, but out
of respect to religion. You have been told many
times, ladies—and no one ought to know it better
than yourselves—in God's presence you recognize
how this profane luxury is opposed to the humility
of your religion, of how many sins it is the source,
to how many occasions of falling it exposes you.
But what I cannot understand is that with you,
zealous as you are for everything which concerns
true piety, so much persuasion should be required
to induce you to renounce these things. What

I cannot understand is, that after you have so often been remonstrated with; after the rules which S. Paul hath laid down for you—S. Paul who is the mouthpiece and interpreter of the Holy Spirit; after the urgent exhortations of the Fathers of the Church, who have treated on this point of morality, as one most important to people of your rank; after your own experience, which is better calculated to convince you than all sermons, you should still strive with God to keep these remnants of worldliness, which you cannot be made to lay aside. What astonishes me is, that after so many communions, there are always to be seen among you some who are as enamoured of that vanity, as much affected in your persons, as eager to please as the most reckless and unrestrained souls. That is what surprises me. But will this offence never cease? and will you refuse to Jesus Christ—I say to Jesus Christ, entering into your heart, such a trifling sacrifice, yet one which is so necessary and so pleasing in His eyes as that? Ah, my brethren, exclaims S. Ambrose, what an advantage for you to be able to make your God a triumph of the very things which are the subject of your irregularities! What a consolation to be able to honour Him, not only with your superfluities, but with your very vanities! You must put under the feet of Jesus Christ all that which the pride of the world invents to give itself a false splendour, and to gain itself distinction. It is thus that you will sanctify your communion, and that your communion will sanctify you. For listen what Jesus Christ will do on His part. He will come unto you like a king, but like a triumphant king, and that is what He Himself orders me to proclaim to you. "Tell ye the daughter of Sion, Behold, thy king cometh." But what is that daughter of Sion? In the sense of the prophecy it is the just soul, and it is strictly in the communion that this prophecy has its fulfilment. Yes, Christians, it is then that the Son of God will make His entrance into you as a sovereign and as a king. For faith teaches us that He is a King, and, according to the express words of S. Luke, His kingdom—"the kingdom of God—is within you." Heaven and earth are absolutely subject to Him; but it is in the heart of man, saith S. Augustine, that He is especially pleased to reign. Why? Because He looks upon it, continues this holy Doctor, as a kingdom gained by conquest. He wishes to be received into it, and to fix His abode there. But when I communicate in a state of grace, I say truly, not only that Jesus Christ is in me, but that He is in me as a Sovereign; that He reigns there, that He commands there, that He is obeyed there, that He holds all my passions in subjection under the law of His love; that He there represses my anger, that He there checks my vengeance; that He there rules over my lust; in a word, that He is my King. "Behold, thy King."

If I were to stop at that first view which my religion gives me, I should remain paralyzed with fear, and surprised at the presence of so high a majesty; I should exclaim with S. Peter, "Depart from me; for I am a sinful man, O Lord." But this God of glory, by a wonderful contrivance of His charity, teaches me not to strain this profession of respectful diffidence, plausible as the excuse may seem. For if He come to me, it is in the character of a gracious King, full of gentleness, " Behold, thy King cometh unto thee, meek." No, no, saith S. Chrysostom, His greatness is not a hindrance which prevents Him from identifyng Himself with us, and in some manner becoming incarnate in us; and we have not grasped the first ideas of the mystery of His Body and Blood, if we be ignorant that He makes that infinite condescension minister to His greatness. His Divinity was a flood of light wherewith we should have been dazzled: so as to enable us to bear it, He hath covered it with the veil of His Humanity. His Humanity would have had too much brightness: He hath hidden it under the elements of the Sacrament, which outwardly are ordinary and simple. This Sacrament, by what it contains, might have kept us away from it: but He sets it before us as bread and wine, which ought to nourish us, and whereof we ought to partake. All that, to prove to us what He saith in the Scripture, that His delights, God though He is, are to dwell with the sons of men, and that He wishes to be our King, that He may have a right to anticipate us and to shower upon us the blessings of His gentleness, " Behold, thy King cometh unto thee, meek." When He entered into Jerusalem, around Him was nothing but pomp and magnificence, and that magnificence was well bestowed on so great a God as He: but in His Person there was only modesty, poverty, humility. So when He cometh down upon the altar, millions of angels come down with Him to escort and accompany Him. This is not one of those pious thoughts which are based only upon conjecture. S. John Chrysostom was no weak-minded man, and he himself testifies to us that he saw these heavenly legions; that he hath seen them, I say, encircling and surrounding Jesus Christ.* "I myself have seen crowds of angels coming down from heaven." But yet, it is upon this same altar that the God of love veils all His splendour; it is here that He abases Himself, here that He makes Himself small and lowly, in order that we may be able more easily to have access to Him. For if He had not humbled Himself, saith S. Augustine,† we should never have dared to take that divine nourishment nor to touch it. Ah! Lord, I perceive this, and henceforth I will render Thee all the homage which respect, obedience and gratitude constrain me to render Thee in my communion. It is only Thou who canst unite such boundless majesty with abasement so profound. If the kings of the earth only appeared in humiliation and entirely stripped of outward tokens, they could not maintain their royalty: but Thine maintains itself by itself, since Thou art King in Thyself, and Thy sovereign power is inseparable from Thy Being: "Tell ye the daughter of Sion, behold, thy King cometh unto thee, meek."

Now, Christians, let me direct your attention to that word, "Thy King cometh unto thee." Perhaps you do not think of it; but consider the

---

* "Vidi ipse turbas angelorum e cœlo descendentium."
† "Nisi enim esset humilis, non manducaretur."

excellent gift that it refers to. It teaches you that the God-Man cometh in communion, not only to us and for us, but for us in a singular and special manner; so that if we alone in this world were capable of participating in this mystery, He would come out again from the sanctuary where He resides, and the tabernacles where He reposes, to come with all the fulness of His Divinity to take a place in our heart. And indeed, how many times hath He honoured you with that grace, when others have not presented themselves to share it? And how many times can it be said that He left the altar for you alone, and that He was borne, as it were, triumphantly in the hands of His priest: "Behold, thy King cometh unto thee?" To unfold unto you in detail all the advantages which you ought to draw from so intimate a union with Him would require a whole sermon to itself. But I should fail to take advantage of my subject, and of the most remarkable point it furnishes me for your instruction, if I did not tell you that the Saviour comes to work invisibly in our souls the same miracles which He worked visibly on men's bodies after His entry into Jerusalem. For the Evangelist adds: "The blind and the lame came to Him and He healed them." But this is no conjecture, it is a point of faith, that the special effect of the Holy Communion, or rather, of the presence of Jesus Christ in the Communion, is to heal our spiritual infirmities, those weaknesses, those languors, those distastes for what is good, those inclinations to evil, to which a just and converted soul may still be subject. And why should He not do it? He healed completely the most desperate sicknesses by the simple touching of His robe: can He have less virtue when He is so really and closely united to us? Yes, Christians, He wishes to heal those traces of corruption that sin, although blotted out by penitence, hath left in your heart; and if you do not hinder His working, He will accomplish in you marvels which will edify the whole Church, and will surprise you yourselves. However violent and hasty you may be, He will make you gentle and moderate; however sensual and fond of pleasure, He will make you forbearing and self-controlled; however vain and ambitious, He will make you humble and submissive; in short, He will transform you into other men. Let us come then to Him, my brethren; let us come to make known to Him all the wounds of our souls, and to say to Him, as the prophet said: "Heal me, O Lord, and I shall be healed." Lord, Thou seest in what state I am, attacked with many evils: but heal me, and I shall begin to enjoy perfect health. I am blind, enlighten me; I am fickle, make me steadfast; I am weak, strengthen me. Only Thou, O my God! canst work this miracle; and every other healing, which cometh not from Thy hand, would only be an apparent healing: "Heal me, O Lord, and I shall be healed." You must then strive for that yourselves: but, to strive effectually, Lord, it is enough that Thou speakest one word. "Speak the word only," that word of grace, "Say unto my soul, I am thy salvation," and it will be saved. He will do it, Christians, He will save you. But now, after having given you the idea of a good communion in the manner in which the disciples received the Son of God, let me also set before you the idea of a bad communion in the manner in which He was received by the Scribes and Pharisees. That is the second part.

II. If the prophecy of Simeon was ever accomplished in the person of the Saviour, so that the God-Man, who is at once a source of division and of blessing among men, hath been at the same time the resurrection of some and the ruin of others, we might say, Christians, that it is especially in the mystery of this day, or rather in what is represented to us in the mystery of this day; namely, in the extreme antagonism which appears between the communion of the just and the communion of sinners. Can we indeed picture to ourselves anything more holy than this triumph in which I have just represented to you the Son of God, blessed by a whole nation and blessing a whole nation, receiving honour and conferring favours, recognized as the Lord's Messiah and as Himself Lord, acting in that twofold character, working miracles, converting souls, healing the sick, raising the dead? In that you see the first part of the prediction fulfilled; and it is also the type of the communion of the faithful, who in a state of grace partake of the Body of Jesus Christ. But look, on the other hand, at the sad type of an unworthy and sacrilegious communion in the way the Pharisees and their partisans received the Saviour, when He entered into Jerusalem; and by all the circumstances which I am going to point out to you, judge if the fulfilment have not completely answered to the prophecy: " Behold, this child is set for the fall and rising again of many in Israel; and for a sign which shall be spoken against." For in the first place the Pharisees and those of their faction receive the Saviour of the world to-day only by a kind of hypocrisy, by dissimulation, and on account of some necessity which compels them to do so; they receive Him on account of fear, or because of the opinion of others. If they had had it in their power to forbid Him ever entering into their town, that is what they would have liked to do; but the Evangelist observes, " they feared the people:" and that is the reason why, in spite of themselves, they joined the bands of disciples, and outwardly conformed with them. Secondly, as soon as Jesus Christ appeared in Jerusalem, they began to form plots against Him, they conspired together to take away His life, and took steps to get rid of Him; for it was on that day they assembled the detestable council, in which the death of Jesus, after much deliberation, was at length determined upon. Thirdly, they contradict His miracles, however incontestable, however glorious; they shut their eyes so as not to recognize them; far from being touched by them, they show indignation at them : " When the chief priests and scribes saw the wonderful things that He did . . . . they were sore displeased." It is thus they received the Son of God : and how did the Son of God come to them? Ah, Christians! mark it well. At the sight of these infidels Jesus Christ was filled with grief, and shed tears: " When He was come near, He beheld the city, and wept over it;" for the latter part of the mystery shows all this. He enters no longer as a gracious king as regards them; but as a terrible enemy, because they despised His grace; He comes to be the cause of their rejection and of the destruction of their city: "they shall not leave in thee one stone upon another;" why? "because thou knewest not the time of thy visitation," wherein thy God hath visited thee. In short, He enters to exercise already on the Pharisees the severity of His justice, condemning them beforehand, and pronouncing against them that terrible sentence: "I say unto you that the stones will cry out," the stones of the Temple will one day bear witness against you. What a similarity there is in this to the communion of sinners! Permit me to add a few words of application.

For that which these Pharisees and ministers of the synagogue did, is just what certain sinners do now, who, through policy and fear of the people, receive the Saviour of the world—sinners who are hardened in sin and by no means disposed to renounce it, but who nevertheless wish to keep up the appearance and externals of religion; men who at heart are enemies of Jesus Christ, but who dare not admit it to others, and who shut their eyes sometimes so as to hide it from themselves. They would be well content never to communicate, but they are pledged to do so by their condition and state, and do not know how to set aside these obligations. One man is a magistrate, and the offence which he would cause would fall upon himself; another is a father, and he would certainly be the subject of remark; another is a lady of rank, who would injure her reputation; another is a churchman who would lose respect and be counted a careless liver. They must guard against these consequences, and to that end present themselves, like others, at the table of the faithful, at least during this holy season. Otherwise they would meet with a clergyman who, to satisfy his ministerial obligation, would rise up against them, speak with, mark, and rebuke them: and that is a thing they do not wish to draw down upon themselves. Bold enough to shake off the yoke of the fear of God, they have not enough courage to free themselves from the fear of man. So they make up their mind, to do what?—to communicate; but how? By a kind of constraint: "for they fear the people."

You can judge from this, Christians, what is the general accompaniment of such communions: at the very moment when these lost and impious men receive the sacrament of Jesus Christ, they set themselves against Him in their hearts; they form plans to satisfy their brutal passions, and the day of their communion becomes for them a day of excess and debauchery. You see, my dear listeners, what is the consequence; and it is better to tell you it to give you a horror of it than to be silent about it, while you are exposed to the contagion of that impiety. Every day other disorders are preached against, but not this; yet it is this nevertheless which directly attacks religion. Light imperfections, which are remarked in the devout souls which frequent the sacraments, are insisted on; but scarcely anything is said about the sacrilegious Christians who profane the Body of Jesus Christ ; yet against them that evangelic zeal ought to be directed. If from time to time the wretchedness of their state were put before them, perhaps at last they would become aware of it ; and sharp, but healthful remonstrances would awaken them from their drowsiness.

Besides, do not expect that God will work miracles for their sake, since they oppose to these miracles an almost invincible obstacle. For after the example of the Pharisees, and as a last feature of resemblance, they treat all these miracles as illusions : and when we tell them that a communion well made is capable of healing them of their weaknesses, they mock at the statement, and only reply by cutting and unseemly raillery. There is but one miracle which the Communion accomplishes in them, and which they cannot hinder. But what is that miracle ? Ah, Christians ! it is that this Sacrament, which ought to be for them a source of light, serves only to blind them ; it is that this Sacrament, which ought to be for them a means of conversion, only serves to harden them ; it is that this Sacrament of life becomes for them a Sacrament of death, of death eternal. I have, therefore, no difficulty in understanding why the Son of God only came to them in tears : " He beheld the city, and wept over it." How could He help weeping ? He sees that the same Sacrament which He hath instituted for the sanctification of souls, is going to cause their reprobation. He sees that these sinners, whom He would have saved, instead of taking advantage of this most excellent gift, and of the visit of their God, are going to draw upon themselves, as well as on Jerusalem, all the wrath of Heaven and its terrible vengeance. Is there a subject more deserving of His tears? "He beheld the city, and wept over it."

But that being the case, would it not be better not to communicate at all, than to communicate unworthily? This is another irregularity, and one all the more dangerous, in that it is made use of by the libertinism which introduced it, as a pretext to justify and uphold itself. It is better, you say, never to communicate, than to communicate unworthily: as if there could be anything better in a thing which causes offence, and offence of the most flagrant nature. No, my dear listeners, the one alternative is not better than the other; and that comparison made by those of whom I am speaking—I mean the libertines—betrays a still more vicious and corrupt principle, than are the results even of an unworthy communion. For they reason in this way only because they are impious and determined to live in their impiety. It is not out of respect for Jesus Christ; they make it very plain by their conduct in other matters that they are little influenced by this motive. It is not in consideration of the holiness of the Sacrament; they scarcely believe this truth. It is not with the purpose of a speedy return; they are far from it, and do not think of it. It is then only because they are urged by a spirit of irreligion, they make this plea. But, to say out of a spirit of irreligion, it is better not to communicate at all than to communicate badly, is, I maintain, the argument of an atheist.

To this I add an assertion which I submit to your judgment, but which I believe to be true, namely, that not to communicate at all because of this principle of recklessness and of irreligion, is a more abominable irregularity in God's sight than to communicate unworthily through negligence or frailty. And indeed, it hath always been believed that to fail in the duty laid upon you at Easter in the way I have just described, was of the nature of apostasy from the faith, because one of the most distinctive marks of Christianity is communion; and to fail in this duty at Easter is to excommunicate ourselves, and by a much more fatal excommunication than by the formal sentence of the Church. For to be excommunicated by the Church is a punishment which even S. Paul declares to be useful, but to excommunicate oneself is a crime which tends to loss of salvation and to damnation. It hath always been believed that a Christian who did not observe Easter ought to be considered as a pagan and as a publican, according to the words of the Saviour Himself, because that man doth not listen to the voice of the Church, and despises her orders. And I, not only do I look upon him as a publican and a pagan, but he seems to me worse than a pagan, because I am convinced that a good pagan—I say good so far as his religion permits—is better than a nominal Christian—one who is at heart without religion. Such is the irregularity which I am combating (and would to Heaven that it existed only in my imagination), but this irregularity is not so rare as you may think. It is only too well known how many of these libertines there are—

libertines distinguished by their gifts and their occupations, who flatter themselves with a pretended good faith in that they never communicate, because they do not wish, they say, to make themselves sacrilegious by communicating. I conjure them not to offend Jesus Christ their Saviour by contempt of His Sacrament ; not to offend the Church, their mother, by an obstinate disobedience ; not to offend the faithful, their brethren, by their bad example ; not to offend themselves by their unrestrained conduct. What, then, shall they do? Shall they communicate unworthily ? God forbid ! but between these two extremes there is a mean ; it is to communicate and to communicate worthily. All devotion which leads men not to communicate is false devotion ; and every maxim which would lead them to communicate in a state of sin is an abomination. But the important point is to draw near to the Table of Jesus Christ, and to draw near with feelings of religion, of penitence, of piety, of warmth ; feelings which sanctify a soul, and dispose it to eat of that heavenly bread which ought to be for us the pledge of a happy eternity. This is my wish for every one here present.

II.

THE PASSION OF JESUS CHRIST.

1 COR. i. 22-24.—"The Jews require a sign, and the Greeks seek after wisdom: but we preach Christ crucified, unto the Jews a stumbling block, and unto the Greeks foolishness; but unto them which are called, both Jews and Greeks, Christ the power of God, and the wisdom of God."

SIRE,—If ever preachers should have any good reason to be ashamed of their ministry, might it not well be so to-day, when they see themselves obliged to make known the astonishing humiliations of the God they preach, the outrages He received, the weaknesses He felt, His weariness, His sufferings, His passion, His death? Nevertheless, said the great Apostle, notwithstanding the shame of the cross, I will never be ashamed of the Gospel of my Saviour: and the reason which he adduces for this is as surprising, and even still more surprising, than the assertion itself: it is because I know, he adds, that the Gospel of the Cross is the power of God to all those who are enlightened with the beams of faith, "I am not ashamed of the Gospel of Christ: for it is the power of God unto salvation to every one that believeth." Not only was S. Paul not ashamed of it, but he gloried in it. "God forbid," my brethren, he wrote to the Galatians, "that I should glory, save in the cross of our Lord Jesus Christ." Far, then, from the cross disconcerting him in the discharge of his ministerial office, he maintained that the preaching of the cross of the God-Man was the surest way to maintain the honour of that office; and that, in fact, there was nothing in the whole Gospel grander, more wonderful, better calculated to satisfy reasonable and sensible minds, than this deep and adorable mystery. This is the literal meaning of the divine passage which I have chosen for my text, "the Jews require a sign, and the Greeks seek after wisdom." The unbelieving Jews ask that miracles be shown to them. The proud and vain Greeks boast that they seek for wisdom: and both obstinately refuse to believe in Jesus Christ, except on these conditions: but as for me, says the Apostle, that I may put to shame both the unbelief of the former and the vanity of the latter, I content myself with preaching to them "Jesus Christ, and Him crucified." Why? Because that above everything else is the miracle of the power of God, and at the same time the highest possible example of the wisdom of God. It is the miracle of the power of God, which ought, for the Jews, to serve instead of all other miracles. "Christ crucified, the power of God:" the highest possible example of the wisdom of God, which is by itself more than sufficient to subjugate the Gentiles to the yoke of the faith, and so make them renounce all earthly wisdom, " Christ crucified, ... the wisdom of God."

The idea of this teacher of the nations, who always represented to himself the Passion of the Saviour of men as a mystery of power and of wisdom, is admirable. Now, I have resolved to unfold this idea, my Christian brethren, partly because it appeared to me calculated to edify you, and partly because it appeared so worthy of Jesus Christ, whose funeral oration I have to deliver in your hearing to-day. For it is not a question here of weeping for the death of that God-Man. Our tears, if we have any to shed, ought to be reserved for another use, and we cannot but know what use we ought to make of them, since Jesus Christ has so clearly and positively pointed it out to us, when on His way to Calvary He said to the daughters of Jerusalem, "Weep not for Me, but weep for yourselves." It is not a question, I say, of weeping for His death, but of meditating on it: the question is to fathom the mystery of it, to discover in it the purpose, or rather the work, of God; the question is to find in it the establishment or confirmation of our faith: and this is the task which, with the grace of God, I now undertake. You have often been touched and softened by the sad story of the Passion of Jesus Christ, and my wish is to instruct you. The pathetic and affecting sermons which have been preached to you have often roused your emotions; but perhaps only with an unfruitful compassion, or, at the most, with a transitory compunction, which has had no effect on your after life. My purpose is to convince your reason, and to tell you something more substantial, which may henceforth serve as a basis for all the pious sentiments which this mystery may inspire. In short, my dear hearers, you who are listening to my words, you have perhaps hitherto considered the Saviour's death only as the mystery of His humility and of His weakness; and I wish to show you that it is in this mystery that He has displayed the full extent of His power: that will be the first head of the sermon. Up to the present time the world has looked upon this mystery only as foolishness; and I wish to show you that it is in this mystery that God has given the most striking token of His wisdom: that will be the second head.

Grant, O Lord, that I may treat so lofty a theme in a worthy manner; give me that zeal with which Thine Apostle was filled, when Thou didst choose him to bear Thy name before kings, and to make them, even in the humiliation of Thy death, revere the Divinity of Thy Person. I do not speak here, as S. Paul did, to Jews nor to Gentiles; I speak to professed Christians, amongst whom, alas! we see every day those who are weak in the faith, and who, full of the maxims of the age, and paying too much attention to worldly prudence, although they be Christians, are none the less at times troubled and even tempted as to question the truth of their religion, when the God whom they adore is represented to them overwhelmed with disgrace, and expiring on the cross. But that is a reason why I ought to strengthen them by making them sensible of the gift of God, which is concealed in the mystery of Thy death, and by giving them a higher idea of Thine apparent weaknesses. O my God, be Thou my stay; but at the same time give my hearers that willingness with which they ought to hear Thy word, so that they may be not only persuaded, but converted and sanctified. I pray, O Lord, for that grace, and I will obtain it by the merits of Thy cross itself. For I look only to Thy cross, our sovereign hope; and, as an act of faith with which to invoke Thy blessing, I solemnly venerate it with the whole Church.

> "Faithful Cross, above all other,
> One and only noble Tree,
> None in foliage, none in blossom,
> None in fruit thy peer may be;
> Sweetest wood, and sweetest iron,
> Sweetest weight is hung on thee."

I. That a God, as God, should act like a Master and a Sovereign; that He should with a single word have created the heavens and the earth, that He should work miracles in the universe, and that nothing should resist His power; that is so natural a thing for Him, that it is scarcely a subject of wonder to us. But that a God should suffer; that a God should expire in torments; that a God, as the Scripture says, should taste death; He who alone possesses immortality; this is what angels and men will never understand. I may, therefore, well exclaim with the prophet: "Be astonished, O ye heavens, at this!" for, lo, here is a matter which is above our comprehension, and which demands all the submission and obedience of our faith; but it is also by this great mystery that our faith has triumphed over the world: "This is the victory that overcometh the world, even our faith." It is true, Christians, that Jesus Christ has suffered, and that He died. But, in speaking to you of His death and His sufferings, I am not afraid of bringing forward a proposition which you would treat as paradoxical, if the words of my text had not disposed you to listen to it with respect; and I maintain that Jesus Christ has suffered and died as a God, that is to say, in a manner in which only a God could suffer and die—in a manner so peculiarly that of a God, that S. Paul, without any other reason, believed he could say to the Gentiles: Yes, my brethren, this Crucified One, whom we preach, this Man, whose death shocks you, this Christ, who appeared to you on Calvary struck by the hand of God and reduced to the uttermost weakness, is even the Power of God. That which you despise in Him is what makes us revere Him: He is our God, and we ask for no other token or proof than His cross. This is the sum of S. Paul's theology, which, perhaps, you have never quite understood, and which I intend to unfold to you. Let us enter, Christians, into the meaning of these divine words, "Christ crucified, the power of God," and let us draw from them all the profit which they ought to yield our souls for our edification. I say that Jesus Christ died in a way in which only a God-Man could die. The explanation of the circumstances of His death will convince you of it. A Man who dies after having Himself clearly and expressly foretold all the circumstances of His death; a Man who, in the very moment of His death, performs miracles, great miracles, to show that there is nothing but what is superhuman and divine in His death; a Man, whose death, when well considered, is itself the greatest of miracles, since, far from dying of exhaustion of Nature, like the rest of men, He, on the contrary, died by an effort of His almighty power; but what surpasses everything else, a Man who, by the infamy of His death, attains the highest glory, and who, expiring on the cross, triumphs by His very cross over the Prince of the World, subdues by His cross the pride of the world, sets up His cross upon the ruins of the idolatry and infidelity of the world, is not that a Man who dies like a God, or, if you prefer it, like a God-Man? And it is on this fact the Apostle took his stand when he said that the Man who died on the cross was, not the minister of the power of God, but the Incarnate Power of God itself: "Christ crucified, the power of God." Let us not separate these four proofs, and you will allow that there is no reasonable mind, nor even obstinate mind, but ought to be influenced by them. Let us proceed to a detailed examination of them.

No, Christians, it belongs to a God alone to penetrate into the future so as to have it absolutely in His power, and to be able to say infallibly and like a Master: "That will be," although the thing depend upon an infinity of free causes which must combine to produce it. It belongs to a God alone to know distinctly and of Himself the bottom of the heart, and to reveal its inmost secrets, its most hidden intentions, so as to know better than man himself knows, what is or what will be in the thought and in the will of man. But this is what Jesus Christ has done in respect to His Passion and His death. Let me explain what I mean. Even long before His Passion, and before the Jews had yet formed any definite plan against Him, you would have said, to have heard

Him speak of His Passion, that He spoke of it as of an event which had already happened, the history of which He was relating; He was so precise in indicating even the least circumstances: to have seen Him on the day of His death undergoing the different punishments which He suffered, you would have thought that the executioners who tormented Him were trying to fulfil His predictions, rather than the judgments against His Person. Lastly, to prepare his Apostles for that sad mystery, He said to them: We go to Jerusalem, and all that which has been spoken of the Son of Man is about to be accomplished: for this Son of Man (it was the title He gave Himself), the Son of Man, whom you see, and who is speaking to you, will be delivered to the Gentiles; He will be outraged, insulted, scourged, crucified; they will spit on His face, He will die in shame, and He will rise again the third day. Mark well, Christians, the reflection of S. Chrysostom on this point. Whole centuries before, the prophets, who during the ancient law were the heralds of the Messiah, had published these minute particulars. Since the chief obstacle which should one day turn aside worldly minds from believing in Jesus Christ was the pretended offence which the ignominy of His death would cause, God had by a singular providence revealed to the prophets that the death of the Messiah, ignominious though it was, would yet, in the fulness of time, be the sovereign remedy for sin, the solemn satisfaction for sin, the excellent means of the salvation and of the redemption of the world; so that prophecy, a witness to His Divinity which cannot be set aside, might render the very ignominy of that death not only worthy of reverence, but even of adoration ; and that men, regarding it thus, far from being offended at it, might be persuaded that there was nothing in the Saviour's passion which was not superhuman : For, behold, says S. Chrysostom, what God's purpose was, when in the Old Testament He made Isaiah speak of the sufferings of Jesus Christ with as much assurance, and in as exact terms as the Evangelists afterwards spoke of them in the New Testament. But the purpose of God made itself more felt, and we have a more convincing and touching proof, in the immediate prediction of it which Jesus Christ Himself made. For it is I, He said to His disciples when He was telling them of His death, now near at hand, I who am that Man of sorrows, spoken of by Isaiah ; it is I who am going to fulfil in every point what is written of Him ; we are close upon the time when all things shall be accomplished, and you are going to be spectators and witnesses of them ; but henceforth it is a matter of great moment to me that you should be warned of them so that you may not be troubled at their accomplishment.

Thus, all that the adorable Saviour had pointed out to them from the books of Moses, and from the Prophets, relating to Himself, was soon afterwards literally fulfilled in the piteous scenes of His passion and death. It was in consequence of and by reason of these divine prophecies, of which He was personally the subject, that the Jews, instead of judging Him according to their law, because He was a Jew, delivered Him to Pilate, who was a Gentile: for the same reason that the soldiers, contrary to all forms of justice, adding insult and cruelty to the decree of His judge, spat on His face, and bruised it with blows: that even to the veriest details, the price for which He was to be sold, the use that was to be made of the money, the parting of His garments and casting lots for His vesture, the gall which they offered Him, the Scriptures which He had applied to Himself might apparently be the measure of all that His enemies attempted against Him; as if He had suffered only to justify these revelations pronounced so many centuries before His appearance in the world: " That the Scriptures might be fulfilled;" " That the saying might be fulfilled, which He spake." This is so well founded and so strong an argument, that, as we read in the book of the Acts, no other was needed to convert that famous eunuch, the treasurer of the Ethiopian Queen, to whom S. Philip, the Deacon, explained the wonder, which is the subject of my sermon. All these prophecies, and many others, literally and exactly fulfilled in the Passion of Jesus Christ, compelled that Ethiopian to recognize in Him the Messiah promised by God, and sent in the fulness of time. Should we, my dear hearers, we, who bear the character of Christians, allow them to have less influence on us? And shall that which sufficed to convince a man, on whom the light of the Gospel had not yet shined, be too weak to confirm us in the faith which we profess? With respect to the knowledge of the heart, of which Jesus Christ in His Passion clearly showed Himself the Master, I would ask again, should not that too convince us? He foretold to His Apostles that one of them would betray Him; and Judas was even then thinking of it, and did betray Him. He foretold that S. Peter would deny him, and S. Peter really did deny Him. He foretold to him also that, notwithstanding his fall, his faith should not fail; and the faith of S. Peter did not fail. He foretold that after his conversion he should strengthen his brethren; and the result of his conversion was to strengthen them all. He foretold to the Magdalene that the action she had just performed in anointing His head with a precious perfume, should be praised and spoken of in all the world; and throughout the whole world it is spoken of to this day. He foretold of Jerusalem, when He wept over it, that it should be utterly destroyed; and Jerusalem was besieged, pillaged, overthrown by the Romans, so that there did not remain one stone upon another. Was not this knowledge of future things, and of things which were secret and most unsearchable, the knowledge of a God, "God who searcheth the hearts and reins?" And a Man who died in this manner, revealing and making known that which could only be known by God, had not He all the authority and all the power of the very God? "Christ crucified, the power of God."

But what I now add ought to make still more impression upon you. He dies, this God-Man, working miracles; and what miracles? Ah! Christians, were there ever any, and will there ever be any, more striking? At the point of death as He is, He makes the earth quake, the graves open; He quickens the dead, rends the veil of the Temple, darkens the sun—wonders so surprising, so unheard of—wonders at which the soldiers were so moved that they returned converted; nay, more converted, as S. Augustine* remarks, by the efficacy of the very blood which they had shed. What do I say which S. Matthew has not related in so many words?—"When the centurion, and they that were with him, watching Jesus, saw the earthquake, and those things that were done, they feared greatly, saying, Truly this was the Son of God." I know that even in Christian countries there are to be found enemies of Jesus Christ more impious than the Jews and pagans themselves, who have not been ashamed to dispute the truth of these miracles, maintaining that they might be imaginary; that, by a preconcerted scheme, the Evangelists might have agreed amongst themselves to publish them for the glory of their Master. But, to make use of a Scriptural expression, impiety here confounds itself, and in setting itself up against God displays as much ignorance as malignity; for, not to inquire how rash this doubt is, since it has no other foundation than prejudice and free-thought, it must be shown, says S. Augustine, what interest the Evangelists could have had in publishing these miracles, if they had been persuaded that they were false. Is it not evident that the only fruit they could expect from them, and which they did reap, was public hatred, persecution, fetters, and the most cruel torments? Far, then, from believing

---

* Ipso redempti sanguine quem fuderunt.

that they would have taken pleasure in inventing and retailing these miracles, of which they must have known the falsehood, we ought rather to be astonished that, even though they knew them to be true, they had courage enough to bear witness to them as they did at the expense of their own lives. Moreover, continues S. Augustine, the mere style in which the Evangelists have written the story of Jesus Christ and of His passion, their simplicity, their ingenuousness, giving no token of indignation against the Jews, nor of compassion for their Master, speaking of Him as the most indifferent men of the world and those least interested in His cause would have spoken, relating His weakness in the Garden, His aversion, His weariness, His fears, the cruel affront to which He was subjected in the palace of Herod, and the contempt which that prince manifested for Him, the unworthy treatment He received in the houses of Annas, Caiaphas, and Pilate, and relating all this more exactly and at greater length than His miracles themselves; that sincerity, I say, makes it very plain that they did not write as prejudiced and impassioned men, but as faithful and irreproachable witnesses of the truth, for which they were martyrs even to the shedding of their blood. Nor is this all; for, if these miracles were imaginary, would not the Jews, to whom it was of such consequence to expose the imposture, and who at that time did not lack celebrated writers, have taken care to have undeceived the world? Would they not in writing have registered their decision against them? And yet this they never did, and do not even now do, since their own writers, and amongst others Josephus, would give them the lie. That general eclipse, which took place contrary to the course of Nature, had in it something so wonderful and remarkable, that two centuries afterwards Tertullian* spoke of it to the pagan magistrates of Rome, as of a fact of which they recorded the tradition in their archives. This very fact, which they looked upon as so certain and well attested, so surprised Dionysius, the Areopagite, that sage of the pagan world, who afterwards became one of the firmest supporters and one of the greatest ornaments of our religion, so that, far away as he was from Judea, and still further from all knowledge of our mysteries, he was so struck by it as to acknowledge that darkness had been for him a source of light, or had at least disposed him to receive with submission the truths of the faith and the divine instructions of S. Paul. What shall I say of that famous malefactor crucified with Jesus Christ, and suddenly converted by this same Saviour? Could this sudden change, which made of a criminal a chosen vessel and a vessel of mercy, be the effect of human persuasion? Did it not clearly proceed from a supernatural and divine source? If Jesus Christ had not acted as God, could He, dying on the cross, have made known to this wretched man, and made him confess, His Divinity? And does not this miracle of grace further serve to confirm all the wonders of Nature, wherewith heaven and earth, acting as it were in concert, honoured this suffering and expiring God? But will you remind me that,

---

* Cum mundi casum relatum habetis in archivis vestris.

in spite of these miracles, the Pharisees did not cease to persist in their unbelief. I admit it, my dear listeners; but, without entering on this point into the depth of the judgments of God, which are always just and holy, although they are terrible and dreadful, you know what the envy of the Pharisees was against Jesus Christ, and you are aware what power such a passion may have in blinding men's minds and hardening their hearts. However hard the obstinacy of the Pharisees may be to understand, perhaps we should still find in the world, even in the Christian world, men as incredulous, who, if they were to see their enemies work miracles, men would rather attribute these miracles to the powers of darkness, as the Pharisees attributed those of the Saviour of the world to the Prince of it, than give up their prejudices and their hate. Be that as it may, says S. Chrysostom, that is how the reprobation of the Pharisees began; and that mystery of predestination and of divine reprobation showed itself, in that the same miracles which converted the soldiers and a great crowd of people, only served to render the Pharisees more stubborn and self-willed. But it is by this difference that we ought to recognize in Jesus Christ the almighty power of which we are speaking: for, as S. Chrysostom argues, is it not to display, even in His death, the most glorious and the most essential attributes of God, to die saving some, and reproving others; enlightening the blind who were living in the darkness of infidelity, and blinding the most enlightened who abused their light; converting these by mercy, and allowing those to perish by justice?

There was only one miracle that Jesus Christ would not work in His Passion: that was, to save Himself, as His enemies proposed to Him, though they assured Him that they would believe in Him if He came down from the cross:—"If He be the King of Israel, let Him now come down from the cross, and we will believe Him." But why did He not do that miracle? We easily see the reason, saith S. Augustine; and it is, that this one miracle would have destroyed all the others, and put an end to the great work which He had undertaken, and towards the accomplishment of which all the other miracles contributed—namely, the work of the redemption of men, which was to be effected on the cross. Moreover, His enemies, prejudiced by their passions, would have shown no more deference to that miracle than to the raising of Lazarus; for if the evidence of the fact which obliged them to admit that Lazarus, who had been dead and buried four days, had undoubtedly been restored to life—if that evidence, instead of disposing them to believe in Jesus Christ, made them resolve to kill Him, since they were no longer governed by reason, but by passion, can we suppose that, if they saw Him come down from the cross, they would have been better disposed to render Him the glory which was His due? But, not to dwell on the conduct of the Pharisees, answer, my dear listeners, and tell me: if Jesus Christ, able, as He indisputably was, at that critical moment to save Himself, willed not to do it; was not that something much greater and more above man than if He had in fact willed to do so? Miracle for miracle (give your attention to this, which perhaps you have never well understood, and which appears to me more edifying), miracle for miracle, the meekness with which He permitted the soldiers to seize His person, after having cast them all to the ground when He presented Himself to them and spoke that word: "It is I;" the reproof to S. Peter for the indiscretion of his zeal, blaming him for having drawn his sword against a servant of the high-priest, when, as He told him, He had only to pray to His Father, and His Father would send Him legions of angels who would fight in his defence; and in order to convince him that He did not speak in vain, He actually healed by a miracle the servant whom S. Peter had wounded; that silence before His judges, so wonderful and so constantly maintained, especially before Pilate, who, convinced of His innocence, only questioned Him, that He might have a reason to give for acquitting Him; that refusal to gratify Herod's curiosity, whose protection it would have been so easy for Him to secure; that abandonment of His own cause, and consequently of His life; that calmness and peace in the midst of the most outrageous insults; that determination to endure all without asking for justice, without taking any one into His confidence, without uttering the least complaint; that heroic charity which made Him, when dying, excuse His persecutors; all that, all these miracles of patience, I say, in a Man, whose conduct, moreover, was irreproachable and full of wisdom; was not all that more miraculous than if He had thought of escaping from the hands of His executioners, and had set Himself free from the cross? "Christ crucified, the power of God."

He died then only because He willed, and in the way in which He willed to die, a privilege, which says S. Augustine, belongs only to a God-Man, and by which, even in His death, He exhibits the sovereignty and independence of God. You see now, Christians, on what I founded that other proposition, that the death of Jesus Christ, considered in itself, was not merely a miracle, but the most singular of all miracles. Why? because instead of dying like other men by weakness, by violence, by necessity, He died, I do not say exactly by choice, and by an unfettered determination of His will, but by an effort of His absolute power: so that, as Son of God and as God, He never exerted that almighty power more than at the moment when He consented that His blessed soul should be separated from His body; and theologians give two reasons in justification of this. First, they say that, because Jesus Christ had been exempt from every kind of sin, and was absolutely incapable of sin, He ought to be, and He was, naturally immortal; whence it followed that His body and His soul, which were joined to His Divinity by the Hypostatic Union, could not be disunited without a miracle. To accomplish that separation, therefore, Jesus Christ was obliged to do violence, so to speak, to all the laws of ordinary providence, and employ all the power which God had given Him for the destruction of that fair life, which, although human, was at the same time the life of a God. Secondly, that because Jesus Christ, by virtue of His priesthood, was pre-eminently the Sovereign Pontiff of the new law, and there was none but He, who could or who ought to offer to God the sacrifice of the redemption of the world, and immolate the Victim reserved for that purpose. But that Victim was His Body. No other than He ought, then, to immolate that Body : no other than He had the power necessary for that. The executioners who crucified Him were, indeed, the ministers of the justice of God, but they were not the priests who ought to sacrifice that Victim to God. For that purpose there was needed a High-priest who was holy, innocent, spotless, separate from sinners, and endued with a special character. But that character could only belong to Jesus Christ; whence S. Augustine,* with his marvellous power of reasoning, concludes that Jesus Christ was at once both the Priest and Victim of His sacrifice. Therefore it was He Himself who sacrificed Himself, He Himself who exercised on His own Person that function of Priest and of Pontiff, He Himself who annulled, at least for some days, that adorable union of a suffering body with a glorified soul ; in a word, He Himself who made Himself die ; for it was not the executioners who took away His life, but He laid it down of His own accord : " No man taketh it from Me, but I lay it down of Myself." He died on the cross, says S. Augustine ; but, to speak properly and strictly, He did not die by the punishment of the cross. And to enable you to understand this, it is certain, on the testimony of

---

* Idem sacerdos et hostia.

the Jews, that the punishment of crucifixion, or rather what made criminals condemned to the cross die, was not due merely to their being attached to it, but because their bones were broken whilst they were yet alive. But, according to the prophecy, Jesus Christ had already yielded up the last sigh when they wished to break His bones; and, therefore, "Pilate marvelled if He were already dead." That He cried with a loud voice when expiring, shows also that He did not die by exhaustion of Nature. "Jesus cried with a loud voice, and gave up the ghost." This was so extraordinary a circumstance that, as the Evangelist relates, "when the centurion, which stood over against Him, saw that He so cried out, and gave up the ghost, he said: Surely this Man was the Son of God." If the centurion had been one of the Saviour's disciples, and had reasoned in this way, perhaps his reasoning and his evidence might have been suspected; but he was an infidel, a pagan, who, from the way in which he saw Jesus Christ die, concluded without hesitation that he died by a miracle, and from that miracle immediately drew the inference that He was indeed the Son of God. Need we anything more to justify those words of the Apostle, "Christ crucified, the power of God."

It is true that this dying Saviour had His weaknesses and His infirmities; and I might forthwith reply, with Isaiah, that the weaknesses and infirmities which He showed in His death were not His own, but ours, and that the wonder is that He bore by Himself the weaknesses and infirmities of all men: "Surely He hath borne our griefs, and carried our sorrows." But, because that thought, although well founded, might perhaps be too refined for worldly and incredulous minds, I answer otherwise, with S. Chrysostom, and say, that dying Saviour had his weaknesses; but the wonder is, that His very weaknesses, His very infirmities, His seasons of exhaustion, were so many miracles in the course of His Passion. For if He sweat whilst praying in the garden, it is a sweat of blood, and so abundant that the ground is soaked with it ; if, some minutes after His death, they pierce His side, by another equally miraculous result, blood and water come forth ; and he who records this assures us that He saw it, and that it ought to be believed : "He that saw it bare record, and his record is true." We might say that He suffers and dies only to display in His own Person the power of God, "Christ crucified, the power of God."

Let us give one last but essential proof in conclusion : that is to see a Man whom the ignominy of His death, whom the confusion, the disgrace, the infinite humility of His death raise to the greatest height of glory a God can claim ; so that at His name only, and at the sight of His cross, the highest powers of the world bend their knees, and prostrate themselves to do Him homage with their greatness : "He humbled Himself, and became obedient unto death, even the death of the cross. Wherefore God also hath highly exalted Him, and given Him a name which is above every name : that at the name of Jesus every knee should bow, of things in heaven, and things in earth, and things

under the earth." That was what God revealed
to S. Paul in a time (the thought is an important
one) when everything seemed to be opposed to
the accomplishment of this prediction; in a time
when, according to all the calculations of human
foresight, this prediction ought to pass for a fancy;
in a time when the name of Jesus Christ was
abhorred. Nevertheless, what the Apostle said
has come to pass; that which was for the Christians
of that time a point of faith has ceased to be so
for us, since we can now behold the fact, and it
needs no effort to make our minds believe it. The
powers of the earth now bend their knees before
that crucified One. The princes, even the greatest
of our princes, are the first to set us the example;
and it only remains for us, seeing them at the foot
of the altar adore Jesus Christ on this holy day,
to console ourselves and to say to ourselves: That
is what S. Paul had foretold to me; and what at
the time of S. Paul I should have rejected as a
dream, that is what I see and cannot doubt. Now.
a Man, my dear listeners, whose cross, according
to the beautiful expression of S. Augustine,* has
passed from the infamous place of punishment
on to the brow of monarchs and emperors: a Man
who, without any other aid, without any other
arms, by the virtue of His cross alone, has overcome idolatry, and triumphed over superstition,
has destroyed the worship of false gods, has conquered the whole universe; whereas the greatest
kings of the universe have for the least conquests

---

* A locis suppliciorum ad frontes imperatorum.

needed so much help: a Man, who, as the Church chants to His praise, has found out the means of reigning where others cease to live, that is to say, from the wood which was the instrument of His death:—

"For God is reigning from the Tree;"*

and, what is still more wonderful, a Man, who during His life had expressly pointed out that all this would take place, and that from the moment when He should be lifted up from the earth, He would draw all men unto Him. "This He said," observes the Evangelist, "signifying what death He should die," is not such a man more than a man? Is He not God and Man both in one? Has not the cross, as we contemplate it, had a wonderful virtue to make all people adore it? How many Apostles of His Gospel, how many imitators of His virtues, how many confessors, how many martyrs, how many holy souls devoted to His service, how many disciples zealous for His glory, or, better still, how many nations, how many kingdoms, how many empires has not He drawn to Himself by the secret but all-powerful charm of His cross! "Christ crucified, the power of God."

Ah! my brethren, the Pharisees saw the miracles of this crucified God, and were not converted: this is what we find so hard to understand. But is what takes place in ourselves less difficult to

---

* "Quia Dominus regnavit a ligno." S. Justin Martyr accused the Jews of erasing from Psalm xcvi. (Vulg. xcv.) 10, the words, "from the tree." Cf. Dial. Tryph. § 73.

understand? For we actually see a miracle of the death of Jesus Christ still greater, a continual miracle, a miracle which is admitted and is indisputable, I mean the triumph of His cross; the world converted, the world become Christian, the world sanctified by His cross: "I, if I be lifted up from the earth, will draw all men unto Me." We see it, and our faith, notwithstanding this miracle, is always languishing and tottering. This is what ought to make us weep and tremble. But, that this mystery may benefit us, let us, instead of trembling and weeping through a feeling of passing and shallow devotion, let us tremble and weep in a spirit of healthful remorse. Jesus Christ in dying worked miracles; He must work yet one more which ought to be the crown of all the others—namely, the miracle of our conversion. He clove the rocks, opened the tombs, rent the veil of the Temple. The sight of His cross must cleave our hearts, which are, it may be, as hard as stones; it must open our consciences, which are, it may be, as firmly closed as the tombs; it must rend our flesh, that flesh of sin, with the stern discipline of penitence. For why shall this dying God not convert us, since He converted the authors of His death? And when shall He convert us, if not on this great day, when His blood flows abundantly for our salvation and our sanctification?

Sinners, you who are listening to me, this is what ought to fill you with confidence. Whilst you are sinners, you are as sinners the enemies of Jesus Christ; you are His persecutors, shall I say? But, since it is only repeating what S. Paul said, why should I not say it? You are even His executioners. For, as often as you yield to temptation, and commit sin, you crucify afresh within yourselves this Saviour. But recollect that the blood of this God-Man had the power to blot out even the sin of the Jews who shed it:* "The blood of Christ was so poured forth, that it could blot out the very sin by which it was poured forth." In that, says S. Augustine, appeared the all-divine power of the redemption of Jesus Christ. It is in that He appeared a Saviour. Of His enemies He made His elect people, He made of His persecutors saints; all sinful as you are, have you not the right to claim His mercy? Draw near to the throne of grace, that is His cross; but draw near to it with contrite and humble hearts, with hearts submissive and purified from the corruption of the world, with teachable hearts, susceptible of all the impressions of the heavenly spirit; for such is the miracle which God the Saviour wishes to work in you to-day by the power of His cross. Your return to God, a perfect return, after such long straying; your penitence, an exemplary penitence, after so many irregularities and causes of offence; your profession of amendment, an open and public profession to live as Christians, after having so long lived as libertines: that is the miracle which will prove that Jesus Christ crucified is personally the

---

* "Christi sanguis sic fusus est, ut ipsum peccatum potuerit delere quo fusus est."—S. AUGUSTINE.

Strength and Power of God. Ah! Lord, shall I be fortunate enough to obtain the visible accomplishment of this miracle in my hearers, as it was in fact accomplished in the soldiers who were present at Thy death, and several of whom attached themselves to Thee as the Author of their salvation? Wilt thou, Lord, bless my words sufficiently for that; and may I hope that among those who hear me, some will be touched as deeply as was the centurion, and go forth from this sermon not only softened, but converted; not only bathed in tears, but to begin to glorify God by their works; not only persuaded but sanctified, and filled with the Christian feelings with which that first truth ought to impress them. Let the unbelieving Jew be offended at the cross; Jesus Christ dying is the Might and Strength of the Incarnate God: "Christ crucified, the power of God," this you have seen. Let the Gentile mock, and let him treat the cross as foolishness; Jesus Christ dying is the Wisdom of God Himself, " Christ crucified, the wisdom of God," this you are going to see in the second part.

II. However just, however holy, however irreproachable God may be in His plans and in their execution, we must not be astonished that man, by reason of his ignorance and his pride, has often undertaken to find fault with the Lord's works, and that he is rash enough to be offended at them. The thoughts of man and those of God being, as the Scripture says, so opposed as they are since the intervention of sin, this offence was an almost necessary consequence. What ought to surprise us most is that, by an extreme blindness, man should be offended against God even for His very acts of kindness, for the marvels of His love, and for the abundance and excess of His mercies. For that, Christians, is the frightful confusion which S. Gregory* deplored in those excellent words of his sixth homily on the Gospels: "For the very reason, which ought rather to have made him a debtor to the Saviour, man assumed an attitude of offence towards Him." That is the confusion into which the heretic Marcion fell, when, under the pretext of a false zeal for the Son of God, he would not believe that this Son of God had truly suffered on the cross, nor that he had truly died there; as if the cross and death had been altogether unworthy of the majesty and holiness of God. To testify against which error God raised up Tertullian, who combated it vigorously and became in that way the defender of the sufferings and Passion of Jesus Christ; and it is an error which, notwithstanding the establishment of Christianity, is perhaps only too common in the present day, and against which it is my duty to employ here all the might of the Word of God. Please to give me your attention again. The mystery of a crucified God appears to be a folly to the worldly as well as to the Gentiles, "to the Gentiles foolishness:" and S. Paul maintains on the contrary that, in respect to the predestinated and the elect, it is pre-eminently the mystery of the wisdom of God: "But

---

* "Inde homo adversus Salvatorem scandalum sumpsit, unde ei magis debitor esse debuit."

unto them which are called . . . . Christ crucified, the wisdom of God." But let us see which of the two has judged better, the Apostle or the worldling: the Apostle, after having been instructed about it in a wholly miraculous manner by the Saviour Himself; the worldling, who knows and understands nothing more about it than flesh and blood have revealed to him. Let us see if in this mystery of the cross, so far above our reason as it seems, there be in reality anything which does violence to our reason. For to-day God is willing not to reject the judgment of our reason, and, provided that our reason be not prejudiced nor obstinate, He does not refuse to admit it into the counsel of His wisdom, and to reply to the difficulties it may suggest.

But what was God's purpose in the great mystery that we are celebrating? It included, says S. Leo, two things equally difficult and equally necessary; the satisfaction of a God offended at, and dishonoured by, the sin of man, and the restoration of man who had been perverted and corrupted. This was why Jesus Christ was sent, and the end He kept in view until He had completed His mission. But, I ask you, could He, God as He is, in order that He might accomplish this twofold purpose, have adopted a more powerful, a more efficacious, a surer means than the cross? And could we, with all our pretended reason, imagine any other means whereby the balance should have been kept, I will not say more exactly, but in such due proportions? Let us go to Calvary, and, witnessing what takes place there, let us consider our religion, the height and depth whereof, which S. Paul wished to be able to understand, there present themselves to us. God must be satisfied, and no other than a God-Man could satisfy Him; even reason must agree to that. What did that God-Man do? Ah, Christians! what did He not do to pay our debts? What care did He omit in choosing that which might in a singular and sovereign manner fulfil the measure of satisfaction which God expected, and had a right to expect? In what did the offence towards God consist? In that man, forgetting himself, had affected to be like God: "Ye shall be as gods." And I, said the God-Man, I, who am not only like God, but equal and of one substance with God, by a very different kind of self-forgetfulness, will humble Myself below all men; I will become rejected of men, a worm of the earth, and not a man: for these are the very words which the prophet represents Him as speaking from the cross: "But as for Me, I am a worm and no man." Can we imagine a more thorough reparation? Man, revolting against God, had shaken off the yoke of obedience, and broken his Sovereign's command, and I, said the God-Man, independent as I am by Myself, I will reduce Myself to the most painful and humiliating subjection; I will make Myself obedient: "He became obedient," obedient even unto death, and that death the death of the cross. Not only will I obey God, but men, even the most criminal, the most vicious, the most sacrilegious of men, who are My persecutors and executioners. Not only will I obey the decrees of Heaven, which are always wise and just, but those of earth which are full of injustice and cruelty. Not only will I obey powers which have no lawful authority over Me, but powers which are banded against Me, powers which oppress Me; and by that voluntary subjection I will do away with the crime of man, rebellious to the law of his Creator. It was for that same reason, says S. Bernard, that He would not come down from the cross, having preferred, remarks that Father, to leave the Jews in their unbelief rather than convince them by a miracle of His own will, choosing rather to accomplish His Father's order and to obey, than to convert and save them by not obeying. Man, urged by sinful want of self-restraint, in tasting the fruit of that tree had indulged his senses with a forbidden pleasure; and I, said the God-Man, who have at My command all the delights of life, and need not refuse Myself any one of them, present Myself to My Father as a Man of Sorrows, a victim of penitence, a Lamb appointed for the most cruel sacrifice. For it was in His Holy Passion that, animated with a fervent zeal for the glory and interests of God, He conceived and executed this purpose: " Sacrifice and offering Thou wouldest not, but a body hast Thou prepared Me: in burnt-offerings and sacrifices for sin Thou hast had no pleasure. Then said I, Lo, I come." O my God, no longer dost Thou wish, said He, in His inmost heart, at the moment of His crucifixion; as, according to S. Paul's testimony, He said on His coming into the world (and Christians, I would have you mark this well, for it explains the hidden purpose of this mystery); "sacrifice and offering Thou wouldest not, but a body hast Thou prepared Me." The sacrifices of animals have ceased to be acceptable to Thee; that is why I have said, "Lo, I come;" I offer Myself in sacrifice. Words worthy of reverence, and which, to the very letter, ought to be understood of what took place on Calvary, since it is there that Jesus Christ as High Priest put an end to the sacrifices of the old Law by the consummation of the sacrifice of the law of grace; there that— the cross serving Him for an altar—by a solemn rite, He presented His Divine Person; there that He offered, no longer the blood of bulls and goats, but His own blood; and to speak simply and exactly, there that He disposed Himself to satisfy God, no longer by other things, but by Himself, and at His own expense. That is what I call the work of the wisdom of a God.

I have not yet said enough; for I add that the Saviour of men has made us understand completely what was of itself incomprehensible, and what without Him we should have never known. And what is that? We should never have known what God is, what sin is, what salvation is; three things, to understand which man ought to employ all his wisdom; three things, the knowledge of which was for you and for me essentially connected with the mystery of Jesus Christ dying upon the cross. What is God? A being for whose glory it was necessary that a God-Man should be humbled and emptied of glory even to enduring the cross. That is the idea I form of Him to-day; all things else do not make me know God sufficiently; all that I discover in Nature, all that theology tells me about Him, all that the Scriptures teach me, all that the light of glory will reveal to me about Him —these are in reality only shadows. It is on Calvary where faith, as in the full light of day, shows me God as He is in all His greatness, because I there see a God-Man sacrificed, that I recognize what He is; and God Himself—shall I venture to say it?—has no more sublime idea of the Divinity of His Being than that of deserving to be glorified by the cross of a God-Man; I say more, that He can have no more sublime idea of it, than that His Divinity could not be satisfied except by the cross of a God-Man. What is sin? An evil for the expiation of which it was necessary that a God-Man should be made a curse, and become an object of malediction: "He was made a curse for us." That is what the mystery of the cross preaches to me. I did not understand how sin could draw down upon us such terrible chastisements; and setting myself up for a censor of the decrees of God, I demanded from Him the reason of that frightful eternity of pain that His justice prepares for the reprobate souls in hell; but my ignorance came from not having well considered the mystery of Jesus Christ dying, for the death of a God, appointed as a necessary means for doing away with sin, made me understand but too well what a just proportion there is between sin, which is an offence against God, and an eternity of unhappiness, which is the punishment of the creature. The one admitted, I no longer find any difficulty in the other, and convinced by the reasoning of Jesus Christ Himself: "If they do these things in a green tree what shall be done in the dry?" If I, the Son, who am innocent, be thus treated, what may the slave and the guilty man expect? I am no longer astonished at the severity of God's judgments, nor at the excess of His vengeance; but I am astonished at my own astonishment. What is the salvation of man? A benefit which has cost a God His life, and for which a God-Man did not think that He was giving too much, or was too lavish when He sacrificed Himself.

That is the great lesson which this Divine Master expiring on the cross teaches me. I counted this salvation for nothing, neglected it, endangered it, risked the loss of it; a vain interest, a false honour, a moment of pleasure, of the most shameful pleasure, made me cast it aside. But draw near, said the voice of the Blood of this crucified God to me, draw near, and by My sufferings, teach thyself the value of thy soul; thou esteemest thyself, but thou dost not yet esteem thyself enough. Contemplate thyself in Me; thou wilt see what thou art, and what thou art worth. It is by Me that thou oughtest to measure thyself: for I am thy price: and this salvation which thou renouncest on so many occasions is nothing less than what I am Myself, since I give up Myself to assure this salvation to thee. It is thus, I say that He speaks to me. Now that alone would be enough to make me conclude with S. Paul that the mystery of the cross is the mystery of Divine Wisdom. For, as S. Chrysostom reasons, a mystery, which gives me high ideas of God, a mystery which inspires me with an infinite horror of sin, a mystery which makes me, on whichever side I regard it,

F

prize my own salvation in preference to all other past, present, future and even possible advantages, ought to be for me a mystery of wisdom. Thoughts so reasonable, so lofty, so sublime cannot emanate from a false and deceitful source: only wisdom, the wisdom of a God, can give them to me. And that is why the Apostle of the Gentiles, filled with the faith of this mystery, made the profession, but an open profession that He would fain be ignorant of everything else except Jesus, Jesus crucified: "I determined not to know anything among you, save Jesus Christ, and Him crucified." For in Jesus crucified he found in an excellent degree the sum of all that he ought to know, and all that it was his interest to know, that is to say, the eminent knowledge of God and the healthful knowledge of self. But with these two kinds of knowledge, he rightly thought that he could dispense with all other knowledge: "For I determined not to know anything among you, save Jesus Christ, and Him crucified."

But let us probe more deeply a truth so edifying, and let us unfold the second motive of the mission of Jesus Christ and of His function of Saviour. After having satisfied God, there lay on Him the task of reforming man, who was not only fallen into disorder, but into the extremity and the abyss of all disorders. This disorder of man, says the beloved disciple S. John, comes from three sources; the lust of the eyes, the lust of the flesh, and the pride of life; that is, from an insatiable thirst for temporal advantages, a passionate striving for the honours of the world, and an inordinate attachment to pleasures of sense. The problem was how to heal ourselves of these three great sicknesses; and here are the remedies that the Son of God has brought us from heaven, and which He presents to us in His Passion to-day; the stripping off of all things and His nakedness in death, against the love of wealth and the cupidity which consumes us; the excessive abasement to which He stooped, against the ambitious schemes which devour us; the austerities inflicted on flesh of virgin purity, made to bleed and lacerated with blows, against the enervation and sensuality which corrupt us; sure and infallible remedies, remedies which it only remains for us to apply and to take advantage of, remedies in which is apparent all the wisdom of the Physician who has prepared them for us. Do not let us prejudice ourselves, and let us this once do ourselves justice, that we may for ever do justice to God. Is it not clear, my dear listeners, that the mystery of the cross is essentially opposed to these three principles whence flow all the irregularities of our life? Is it not clear that this mystery alone condemns all your acts of injustice, of violence, of hatred, all your offensive habits, all your wantonness and dissipation; and may we not therefore gather that it is a mystery in which the wisdom of God has presided? That which moderates our desires, regulates our passions, confounds our pride, snatches self-love out of our hearts, in a word, that which corrects all our vices and keeps us in order, must it not be the effect of order, and consequently of that supreme wisdom which is in God? What would happen, said the learned

Pic de la Mirande, if men by one consent agreed together to live according to the examples that Jesus Christ gave them, and the lessons which He taught them in His Passion, so that this crucified God should be the universal rule whereby the world governed itself in its practices? To what height of perfection would not the world, which to-day is so corrupt, find itself suddenly raised? In what modesty would it keep the great, and to what submission would it inspire in those of no reputation, to be living constantly in sight of, and to keep their eyes fixed on the cross! Would the rich abuse their riches, and would the poor complain of their poverty? Would those who suffer turn against God in their sufferings, and would those who count themselves the fortunate ones of the world forget God, by forgetting themselves in their prosperity? Should we see vengeance and treason in human society? Would the spirit of interest reign there? Would jealousy and ambition cause divisions and troubles there? Would good faith and uprightness be banished thence? In proportion as men are irregular in their lives now, so would their conduct then be wise and straightforward, and their life innocent and pure.

But why must Jesus Christ, who was not subject to our evils, experience in His own person the remedies for them? Ah! my brethren, replies S. Augustine, these remedies being as bitter as they are, could He do better than experience them in His own person, so as to soften them for us and persuade us to make use of them? But for that, could we ever have tasted them? and, to induce us to adopt them, did we not need the example of a God? Let us suppose that God-Man had chosen for our salvation, instead of the cross, all the sweetnesses of life; what advantage would our self-love, the source of all corruption, have drawn from that, and to what a degree it would have prevailed! Should I then have presumed to advise you, as I do to-day, to practise mortification of the senses, crucifixion of the flesh, self-renunciation, the humility of penitence? Would you listen to me? And would not the mere idea of your God in the brightness of honour and pleasure have formed an insurmountable prejudice against all my reasons? But what strength, too, does this example of a God dying on the cross give to my ministry and my words! And with what authority do I now say you must be humble, mortified, detached from the world, which otherwise I should only have said trembling and despairing to be believed? But was it not then an act of God's wisdom to furnish the ministers of Jesus Christ and the preachers of His Gospel with an argument to close your mouth, when they preach to you on the most difficult duties of your religion; was it not an act of His wisdom to render you powerless to answer them, when they reprove you for the extreme repugnance you show as to the practice of these duties? Yet why correct excesses by other excesses? The excesses of man by the excesses of God? But I say, what wisdom it shows to have corrected the excesses of malice by those of perfection, the excesses of iniquity by those of holiness, the excesses of ingratitude by those of love! To wean man from the extreme of the vices into which he had fallen, must we not make him lean towards the extreme of the opposite virtues? Could he, in the violence of his passion, have always maintained the happy medium? and, to extinguish in him the fire of avarice, ambition, and impurity, was it not necessary to make him love poverty, humiliation, and austerity? Again, to save us perfectly, it was not enough for Jesus Christ to come and tell us that these three lusts would be our destruction, He must needs come in a state which should pledge us to combat them, to contradict them, to pluck them out of our hearts. They destroyed us only, inasmuch as they seduced our reason and infected our heart; and if we had always preserved the love and esteem of these lusts, we should only be half saved. It was necessary therefore that the virtues opposed to these wretched lusts should become to us not only endurable, but lovable, precious and honourable. But, for that end, what more wonderful means could the Word of God find, than to consecrate them in His own Person, so that, as S. Augustine* appropriately remarks, the humility of man might have the humility of a God for its stay and support against the attacks and insults of pride?

That is too much, Christians, I do not say to convince, but one day to confound our reason in the judgment of God; and may it please Heaven that that judgment of God, by which our reason ought to be convinced of its errors and confounded,

---

* "Ut humilitas humana contra insultantem sibi superbiam divinae humilitatis patrocinio fulciretur."

be not already commenced as far as we are concerned! For this very day this dying Saviour is invested with the right of the judging of the world, and the cross was the first tribunal on which He appeared, pronouncing against men or in favour of men sentences of life or of death. This is not a private opinion such as piety inspires in me, but a truth which faith teaches me, when I tell you that the judgment of the world commenced at the same moment in which the Passion of Jesus Christ commenced, since it is thus that He expresses Himself to His Apostles: "Now is the judgment of this world." It is not to inspire us with groundless fear, that we are told that the cross to which that God-Man was fixed will at the end of the ages be brought forward as the rule of God's judgment towards us and towards all men. "Then shall appear the sign of the Son of Man." Terrible thought for a worldling! It is the cross of Jesus Christ which shall judge me: that cross which is such an enemy to my passions; that cross which I have honoured only in theory, but from which I have always shrunk in practice; that cross of which I have never made any use, and of which in respect to myself I have made void the merits. It is that cross with which I shall be ever confronted. "Then shall appear the sign of the Son of Man." All which will not be found conformed to it will bear the stamp and seal of reprobation. But what features of resemblance can I discover between this cross and my wantonness, between this cross and my foolish vanities, between this cross and my sensual life? Ah! Lord, shall I then be condemned by the greatest of Thy favours and by the very pledge of my salvation? And will that which ought to reconcile me to Thee only serve to render me more guilty and more hateful in Thy sight? But, on the other hand, consoling thought for a faithful and righteous soul: it is the cross of Jesus Christ which shall decide my lot; that cross in which I have placed all my confidence, that cross which has strengthened me, and which still strengthens me in all my troubles; that cross, the symbol of which I reverence before this altar, but of which I myself would be a living symbol. God crucified, receive my homage, accept the feelings of my heart, and grant that Thy cross, after having been the subject of my veneration, and still more the object of my adoration, may for ever be to me a sign of benediction.

III.

S. LUKE xxiii. 27, 28.—" There followed Him a great company of people, and of women, which also bewailed and lamented Him. But Jesus turning unto them said, Daughters of Jerusalem, weep not for Me, but weep for yourselves and for your children."

Is it true then that the majestic, but sad, mystery of the Passion of Jesus Christ, whatever thought faith gives us of it, is not the most touching object which ought to occupy our minds and arouse our grief? Is it true that our tears can be employed in a more holy or more useful way than in bewailing the death of the God-Man? Is it true that another more pressing and necessary duty suspends, as it were, the obligation imposed upon us to sympathize most tenderly with the sufferings of our Divine Redeemer? We should never have thought it; and yet it is Jesus Christ, who, as a last proof of the most generous and disinterested charity which ever was—Jesus Christ, on his way to Calvary, where He was to die for us—bids us bewail something else rather than His death: " Weep not for Me, but weep for yourselves." S. Ambrose, when pronouncing the funeral oration over the young Emperor Valentian, in the presence of all the people of Milan, believed he had well acquitted himself of his task, and had fully satisfied the expectations of his hearers, when he exhorted them* to show, by the tribute of their tears, what they owed to the memory of that incomparable prince, who had exposed his life, and had lost it for their sake. But I, who have to set before you in this sermon the painful death of a Divine Saviour of men, am constrained to address you in a very different manner. Instead of borrowing the words of S. Ambrose, which seem naturally to fit my subject, I ought to say to you on the contrary: No, my brethren, do not give the expiring Son of God tears for which He does not ask. Those tears which you would pour forth are precious; treasure them up carefully; you will need them for a more important matter than you think. Not merely does Jesus Christ permit you not to bewail His death, but He expressly forbids your doing so, if to bewail it shall hinder you from bewailing another evil which more nearly concerns you, and which is, indeed, more deplorable than even the death of the Son of God. I know that all creation became or appeared affected by it, that the sun was darkened, the earth quaked, that the veil of the temple was rent, the rocks split asunder, graves opened, and the ashes of the dead breathed again, that the whole earth was moved; but man alone, I repeat, is dispensed from this duty, if only he acquit himself of another less tender in appearance, but in reality more substantial. Let us leave then to the stars and elements, or, if you wish to associate intelligent

---

* "Solvamus bono principi stipendarias lacrymas, qui pro nobis etiam vitae stipendium solvit."

creatures with them, let us leave to the happy angels the care of honouring with tokens of mourning the death of Jesus Christ.* "These angels of peace," says Isaiah, "have wept bitterly for it." As for us, for whom God's purpose is different, instead of weeping for Jesus Christ, let us weep with Jesus Christ, let us weep like Jesus Christ, let us weep for that which made Him weep; it is thus that we shall sanctify our tears, and that they will be beneficial to us. Adorable cross, we shed them before you, and you will communicate to them that heavenly virtue, and that character of holiness which you received when you received in your arms the Saint of saints. Full of confidence, we have recourse to you, and with the whole Church we salute you:

> "O Tree of Glory, Tree most fair,
> Ordained those holy limbs to bear,
> How bright in purple robe it stood,
> The purple of a Saviour's blood."

There is an evil greater in the sight of God than the death of the Son of God; an evil to be wept for more than all that He suffered; an evil which has more right to our tears than has the Passion of the God-Man. You are too enlightened, Christian brethren, not at once to understand what it is: it is sin. Of all possible things, sin is the only one which concerns us more than the sufferings of Jesus Christ; the only thing which could justify that speech of the Saviour: "Weep not for Me, but weep for yourselves." To obey this command of

---

* Isa. xxxiii. 7. Vulg. "Angeli pacis amare flebunt."

our Divine Master, and to profit by such important advice, let us consider to-day the mystery of His holy Passion, only to weep for the disorder of our sins, and let us weep for the disorder of our sins only in the sight of the mystery of His holy Passion. If Jesus Christ had suffered independently of our sin, His Passion, severe as it was for Him, would no longer have had in it anything so frightful for us; and if our sin had had no connection with the sufferings of Jesus Christ, sin though it is, it would be less hateful to us. It is, then, by sin that we ought to measure the inestimable benefit of the Passion of the Son of God; and it is by the inestimable benefit of the Passion of the Son of God that we ought to measure the grievousness of sin.

Note well the three points that I put forth, and which will form the divisions of this sermon. Sin was the essential cause of the Passion of Jesus Christ; sin is a constant renewing of the Passion of Jesus Christ; lastly, sin makes the Passion of Jesus Christ of none effect. In three words:—

(1) The Passion of Jesus Christ caused by sin;

(2) The Passion of Jesus Christ renewed by sin;

(3) The Passion of Jesus Christ rendered useless and even hurtful by sin.

That is what deserves all our tears and demands all our attention.

What is to-day set before us by faith is something very marvellous in the order of Nature, to wit, a Divine Sufferer; but I am bold enough to say that this marvel, surprising as it is, is not to be compared with that which faith discovers to us in the order of grace, when it puts before our eyes a

Divine Penitent. Such, nevertheless (oh, the depth of the counsel of God!), is the character which the Saviour of the world has willed to assume, and which He has supported in such a holy and consistent manner all through His adorable Passion. Such is the mystery that we are celebrating: and, because, according to Scripture, true penitence consists chiefly of two things, contrition which makes us hate sin, and satisfaction which makes amends for sin, when I speak of a Divine Penitent, I mean a God touched with the most lively contrition at the sight of the sin of man; and I mean a God making satisfaction for the sin of man at His own expense and with strict justice. From the first moment of His life Jesus Christ burdened Himself with these two obligations, and you will see how exactly He acquitted Himself of them on the day of His Passion. For see how these two conditions were fulfilled by this Mediator between God and men in two scenes to which I wish to direct your attention: His agony in the Garden and His death on Calvary. The Garden of the Agony, it is there that I am going to show you a contrite God, keenly alive to all the bitterness of sin: the Cross of Calvary, it is there that I am going to ask you to contemplate in His person a God offered to atone for sin. Hence, we may conclude with S. Leo that the Passion of the Son of God was a universal penitence, a public and authentic penitence, a perfect and complete penitence for all the sins of men: and we may conclude too that the sins of men have caused that Passion. What more is needed to compel you and me to shed tears, not because of our empty or barren compassion, but because of our efficacious and holy compunction? "Weep not for Me, but weep for yourselves." Let us attend, beginning with the inner griefs of Jesus Christ, so as to learn what it is that we ought always to lament.

Hardly had He entered the garden whither He went to pray before He fell into a profound sadness. He "began to be sorrowful." The feeling was so piercing that He could not hide it. He made it known to His disciples: "My soul is exceeding sorrowful, even unto death." Fear seized Him: loneliness overwhelmed Him: by His struggle against Himself, He already suffered a kind of agony beforehand; and by the violence of that struggle His sweat was even unto blood. What is the meaning of all that, asks S. Chrysostom, in a God who was strength Himself, and whose apparent weaknesses could only be so many miracles of His almighty charity? What does He fear? What troubles Him? Why is this soul overwhelmed, which, enjoying in other respects the clear sight of God, did not cease to be filled with the pure joys of blessedness? Whence that internal war, and that rising of the passions in a spirit incapable of being influenced by other motives than those of sovereign reason? Ah, Christians, that is the very point on which we must meditate, a point that we can never understand too well for our edification. For, to say that the Saviour of the world was in agony only because He was about to die; to say that the shame of the cross alone, or the harshness of the punishment that was awaiting Him caused in Him this agitation, this aversion, these mortal fears, this would not be a very high opinion to entertain of the Passion of God. No, no, my brethren, continues S. Chrysostom, that is not the reason why this great soul was so troubled. The cross that Jesus Christ had chosen as the instrument of our redemption, did not appear to Him so terrible an object. That cross which was to be the foundation of His glory did not become to Him a source of shame. The cup which His Father had given Him, and which for that very reason was so precious, was not the bitter cup of which He manifested so much horror, and it was not the nearness of the mysterious baptism of His death which made every limb of His body sweat blood. For, however terrible that baptism of blood was to be, He Himself had earnestly wished for it, and had sought it with a holy eagerness. He had said to His Apostles: "I have a baptism to be baptized with: and how am I straitened till it be accomplished." It was then something else than the presence of death which caused these feelings of desolateness and consternation. And what else? I have already pointed out to you what it was: but, O Lord, in order to imprint it well on both the minds and the hearts of those who are listening to me, I need all the zeal with which Thou wert consumed. What was it? I ask: sin, the only thing opposed to God, the only evil capable of saddening the God-Man, and of making of that God of Glory a suffering and penitent God. Christians, lift up your minds above all human thoughts, and once more fix them on that great truth. This is a faithful exposition of it taken from the Fathers of the Church, but especially from S. Augustine.

For, whilst the chief priests and Pharisees were holding a council in the house of Caiaphas, and were preparing to overwhelm Him with false accusations and imaginary crimes, Jesus Christ Himself in the Garden, bowing in lowly submission before His Father, regarded Himself, yet without prejudice to His innocence, as loaded with real crimes. In this He fulfilled exactly the words of Isaiah: "God hath laid on Him the iniquity of us all." But in consequence of this transference of our guilt by God the Father to His adorable Son, this Just One, who had never known sin, found Himself covered with the sins of all nations, the sins of every age, the sins of every state and condition of life. Yes, all the sacrileges which should ever be committed, and which His infinite foreknowledge distinctly showed to Him beforehand, all the blasphemies which should be uttered against Heaven, all the abominations which should make earth blush, all the causes of offence which should break forth in the universe, all the monsters that hell should produce, and the dreadful deeds of which men would be authors, came in a crowd to afflict Him, even then, with excruciating torture. Who tells us all this? He, Himself, the only witness and only judge of what He suffered in that cruel terror. He tells us: for, according to S. Augustine, it is of Jesus Christ in His own Person that we must understand the words of the Psalm:

> "The snares of death compassed me round about:
> And the pains of hell gat hold upon me."

It was, then, in view of this happy, and at the

same time this sad moment, that Jeremiah prophetically said of Jesus : * " Thy contrition is great like the sea." Ah, Lord, Thy grief is like a vast sea, of which men can neither sound the depth, nor measure the immensity. It was to swell that sea, and make it larger that all the sins of men, as the Scripture says, flowed like rivers into the soul of the Son of God ; for it is still of His Passion and of the excess of His sadness that we must explain the passage, " Save me, O God ; for the waters are come in, even unto my soul," with this difference, however, in the comparison, that whereas the rivers which flow into the sea are there mingled and lost, so that it is no longer possible to distinguish one from another; here, on the contrary, in that abyss of sins and in that sea of griefs with which the soul of the Saviour was inundated—He discerned without confusion and without any blending all the classes of sins for which He was going to suffer; the sins of kings and those of the people ; the sins of the rich and those of the poor ; the sins of the fathers and those of the children ; the sins of the clergy and those of the laity. In this flood of iniquity He disentangled slanders and calumnies, immodesties and adulteries, simonies and usuries, treasons and revenges. He pictured to Himself, but with all the vividness of His divine penetration, the tempers of the proud and the ambitious, the dissoluteness of the libertines and evil livers, the impieties of atheists, the impostures and the malice of hypocrites. Can we be astonished if

---

* Lam. ii. 13, Vulg. "Magna est velut mare contritio tua."

all that, according to the metaphor of the Holy Spirit, deluged His happy soul so that it remained overwhelmed in it, and if, in the pangs of His heart, and in His sadness, caused by His zeal for God and His charity for us, this flood of waters was followed by a sweat of blood?

Here, Christians, is what I call the contrition of a God and the first act of His penitence. Do we look at sin in this way? And is the grief which we feel for sin in proportion to its effects? Let us enter to-day into the secret of our consciences, and, profiting by the model which God places before us, let us see if our dispositions in Christian penitence reach far enough to make it effectual. Do we look at sin in this way? I ask. Have we the same horror of it? Does it disturb our peace of mind? Are we distressed at it? In the estimation which we form of sin, do we regard it in some sense a punishment to Jesus Christ? Do we dread it, as Jesus Christ did, more than all the evils of the world? Does it reduce us by remorse for it to a kind of agony? Ah, my brothers, exclaims S. Chrysostom, touched with that comparison, that is the great disorder with which we have to reproach ourselves, and which we ought ever to bewail. A God is troubled at the sight of our sin, and we are unmoved; a God afflicts Himself because of it, and we console ourselves; for that reason a God is humiliated, and we walk with head erect; a God sweats until blood exudes, and we shed not a single tear for our sins; it is this which ought to terrify us. We sin, and, far from being sorrowful unto death on that account, perhaps after we sin we again insult the justice and providence of God, and like the wicked man, say within ourselves: "I have sinned, and what harm hath happened unto me?" Am I less at my ease on that account? Does the world think less of me? Have I less credit and authority? Hence comes that false peace, so directly opposed to the agony of the Son of God; that peace which men enjoy who are in the most frightful of states—the state of sin. Although enemies of God, we still appear contented. It is not merely that we pretend to be contented, but we are capable of being so, going to such a length as to throw ourselves into the dissipations and frivolous joys of the age. But such a peace as this is to be reprobated; it can only come from our hardness of heart; it is peace a thousand times more deadly than all the other penalties of sin; it is in a sense worse than sin itself. Hence springs that false confidence which stands in such contrast with the holy fear of Jesus Christ; presumptuous confidence which makes us bold where the God-Man trembled; which makes us hope everything where He believed we ought to fear everything; which flatters us with a mercy, and which falsely assures us of a patience from God on which He did not reckon. Mercy ill understood, a weak and imaginary patience which would not profit, but which, in fact, by the way we abuse it, only serves to encourage sin within us. Hence that boldness of the sinner, and, if I may employ the word, that effrontery which never blushes, and which seems so monstrous when we put it side by side with the uneasiness of Jesus Christ. After sinning against God, we are no less proud before men. We bear our sins with haughtiness, and, far from feeling any confusion because of them, we glory in them, we praise ourselves, and are puffed up because of them, we triumph in them. Yet this is what obliged the Divine Word to empty Himself of His glory. The shameful insolence of some sinners could be repaired by nothing less than the humiliation of Jesus Christ; the blind rashness of so many libertines could be expiated by nothing less than the fear which Jesus Christ suffered; the indifference of so many souls insensible of guilt needed no less a remedy than the holy sensitiveness of Jesus Christ. To the end that God might receive the satisfaction He ought to receive; to the end that sin might for once be detested as much as it was detestable, it was necessary that once some one should feel a grief corresponding to its malignity. Now there was none but the God-Man who could measure that proportion, because there was none but He who could know perfectly in all its extent the malignity of sin; and consequently there was none but He who could make us learn to hate sin. It is for that very purpose that He came into the world, and that in the days of His mortal life, as S. Paul says, He offered with tears His prayers and supplications to Him who could save Him from death, thus giving us the most excellent example of Christian penitence. If, then, we devote ourselves to penitence with sluggish hearts, cold hearts, unfeeling and hard hearts, let us not doubt, my brethren, concludes S. Bernard, but that it is to us our Saviour addresses these words to-day, " Weep not for Me, but weep for yourselves."

Do you, indeed, know what it is which will add most to our condemnation in the judgment of God? Not our sins, but our pretended contritions; those languid contritions which are so far removed from the earnestness of the great penitent, Jesus Christ; these shallow contritions, in which there is no sacrifice of will, no curbing of the heart, no restraining of our pleasures; but in the midst of which we revel in all the delights and comforts of society; those imaginary contritions which, inasmuch as they do not afflict us, do not convert us. If we were moved by the spirit of faith, a single sin would be sufficient to disconcert all the powers of our soul, to throw us into the same fright that Cain endured, to make us lament as Esau did, when he saw himself shut out from his inheritance and deprived of his father's blessing; sufficient to make us shudder like the king of Babylon when he caught sight of the hand which wrote his doom; or better still, according to the words of the Apostle, to make us feel in the depth of our heart what Jesus Christ felt in Himself: "Let this mind be in you, which was also in Christ Jesus." But since habitual sin has little by little changed our hearts into hearts of stone, that which appalled Jesus Christ astonishes us no more, that which aroused all His emotions concerns us no more. Ah! Lord, said David, and we ought to say it with him: "heal my soul." But to heal my soul completely, heal its weak and imperfect contritions, those contritions which make its wounds still more incurable, instead of closing them. "Heal the contritions thereof, for it shaketh." But it is not enough that it be shaken;

it must be converted by the invincible strength of the example and the penitence of God. Let us conform ourselves to this model; sinners though we be, we shall find grace with God. Keeping this model ever before our eyes, the penitence we have so often abused will become to us a source of health. It will no longer be for us, as it has so often been, an empty ceremony; it will be a true return, a true change, a true conversion. It has been said, and it is true, that the grief for sin to be accepted in this sacrament, ought to have qualifications as rare as they are necessary; that the grief ought to be supernatural, unconditional, sincere, strong, thorough; that God ought to be the origin, the aim, the end; that it ought to exceed every other grief, and that, sin being the sovereign evil, it ought to make us abhor sin above every other evil; that there is no possible sin which it ought not to shut out, no temptation which it ought not to have strength to surmount, no opportunity to sin which it ought not to be able to make us avoid, and that, failing in but one of these qualifications, it is nothing but a vain and unreal contrition. But I tell you to-day that all these qualifications together are included in the contrition of Jesus Christ, I tell you that to assure yourself of a substantial and perfect contrition, you have only to copy Jesus Christ, applying to yourselves God's word to Moses: "Look that thou make it after the pattern, which was shewed thee in the Mount." If that be not our rule, let us weep on that account, and so much the more bitterly, in that we can only blame ourselves. Hardened as regards our sins, let us weep at least for our want of feeling; let us weep because we weep not, and let us be concerned because we feel no concern. By this means we may attain to true contrition, and by this means we shall begin to be imitators of the Saviour's penitence.

In addition, moreover, to this inner Passion—if I may so call it—which sin at first caused in Him, there is another Passion more obvious to sense, of which sin, in like manner, was the wretched object and the source. For, from the garden in which Jesus Christ prayed, without lingering at present over other points, I am going to Calvary where He died; and there, contemplating in mind this God crucified, the author and finisher of our faith, who, according to the expression of the great Apostle, instead of the happy and peaceful life He might have enjoyed, died by the most cruel and ignominious of deaths, surprised by an event so strange, I venture to ask God the reason of it, I appeal to His wisdom, justice, and goodness, and, Christian as I am, I am very near following the example of the faithless Jew in making of the mystery of my redemption a stumbling-block. Think what it is to see the most innocent of men treated like the worst criminal, and handed over to pitiless executioners. But God, jealous of the glory of His attributes, and interested in destroying a cause of offence in appearance so specious, but in reality as pernicious as that is, well knows how to check my zeal in its commencement; and how does He do this? By showing to me that death is the punishment of my sins; by obliging me to confess that all which took place on Calvary—

horrible as it seems to me—was justly ordered, wisely planned, and carried out in a divine and holy manner. Why so? Because nothing short of this would have been a sufficient punishment for sin, and it is true, as S. Jerome remarks, that if, in the treasures of the wrath of God, He had not had other ways of punishing sin than those approved by our reason, our reason being limited, and sin having in its nature a sort of infinity, God could never have been fully satisfied.

Our mistake, Christian brethren, is that we consider the Saviour of the world to-day by what He was in Himself, and not by what He willed to become for us. We are deceived by regarding His Passion in relation to the Jews, who were only the instruments of it, and not in relation to God, who was the chief agent and sovereign controller of it. In other words, Jesus Christ in Himself is the Saint of saints, the well-beloved of the Father, the object of His affection, the chief of the elect, the fount of all blessings; incarnate holiness. That is why our reason revolts at seeing Him suffer. But we do not consider that at Calvary He ceased, so to speak, to be all that; and instead of these attributes which were for a time veiled and eclipsed, He was, according to the words of Scripture, made "a curse for us," a "propitiation for our sins;" and, since S. Paul has said it, I will repeat it in the same sense, a substitute for sin, and even sin itself: for God "hath made Him to be sin for us, who knew no sin." Now in that state, remarks S. Chrysostom, there was no punishment which was not due to Jesus Christ; humiliations, outrages, scourges, nails, thorns, the cross; all that, in the language of the Apostle, was the wages and desert of sin: and since the Son of God then represented sin, and had undertaken to be treated by His Father as if He were sin itself, it followed naturally that He should experience all the suffering that fell to His lot. If we understand it so, has He suffered too much? No; His charity, says S. Bernard, was full and abundant, but it was not lavish. He is called the Man of sorrows; but, replies Tertullian, it is the name which belongs to Him since He is the Man of sins. We see Him lacerated and bruised with blows, but the number of blows He receives is not out of proportion to the multitude of the crimes He expiates. He is abandoned to wicked, barbarous, and cruel men, who add to His death-warrant all that their rage can suggest; but, though they add to the warrant of Pilate, they add nothing to that of God. They maltreat and insult Him; but sin, if it assumed a substantial form, would deserve to be maltreated and insulted. He dies on the cross—thus is it the spot where sin must be placed. Correct your opinions, then, my brethren, and whilst this Divine Lamb is sacrificed, instead of occupying yourselves with the merit of His holiness and His virtues, remember it is for your open and your hidden offences that He is sacrificed, that it is for your excesses, your indulgences, for the shameful and infamous pleasures to which you are addicted. If you picture Him to yourself such as He is, burdened with all our debts, that scourging to which He was condemned will no longer be a stumbling-block to you; those thorns which lacerated Him will no longer wound the delicacy of your piety; those nails with which they pierced His hands and His feet will no longer excite your indignation. My sin, you will say, self-accusation, deserved all these pains, and since Jesus Christ is clothed with my sin He must bear them all. So, in view of that, the Eternal Father, by a line of conduct no less adorable than stern, forgetting that He is His Son, and looking upon Him as His enemy (pardon all these expressions) declared Himself His persecutor, or rather the chief of His persecutors. The Jews, professing a zeal for religion, in their hatred, subject that sacred body to all the outrages that cruelty can devise; but the cruelty of the Jews was not enough to punish such a man as that—a man covered with the crimes of the whole human race: necessary, says S. Ambrose, that God should interfere in it, and this is what faith makes plain to ourselves.

Yes, Christians, it was God Himself and not the council of the Jews that delivered Jesus Christ to punishment; that Just One, S. Peter said to the Jews, has not been put into your hands as guilty, except by an express order of God and a decree of His wisdom; an announcement which He made in their assembly without fear that they would take advantage of it, and use it to stifle their remorse at the murder of God, which they had committed. It is true that the Pharisees and doctors of the Law had persecuted Jesus Christ to put Him to death; but they had only persecuted Him, O Father, because Thou hadst struck Him the first. This David, by the spirit of prophecy, attests, "They persecute Him, whom Thou hast smitten." Hitherto, they had respected Him; hitherto, enraged though they were, they had not dared to attack His person; but from the moment that Thou didst turn against Him, and by lifting up Thy hand, and pouring forth Thy wrath, gavest the signal, they threw themselves on that innocent prey reserved for their fury. But reserved by whom, if not by Thee, O my God! who in their unholy vengeance didst find Thine holy vengeance accomplished! For it was Thou Thyself, Lord, changed by justice into a cruel God, who didst make, no longer Thy servant Job, but Thine only Son feel the weight of Thine arm. For a long time Thou hadst been awaiting that victim: Thou didst need Him to re-establish Thy glory and satisfy Thy justice: Thou didst think of such a victim: but seeing in the world only vile and sin-stained creatures, weak men, whose actions and sufferings were devoid of merit in Thy sight, Thou didst find Thyself powerless to avenge Thyself. To-day Thou hast the means of satisfying it fully; for behold a victim worthy of Thee, a victim able to atone for the sins of a thousand worlds, a victim such as Thou didst desire, and such as Thou dost deserve. This Saviour attached to the cross is the object which Thy stern justice has prepared for itself. Strike now, Lord, strike; He is prepared to receive Thy blows; and, without regarding Him as Thy Christ, only look on Him to remind Thyself that He is ours, that He is the victim we offer, and that, by the oblation of Him, that hate of Thine is satisfied, even the divine hate with which Thou hatest sin.

God is not contented with striking Him, but seems to wish to cast Him off by forsaking and abandoning Him in the midst of His punishment: "My God, my God, why hast Thou forsaken Me?" This forsaking by God is in some sort the punishment of the damned, which Jesus Christ had to undergo for us all, as S. Paul says. The reprobation of mankind would have been inadequate to punish sin in the full extent of its evil consequences; something more was needed, and that something (if I may be permitted to use the term, and you will understand how I use it—in no Calvinistic sense), that something was the visible reprobation of the God-Man, His reprobation fulfilling the measure of the curse, and of the punishment due to sin. You have said, O prophet, that you "have never seen the just forsaken;" but here is a memorable example which you cannot gainsay: Jesus Christ abandoned by His Heavenly Father, and scarcely daring any more to claim Him as Father, calling Him only His God: "My God, My God, why hast Thou forsaken Me?" Nevertheless, do not be offended at it, since, after all, God has throughout only acted according to the rules of equity. No, concludes S. Augustine, there was never death more just, nor at the same time more unjust than that of the Redeemer; never death more unjust in relation to the men, who accomplished it; or more just in relation to God, who pronounced the sentence. Believe me, my beloved brethren (it is a remark of the Abbé Rupert, which will perhaps surprise you, but which theologians acknowledge as an indisputable truth), believe me, that to-day is pre-eminently the day foretold by all the Scriptures as "the day of the Lord's vengeance." For it is not in the last judgment that our offended and angry God will satisfy Himself as God; it is not in hell that He declares Himself the God of vengeance; it is on Calvary that He is the "Lord God to whom vengeance belongeth." It is there that His vindictive justice acts freely and without restraint, having nothing to keep it in check, as it has elsewhere, being limited by the meanness of that on which it wreaks its vengeance: "God to whom vengeance belongeth acted freely."* All that the damned will suffer is only a half-vengeance for Him; the gnashing of teeth, the groaning and weeping, the fire which shall never be quenched, all that is nothing, or next to nothing, in comparison to the sacrifice of Jesus Christ in His death.

See, my brethren, what sin has cost a God; but what has it hitherto cost us? And, considering the immense contrariety there is in this matter, Him and us, since we are so guilty and He so holy, has He not the right to say to us: "Weep not for Me, but weep for yourselves." For is it not a most deplorable inversion to see guilty people spared, while the Just One does penance, and a severe penance too: sinners cared for and caressed, whilst the Innocent One is sacrificed; sin itself living in honour and delicacy, while what is, so to speak, the semblance of sin is in disgrace and torments?

---

* Ps. xciv. (Vulg. xciii. 1,) " Deus ultionum libere egit."

Nevertheless, men of this refined and luxurious age, that is the sad contrast which here presents itself to your eyes, and which ought to cover you with confusion. He dies, that Lamb without spot, that God who for us is made the victim of sin. But how? Lacerated and blood-stained, crowned with thorns, and nailed to a cross. And you, who deserve all the plagues and chastisements of Heaven, how are you living? Peacefully, surrounded by every luxury, enjoying at your ease all the pleasures of your condition. Ah! Lord, since sin, that monster which hell formed against Thee, caused Thy death, the death of the cross, that was enough to make hearts touched with compassion conceive against it all the hate of which they are capable! But Thou biddest us not shed our tears for Thee, only for ourselves; and since sin is to us the cause of death, not a natural and temporal death like Thine, but a spiritual and eternal death; what means ought we not to employ for its destruction? Instead, however, of striving to destroy sin in ourselves, we cherish it, nourish it, and allow it to get dominion over us. Is there now any penitence in the Christian world? If there be, what is the penitence of Christians? Is it a penitence which keeps under the body, a penitence which mortifies the feelings, a penitence which crucifies the flesh? You know it, my dear brethren, and what ought to affect you more keenly is to see the Passion of Jesus Christ not only caused by sin, but renewed by sin, as I now proceed to show in the second part of the sermon.

II. However sorrowful and ignominious the Passion of Jesus Christ appears to us, He must have regarded it with something of satisfaction, for in His inscrutable wisdom and marvellous love, He has willed that the mystery should be perpetuated in His Church by the continual memorial of His precious death until His coming again. For what else is the Eucharist but a perpetual representation of the Passion of the Saviour; and what was His intention in instituting it, if not that His Sacrifice on Calvary should be, not merely shadowed forth, but incessantly pleaded and offered on our altars? That is to say, that He Himself, as the victim, is the oblation that is ever being offered; as though it were not enough for Him to have suffered once, unless His extraordinary charity had given His sufferings this character of perpetuity which they have in this sacrament, and from which the sacrament derives its virtue. Behold the means which the love of God has invented, but behold, too, the results of the malignity of men. At the same time that Jesus Christ in the Sacrament of His body continues in a mystical manner His sacred Passion, men, false imitators, or rather corrupters of the works of God, have discovered a means of continuing that same Passion not merely in a profane, but in a criminal, sacrilegious, and horrible manner. Do not suppose that this is only figurative language. Would to heaven that it were only figurative, and that you could justly take exception to the terrible expressions I am forced to employ! My words are literal, and you ought to be the more touched by them, if the statements that I am making appear to you exaggerated; for it is not my words but your deeds which have stamped them with this terrible character. Yes, my brethren, the sinners of the present day, by this irregularity of their lives, renew in the world the cruel and tragic Passion of the Son of God. I mean that the sinners of the present day cause to the Son of God, even in His state of glory, as many new sufferings as they commit outrages against Him by their deeds. To bring this home to you, regard attentively the picture which will astonish you, and recognize what you are, so as to weep bitterly for yourselves. What do we see in the Passion of Jesus Christ? A God betrayed and forsaken by cowardly disciples; a God persecuted by the hypocritical chief priests; a God set at nought and mocked by impious courtiers in the palace of Herod; a God placed on a level with Barabbas, and to whom Barabbas is preferred by a blind and fickle multitude; a God exposed to insults, and treated as a would-be king by soldiers whose brutality was equalled by their insolence; in short, a God crucified by ruthless executioners; for that is a brief summary of all that was most humiliating and most cruel in the death of the Saviour of the world. But tell me if that is not precisely what still presents itself to our sight; and of which we are every day witnesses.

To proceed, we see a God betrayed and forsaken by cowardly disciples; such, O Divine Saviour, has been Thy destiny! It was not enough that the Apostles, those men whom Thou didst choose first to be with Thee, should, in spite of the most sacred ties, have left Thee in the last scene of Thy life; that one of them should have sold, another denied Thee, and all as a body dishonoured Thee by flight, which was perhaps of all Thy wounds the one which made itself most keenly felt in Thy death-agony. This was not enough, but that wound must be re-opened by a million of infidelities more scandalous; throughout the centuries of Christianity we must see men bearing the character of Thy disciples and not resolute enough to sustain that character; Christians equivocating and deserting their faith; Christians ashamed to declare themselves on Thy side, not daring to show what they are, renouncing, at any rate outwardly, the profession they have made, fleeing when they ought to fight; in a word, Christians who adopt the outward rites, and are ready to follow Thee in prosperity even to the Holy Communion, as long as it costs them nothing, but who have made up their mind to quit Thee in the moment of temptation. It is for you, and for myself, my dear brethren, that I say this; and this is what we ought to grieve over.

We see a God persecuted to death by hypocritical priests. Let us not look too closely into that point, by which your piety might perhaps be shocked, since it might lessen the respect that you owe to the ministers of the Saviour. It is for us clergy to meditate on that truth to-day in a spirit of holy compunction; it is for us who are ordained to minister at the altar; for us priests of Jesus Christ, whom God has chosen to be the dispensers of His sacraments in His Church. This is not the place to address remonstrances to the clergy, and

I would rather say with S. Jerome:* " Far be it from me to presume to judge those who, by virtue of their Apostolical succession, can, with the words of their lips, consecrate the body of Jesus Christ ; such conduct is inconsistent with humility." It is inconsistent with humility, especially when I am preaching before many clergy, whose blameless lives contribute so much to the edification of the people ; I have no inclination to make myself the judge, still less the censor, of their conduct. But if it be only in recognition of the graces with which God forearms you, in contrast to the frightful blindness into which He allows others to fall, remember that the Evangelist singles out the priests and the chief priests as the authors of the conspiracy formed against the Saviour of the world ; remember that this scandal is notoriously renewed every day amongst Christians; remember, but with fear and horror, that the greatest persecutors of Jesus Christ are not the dissolute laity, but the bad priests, and that amongst bad priests, those whose corruption and iniquity are covered with the cloak of hypocrisy are still His most dangerous and His most cruel enemies. Envy, disguised under the name of zeal, and coloured by the specious pretext of fidelity to the Law, was the first motive of the persecution which the Pharisees and chief priests stirred up against the Son of God. Let us beware lest the same passion

---

* "Absit hoc a me, ut de his judicem, qui apostolico gradui succedentes, Christi corpus sacro ore conficiunt ; non est hoc humilitatis meae."

blind us. Wretched passion, cries S. Bernard, which allows the venom of its malignity to reach even the most amiable of the children of men, and which could not behold a God upon the earth without hating Him! Envy not merely of prosperity and happiness, but, what is still more strange, envy of the merits and perfection of another; cowardly, shameful passion, which, not content with having caused the death of Jesus Christ, continues to persecute Him by rending His mystical Body—that is, His Church; dividing His members—that is, the faithful; quenching in their hearts charity, which is the bond of unity. That, my brethren, is the subtle temptation against which we must be on our guard, and to which we are only too liable to yield.

We see a God set at nought and mocked in the palace of Herod by impious courtiers. Doubtless this was one of the keenest affronts that Jesus Christ received. But do not think that impiety stopped there; it has passed from the court of Herod, that prince without religion, even into the courts of Christian princes; and is not the Saviour still a butt for the dissolute wits who frequent those courts? He is there adored outwardly; but how do they in reality regard His maxims? What ideas are current there about His humility, His poverty, His sufferings? Is not virtue almost always ignored or despised? And what other course is open to it but to hide itself there, or to come out of the court? It is not hasty zeal which makes me speak in this way: it is only what you can too often behold; it is perhaps what you feel in yourselves: and a little reflection on the way people conduct themselves at court will show you a thousand examples in confirmation of what I say, incidents in which, unfortunately, you are sometimes accomplices.

Herod had earnestly desired to see Jesus Christ. He was stimulated by the reputation which Christ had acquired by His miracles; and expected that a Man, who commanded the whole of nature, would execute some extraordinary stroke to free Himself from the persecution of His enemies. But the Son of God, who had not spared His wonders for the welfare of others, spared them for Himself, and would not utter a single word to save Himself: He considered Herod and His courtiers as profane people, with whom He ought to have nothing to do; and He would rather be thought to be beside Himself, than gratify the false wisdom of the age. Since His kingdom was not of this world, as He explained to Pilate, it was not at the court that He expected to establish it. He knew too well that His doctrine would not commend itself there, in a place where only the rules of a worldly policy were followed; and that all the miracles He might work could not win over men filled with self-love, and rendered obstinate by their greatness. In that corrupt region they only breathe a certain air of vanity, they only esteem the man who makes a display, they only speak of people of rank; and whichever way we turn, we only see what flatters or what kindles ambitious desires in the heart of man. What likelihood is there then of Jesus Christ, the most humble of men, being listened to where pomp and pride reign supreme? If He had brought with Him honours and riches, He would have found partisans near Herod, as He would find them everywhere else; but as He preached only renunciation of the world and of self, let us not be astonished that people have shown so much contempt for Him. That holy man Job had predicted as much of Him, and of every just man after Him: "the just upright man is laughed to scorn." In fact, you know, my brethren, that however much virtue or goodness a man may have, that is not enough to make him considered at court. Go thither, and like Jesus Christ show yourself there only clothed in the robe of innocence, with Jesus Christ walk there only in the path of simplicity, with Jesus Christ speak only to bear witness to the truth, and you will see if you will be treated otherwise than Jesus Christ was. To be well received there, you need pomp and display. To keep your position there, you need artifice and intrigue. To be favourably listened to there, you must bow and flatter. But all that is opposed to Jesus Christ; and the court being what it is, namely, the kingdom of the prince of this world, it is not surprising that the kingdom of Jesus Christ could not establish itself there. But, woe to you, princes of the earth, exclaims Isaiah, woe to you, men of the world, who despise the Incarnate Wisdom; for in turn you will be despised by it, and its despising of you will be to you something more terrible than your despising can be to it :* "Woe, thou

---

* Isa. xxxiii. 1. "Vae qui spernis, nonne et ipse sperneris!" Vulg.

who despisest, shalt not thou be thyself despised?"

We see a God placed on a level with Barabbas, and to whom Barabbas is preferred by a blind and fickle multitude. How many times have we done the same outrage to Jesus Christ that the Jews did? How often, after having triumphantly received the Holy Communion, have we, seduced by cupidity, preferred to this God of glory some pleasure, or some interest, which we have pursued to the dishonour of His law? How often, when conscience, which ought to govern us, and impulse, which would lead us astray, have been at strife within, have not we renewed that abominable decision, that unworthy preference given to the creature over our God? Take note, Christians, of this application, for which I am indebted to S. Chrsyostom, and if you grasp it, you can hardly help being touched by it. Conscience, which in spite of ourselves presides in us as judge, asks us secretly, What art thou going to do? Behold, on the one hand, thy pleasure, on the other, thy God: for which of the two dost thou declare thyself? for thou canst not keep them both; thou must take thy pleasure or thy God: it rests with thee to choose, "Whether of the twain wilt thou that I release unto thee?" And inclination, which has made itself mistress of our heart, by a monstrous infidelity, makes us decide, I will have my pleasure. But what then will become of thy God? conscience silently asks, and what shall I do with Him, since I cannot uphold His interests against thee? "What shall I do with Jesus?" Let what may happen to my God, inclination boldly replies: I wish to please myself, and have already made up my mind to do so. But dost thou know, conscience remorsefully insists, that the granting thyself this pleasure must cost thy God a second death, a crucifixion in thee? No matter to me if He be crucified, provided that I am contented: "Let Him be crucified!" But still, "What evil hath He done?" And what reason hast thou for abandoning Him in this manner? My pleasure, that is my reason; and since my God is the enemy of my pleasure, and my pleasure crucifies Him, I repeat: "Let Him be crucified!" For, my brethren, that is what takes place every day in the consciences of men, that is what takes place in you and me as many times as we fall into the sin which causes death to Jesus Christ, as well as to our own soul; that is what constitutes the grievousness and malignity of this sin. I know that it is not usual to speak so explicitly and frankly, but, after all, even if we did not explain this in words so clear and plain, there is a language of the heart which says the same thing. For as soon as I know this pleasure is criminal, and forbidden by God, I know that it is impossible for me to desire it and seek it without losing God; and consequently, by desiring and seeking for this pleasure, I do prefer it to God. And that suffices to justify the opinion of S. Chrysostom, and the doctrine of theologians as to the nature of deadly sin.

We see a God exposed to insults, and treated as a would-be king by a troop of false adorers; what a sight! Jesus Christ, the Eternal Word, covered with a paltry purple robe, a reed in His hand, a crown of thorns on His head, delivered to an insolent band of soldiers, for them to make of Him, whom the angels adore with trembling, a theatrical king, as S. Clement of Alexandria expressed it. They bow the knee before Him, and in most cruel mockery snatch from Him the reed that He holds to strike Him on the head with it; a too fitting emblem of the many impieties daily committed whilst the most august of mysteries is being celebrated. The Saviour of the world is there concealed under the form of bread and wine, but although hidden, He is always God, and consequently always worthy of our adoration. But what homage do we render Him? No studied reasoning is necessary to teach us what that homage is. Let us open our eyes, let us see what is passing around us, and let us acknowledge with grief one of the greatest disorders in Christendom. I am not surprised that His executioners loaded Him with ignominy and scorn: they regarded Him as a criminal burdened with the public hatred, and an enemy of the nation. But you, Christians, you cannot ignore that He is your God, and that He is present under the symbols which veil Him from your sight. If He were to appear there in all His majesty, and such as He will in His second coming, you would be seized with terror; however, adds S. Bernard, the less He makes Himself, the more worthy is He of our respect; since it is His love and not necessity which makes Him so empty Himself of His glory. But you seem to take pleasure in undoing His work: in opposing your malice to His goodness, you insult Him even upon His throne of grace, and, to use the words of the Apostle, you are not afraid of trampling under your feet the blood of the New Testament. For, in truth, what else is it that you do in so many irreverent actions and scandalous deeds which dishonour alike the sanctuary you enter, and the God whose dwelling it is? Ah, my brethren, I might well ask the majority of Christians, as S. Bernard asked them in his time: "What notion have you got about God? What do you think about Him?"* If He occupied in your mind the position He ought, would you go to such lengths in His presence? Would you come to His feet to insult Him? For I call it insulting Jesus Christ, to come before His altar to amuse yourselves with idle talk and conversation, disturbing the sacred mysteries by unseemly giggling and laughter. I call it insulting the majesty of Jesus Christ, to remain in His presence in an irreverent posture, and with as little restraint as in a public place of amusement. I call it insulting the humility of Jesus Christ, to display ostentatiously in His presence all the luxury and all the vanities of the world. I call it insulting the holiness of Jesus Christ, to bring into His holy house and before His altar a shameful passion, cherishing it whilst there by glances, words, and sometimes sacrilegious abominations. God complained formerly of the infidelity of His people, saying by the mouth of His prophet: "You have profaned My holy name." But it is not only His holy

---

* "Vide jam quid de Deo tuo sentias."

name that we profane, it is His body, His blood, His infinite merits, His Divinity itself, all that there is in Him highest and greatest. Nevertheless, be not deceived; for the Lord will have His turn, and, justly provoked by so many insults, He will not leave them unpunished, but will know how to avenge Himself for them, overwhelming you with eternal confusion.

In short, Christians, you behold a God crucified by ruthless executioners, the last effect of the cruelty of men on the innocent person of the Son of God. It was at the foot of that cross, to which we see Him fixed, that the justice of His Father had been awaiting Him for four thousand years. So, frightful though it was, when He looked at it He felt Himself drawn towards it, because in it He saw the reparation of the divine glory and the punishment of our offences. But, in proportion as that first cross had charms for Him, so did the cross which our sins daily rear for Him inspire Him with horror. So that S. Augustine said: He did not complain of the harshness of the former, yet the severity and weight of the latter appeared to Him intolerable.* He knew that His cross, ignominious as it was, would, as S. Augustine adds, pass from Calvary on to the heads of emperors. He foresaw that His death would be the salvation of the world, and that His Father would one day render His disgrace so glorious that it would become the hope and the joy of all nations. But in that other cross, to

---

* "Cui me graviorum criminum tuorum cruce, quam illa in qua pependeram afflixisti?"

which we ourselves attach Him by our sin, what is there, what can there be, to console Him? He there sees His love despised, His grace rejected, unworthy creatures preferred to the Creator. If then the sun hid itself so as not to shed its light on the barbarous deed of His enemies who crucified Him, with what darkness, sinner, should it not cover itself at the sight of your irregularities and excesses? For it is by that means (grasp the fact now if you have not yet sufficiently done so), it is by that means, my brother, you incessantly renew the Passion of Jesus Christ. It is not I who say this, it is S. Paul in the Epistle to the Hebrews who writes: "They crucify to themselves the Son of God afresh, and put Him to an open shame." And since that great Apostle expresses himself in that way, do not you think, my brethren, that it was the Jews only who stained their hands with the Saviour's Blood. You were accomplices in that murder of God; and how? By your impieties, your sacrileges, your immodesties, your resentments, your vengeances, by all that corrupts your heart and makes it rise against God. Is it not then just that, in weeping for Jesus Christ, you should much rather weep for yourselves, since you are not merely the authors of His death, but by your sins you make it of none effect in relation to yourselves, you render it useless and even hurtful to yourselves, as it remains for me to show in the third part.

III. That there should be men, and Christian men, to whom, by a secret judgment of God, the Passion of Jesus Christ, of saving power as it is in itself, should become useless; this is a truth of our religion too essential to be ignored, and too melancholy not to be the subject of our grief. When about to render up His soul, the Saviour, from the height of His cross, sent forth toward heaven that cry: "My God, My God, why hast Thou forsaken me?" there was no one but believed that the violence of the torture drew from Him that complaint, and perhaps we ourselves are still of that opinion. But the great Bishop Arnold de Chartres, probing more deeply the thoughts and affections of this dying God, saith, with much more justice, that the complaint of Jesus Christ to His Father came from the feeling with which He was affected in picturing to Himself the little fruit produced by His death; in considering the small number of the elect who would take advantage of it; in foreseeing, but with horror, the multitude of the reprobate for whom it would be without effect; as if He would have us understand that His merits were not recompensed in a sufficiently wide and worthy manner, and that after so much travail He might reasonably have promised Himself a very different result in respect to mankind. The words of this author are admirable.* Jesus Christ complains, says the learned prelate, and of what does He complain? He complains that the malignity of sinners has made Him lose the wages of the contest He has maintained; that millions of men,

---

* "Subtracta sibi agonum suorum stipendia Christus queritur, protestans non esse quaestuosos tanti discriminis sudores, si hi quibus tanti laboris impensa est opera, sic derelinquantur."

although He has suffered for them, will yet be excluded all the same from the benefits of His redemption. And, because He looks upon Himself in them as their Head, and He regards them, notwithstanding their unworthy treatment of Him, as members of His mystical Body, seeing them forsaken of God, He complains that it has happened to Himself: "My God, My God, why hast thou forsaken me?" He complains of the same thing which made S. Paul groan when, burning with apostolic zeal, he asked the Galatians, Has Jesus Christ then died in vain? Is the mystery of the cross made of none effect for you? Will not that blood which He has abundantly shed have virtue to sanctify you?

But here, Christians, I am struck with a thought which, although the exact opposite of that of the Apostle, none the less serves to confirm and strengthen it. For S. Paul is distressed in that Jesus Christ seems to have suffered in vain; and I could almost console myself, if it were only in vain that He suffered, and if His Passion were merely rendered useless to us by our sins. But what fills me with consternation is the thought that at the same time that we make His Passion useless, it must inevitably become hurtful to us. For that Passion, says S. Gregory Nazianzen, resembles in its nature those remedies which must either kill or cure, and the effect of which is either to give life or to become a poison. Do not let this thought slip, I pray you. Call to mind, Christians, what took place after the judgment, at the moment when the Son of God was condemned, and when Pilate, washing his hands before the Jews, declared to them that he was not guilty of the blood of that Just One, but that he laid it on them, and that they would have to answer for it; they cried out with one voice that they consented to do so, and were well satisfied that the blood of that Just One should rest on them and on their children: "His blood be on us and on our children." You know what those words cost them; you know the curses which such an imprecation brought on them—the wrath of heaven, which began from that moment to break forth upon this nation; the destruction of Jerusalem, which followed soon after—that is to say, the slaughter of the citizens, the profanation of their temple, the overthrow of the nation; the visible stamp of reprobation, which their wretched posterity still bears; that universal banishment, that exile of sixteen centuries, that slavery throughout the world; and all that in consequence of the sure prediction of these things which Jesus Christ made to them on His way to Calvary; all that, accompanied with circumstances which indisputably prove that so exemplary a punishment can only be ascribed to the murder of God, which they had committed in the person of the Saviour; since it is evident, says S. Augustine, that the Jews were never at any other time further removed from idolatry, nor more religiously observant of their law than they were then, and that, excepting for the crime of the death of Jesus Christ, God must, instead of punishing them, have showered down His blessings on them: you know, I say, all that, and it is a convincing proof that the blood of the God-Man had, indeed, fallen on this sacrilegious people, and that God, condemning them out of their own mouth, had, though unwillingly, made use for their destruction of the very thing by which he had purposed to save them: "His blood be on us, and on our children."

But even that, Christians, according to the Holy Spirit, happened to the Jews only as a type: that is still only the shadow of the fearful curses of which our abuse of the merits and Passion of the Son of God will be the source and measure to us. I will explain what I mean. What is it that we do, my brethren, when, urged by the unbridled impulses of our heart, we consent to a sin from which our conscience would hold us back? And what is it that we do when, filled with a worldly spirit, we resist the grace which prompts us and presses us to obey God? Without thinking of, and without intending it, we secretly pronounce against ourselves the same decree of death that the Jews pronounced against themselves in the presence of Pilate, when they said: "His blood be on us." For that grace which we despise is the price of the blood of Jesus Christ; and the sin which we commit is a real profanation of that same blood. It is as if we were to say to God: I see well, Lord, to what I am pledging myself, and I know the risk that I run; but rather than not gratify myself, I consent that the blood of Thy Son should fall on me: it will rest with me to bear the punishment for it; but I shall satisfy my impulse: Thou wilt be right in exacting a just vengeance; but nevertheless I shall accomplish my enterprise.

Thus we condemn ourselves: and that, Christians,

is one of the fundamental points in respect of that terrible mystery, the eternity of punishment, with which the faith threatens us, and at which our reason is shocked. We despair of understanding it in this life, and we do not consider, says S. Chrysostom, that we find the reason for it in the blood of the Saviour, or rather in the way we profane it every day. For that blood, adds the holy doctor, helps to make that eternity not less frightful but less incredible to us; and you will see how. That blood is of infinite worth : it can only be avenged by an infinite punishment. That blood, if through our own deeds we be lost, will be ever brought against us at the judgment-seat of God : it will therefore eternally arouse against us the wrath of God. That blood, falling upon the reprobate, will imprint upon him a stain which will never wear off; and so his torments can never cease. A reprobate in Hell will always appear in the eyes of God imbued with that blood which he has treated so unworthily : God will always regard him with horror ; and since the horror of God for a being He has created is what makes Hell, it follows that Hell will be eternal. And in this, my God, Thou showest Thyself pre-eminent in equity and holiness, and worthy of our praises and adorations: " Thou art righteous, O Lord, because Thou hast judged thus." It is thus that the beloved disciple, addressing God in the Revelation, expressed himself: Men, said he, have shed the blood of thy servants and of Thy prophets; that is why they deserved to drink it, but to drink it from the chalice of Thine indignation : " For they have shed the blood of saints and prophets, and Thou hast given them blood to drink." By this expression of Holy Scripture is meant the last effort of divine vengeance. Ah! if the blood of the prophets drew on men the plagues of God, what will not the blood of Jesus Christ do? If the blood of the martyrs cried to Heaven against the persecutors of the faith, how will the blood of the Redeemer cry? See, Christians, the strait to which we are reduced. The blood of Jesus Christ which flowed on Calvary either demands pardon for us, or justice against us. When we apply it to ourselves by a lively faith and sincere penitence, it demands pardon; but when by our irregularities and impieties we check its healthful virtue, it demands justice and does not fail to obtain it. It is in this blood, says S. Bernard, that all just souls are purified; but, by a marvel quite contrary, it is also with this same blood that all the sinners of the earth stain themselves, and, if I may say so, render themselves more hateful in the sight of God. Ah! my God, shall I appear to Thine eyes stained with that blood which washes away the crimes of others? Yet if I were only stained with my own sins, perhaps I could expect a less stern judgment; perhaps Thou, considering my sins as weaknesses and ignorances, wouldst hold me less guilty. But now that the sins with which I am covered present themselves to me, in relation to the blood of Thy Son, as so many acts of sacrilege; now that the abuse of that blood is mingled and has its part in all the irregularities of my life, and now that that blood cries against each one of them still louder than Abel's

I

blood cried against Cain; now, O God of my soul! what will become of me in Thy presence? No, Lord, exclaimed S. Bernard with emotion, do not allow the blood of my Saviour to fall on me in that way!* Let it fall on me to sanctify me, and not to condemn me; let it fall on me by the good use I make of the graces which are the divine channels through which it is poured, and not fall on me by the blindness of my understanding and the hardness of my heart, which are troubles most to be dreaded; let it fall on me by my reception of the adorable Eucharist, which is a precious fount of it, and let it not fall on me by the curses attached to the contempt of Thy sacraments: in short, let it fall on me by the regularity of my mode of life, and by my practice of good works, let it not fall on me by my erring and straying, by my unfaithfulness, my obstinacy, and my impenitence. That, my brethren, is what we ought to-day to beg of Jesus Christ crucified, it is with such thoughts as these that we ought to draw nigh to the foot of the cross, and profit by the blood which flows from it. He was the Saviour of the Jews as well as our Saviour; but † that Saviour, says S. Augustine, the Jews made their judge. Let us guard ourselves against this calamity: it rests with us to do so. May this God, who died to save us, be our Saviour. May God, who died to save us, be our Saviour throughout the whole course of our

---

* "In me, non super me."
† "Crucifixerunt Salvatorem suum, et fecerunt damnatorem suum."

life, and may His merits, abundantly shed upon us, lose none of their power through our treatment of them, but preserve that power undiminished in the fruit which they produce in us. May He be our Saviour even unto death; and at that last moment may His cross be our stay, and help us to complete the work of our salvation which it has begun. May He be our Saviour in an eternity of bliss, when He will make us share His glory, as we have shared His sufferings. That is my wish and prayer for each one of you.

IV.

THE PASSION OF JESUS CHRIST.

S. JOHN xii. 31-33.—"Now is the judgment of this world : now shall the prince of this world be cast out. And I, if I be lifted up from the earth, will draw all men unto Me. This He said, signifying what death He should die."

SIRE,—It is thus that the Saviour of the world spake of Himself. When foretelling to His disciples what was going to happen to Him, He at the same time prophetically made known to them the three great mysteries contained in that of His Passion and death, how the judgment of the world had begun, the prince of the world been driven away, and the Son of Man lifted up, drawing all men unto Him. Of these three mysteries, and of these three utterances of Jesus Christ, we already see two plainly accomplished. First, the Son of Man lifted up and drawing all men unto Him ; for has not the cross, as we gaze at it on this holy day, had a wonderful power to attract the hearts of men? By that cross, on which He was lifted up from the earth, how many votaries of His doctrine, how many imitators of His virtues, how many confessors of His name, how many martyrs, irreproachable witnesses of the truth of His religion, how many disciples eager for His glory ; better still, how many peoples, how many kingdoms and states has not He gained and made submissive to His Gospel! "I, if I be lifted up from the earth, will draw all men unto Me." Secondly, the prince of this world cast out; for by virtue of that mystery of the cross, how many temples have been overthrown, how many idols broken down, how many false sacrifices abolished, how many errors confounded, how many superstitions destroyed, how many infidels converted, how many sinners sanctified ! All that, at the expense of the prince of this world, and of that strong one armed, whom the Son of God, stronger and mightier than he, came to overthrow; not, however, by might and by power, but by weakness and infirmity. "Now shall the prince of this world be cast out." There now remains, therefore, only the judgment of the world; and that is the important mystery which I have chosen as the subject of this sermon. Jesus Christ assures us that the judgment of the world began in His Passion : "Now is the judgment of this world ;" and that is what I undertake to prove, after we have rendered the cross, which was the instrument of all these marvels, the usual homage, saluting it in the words of the Church's hymn—

"Hail, Cross ! thou only hope of man."

That He who is God, and without usurpation equal to God, should judge and condemn the world is the natural and inviolable order of things; but that the world should undertake to judge and condemn God, is an upsetting of order, and the crown of all disorder. "It pertains," said S. Ambrose "to the superior to judge, and to the inferior to be judged." To judge, a man must have authority; and to be judged and condemned, he must be dependent and criminal. The world was the criminal and the subject; Jesus Christ was the Just One and the Sovereign. It was, therefore, Jesus Christ who ought to judge the world, and not the world which ought to judge Jesus Christ. However, my dear listeners, we see both here; and the mystery of the sufferings of the Saviour is only a clear and convincing proof of those words which I have taken for my text, which is literally verified in the twofold meaning I am going to give to it. "Now is the judgment of this world." That is to-day; and how so? Because it is to-day that the Son of God, by an unsearchable secret of His wisdom and of His divine charity, hath submitted to be judged and condemned by the world; and because it is to-day that the world, by a necessary and inevitable reaction, hath, in spite of itself, been condemned and judged by the Son of God. Two judges and two guilty at the same time; or rather, the guilty raised to the position of judge, and the Judge degraded to the condition of a guilty person: a false judge and truly guilty, which is the world; One apparently guilty, and a rightful Judge, which is Jesus Christ; both pronouncing sentence, both giving their decision, both, by a strange and surprising contradiction, declaring each other respectively guilty. Two judgments, in the sight of which I may exclaim with the royal prophet: "Thy judgments are like the great deep." Ah! Lord, how profound are Thy judgments! Whether I consider that of the world against Thee, or whether I meditate on Thine against the world, both appear to me great deeps: the one of sin, the other of virtue; the one of horrors and iniquities, the other of grace and holiness. A deep of iniquities in the judgment wherein I behold the Saint of saints condemned by sinners; a deep of holiness in the judgment wherein I see sinners condemned by the pattern of a dying God. In two words, Christians:—

(1) Jesus Christ judged by the world, and
(2) The world judged by Jesus Christ.

These are the subjects to which I would direct your attention.

I. It was not without a special purpose of God that Jesus Christ, who was to be the Judge of all conditions of men, hath willed to be judged by men of all conditions. "The Jew and the Gentile," says S. Chrysostom, "the laic and the priest, the pontiff and the magistrate, the subject and the king, the people and the court, all have condemned Him, because they must all be judged by Him; and when we see that God-Man led from tribunal to tribunal, to experience the injustice of the various judgments of the world, we ought not to consider Him as a guilty one deserving to undergo them' but as a God who is going to confound them. He appeared before three different tribunals, that of Caiaphas, that of Herod and that of Pilate: that of Caiaphas, where His innocence was oppressed; that of Herod, where His holiness was distrusted; that of Pilate, where His cause was betrayed and abandoned: that of Caiaphas, which I call the tribunal of passion; that of Herod, which I call the tribunal of libertinism; that of Pilate, which I call the tribunal of policy. Three judgments of the world, to which Jesus Christ willed to submit Himself, and the injustice of which I am going to represent to you. Please to listen.

The soldiers, says the sacred text, having taken Jesus Christ in the Garden, and got Him into their power, led Him first to Caiaphas; and there the doctors of the Law and the elders of the people were assembled. "They that had laid hold on Jesus led Him away to Caiaphas, the high priest, where the scribes and the elders were assembled." That was the first tribunal before which the Son of God was presented, and where men passed against Him a judgment, which I call a judgment of passion. Why? Try and grasp my thought; because it was a judgment in which passion alone presided; a judgment where no other proceedings were observed than those into which passion entered; and, what is more monstrous still, a judgment which passion alone carried out: "Now is the judgment of this world."

Passion alone presided in it; for it was the enemies of Jesus Christ, who, contrary to all laws of equity, constituted themselves His judges. The same who had persecuted Him with a high hand, the same who, by a preconcerted plan, had undertaken His destruction, the same who were known in Jerusalem for their animosity and their hatred against Him, these were the men who seated themselves to decide His cause. They had rage in their hearts; a malignant envy goaded and irritated them. Possessed by this demon they meditated a notable vengeance, and in that disposition they held a council. What are we thinking about? said they. People talk of nothing else but this Man's miracles, everybody runs after Him, they listen to Him as if He were a prophet, and if we let Him alone, He will be our ruin: better forestall Him; and since His ruin is the one thing necessary to prevent ours, let us make haste and get rid of Him. It was thus these prejudiced and envenomed minds reasoned. The Son of God was for them an offensive rival. The Pharisees were mortally offended that He unveiled their hypocrisy; the wise people of the synagogue, that their teaching was less approved of than His; the pontiffs and the priests, that He was more honoured than they; and, as they despaired of casting a shadow on His reputation, they attacked Him directly, and strove to crush Him. But they needed a pretext. Ah! my dear listeners, does passion ever lack a pretext? And when it has no other, has not the mask of piety always served as a specious veil under which passion may cloak itself? They make their plot pass for a true act of zeal. Caiaphas proposes it to them as a necessary expedient for the welfare and prosperity of the nation, that is to say, he commits them to the greatest of all sacrileges as to an act of religion and charity. Having taken the measures necessary to ensure the success of their scheme, they begin to break out, but with a violence, or, rather, with a fury, which had no equal, wishing that Jesus Christ should be judged and condemned to death the very day on which the Passover was being celebrated, without any respect for the festival, any deference for custom, or any regard for seemliness, because passion had extinguished in them every spark of reason.

But again, what mode of procedure, what form did they observe in that judgment? I have told you; no other than that which passion suggested to them. For mark well, if you please, they are all judges, and their whole industry is to seek false witnesses against Jesus Christ to put Him to death: "the chief priests, and elders, and all the council, sought false witnesses against Jesus, to put Him to death; but found none." Truth failing them, they had recourse to imposture and calumny: of a great number of accusers who spoke neither consistently nor of their own will, they suborn two, whose vain and frivolous testimony is received with applause. They urge the Saviour to say if it were not true that He boasted He would destroy the temple of God and restore it after three days. And although He explained Himself in such a way as to make the dullest of them understand that He referred to the temple of His body, they pretend to make that a crime which He wished to give as a token of His power. They question Him as to His teaching and His disciples, and, because He replies that He has said nothing in secret, that He has always spoken in public, and that He is content to appeal to those who heard Him (an answer full of wisdom, humility, and modesty) they treat Him as an insolent fellow, as if He had forgotten the respect due to the sovereign pontiff. The high priest charges Him by the living God to declare if He be in reality the Christ, the Son of

God; and, without any other examination, having drawn from Him that avowal, he accuses Him of blasphemy, rends his clothes, and judges Him to be worthy of death. Did passion ever pronounce a more irregular judgment? But it did not content itself with having pronounced it, since, at the same time, in defiance of all the laws of humanity, it proceeds to carry it out. Scarcely had Caiaphas, as the spokesman of all, delivered sentence against Jesus Christ, ere each one of them, forgetting his character of judge, thought only of outraging and insulting Him: some spit in His face, others attack Him with blows; these buffet Him, those blindfold and strike Him, challenging Him to point out which one of them smote Him: "Then did they spit in His face, and buffeted Him; and others smote Him with the palms of their hands, saying, Prophesy unto us, Thou Christ, who is he that smote Thee?"

It seems as if nothing could be added to this transport of passion. You are mistaken, Christians, a new circumstance had something still more poignant, and surpassed all the rest. It was the custom at the time of the Passover to release a criminal, and, in the choice that was placed before them, either of Jesus called the Christ, or of Barabbas, one of the most abandoned men in Judea, they, being still full of spleen, and blinded with passion until they were beside themselves, persuade the people to ask for Barabbas and to give up Jesus. "Be astonished, O ye heavens, at this," cried the prophet, at the sight of this iniquity. The Saint of saints is put on a level with a seditious man and an homicide. What an estimation we ought after that to form of the false opinion of the world. But at the expense of the Saviour, the extravagance of the world's opinion was carried further, for when the matter was under discussion, without any dissension of opinions and votes, it was unanimously agreed to give up Jesus Christ and set Barabbas free. An infamous wretch is preferred to innocence itself; and that people, whose cries of welcome resounded a few days before to the glory of the Son of David, that people who received Him as the Messiah, sent by His Father, as the King of Israel, by a change as startling as it is extreme, placed Him beneath Barabbas, overwhelmed Him with curses, begged for His death, and eagerly demanded with repeated cries that He should be crucified.

Once more, Christians, that is the judgment of the world; the judgment of passion, and therefore corrupt and reprobate judgment. Were I to tell you that it is thus we judge every day, that the majority of men's judgments are still of this character; judgments in which passion is the ruling motive, in which passion pronounces sentence and decides in a sovereign manner, but cruelly to our neighbour's disadvantage; judgments formed by aversion or envy, the hurtful consequences of which contribute, no less than did that judgment of the Jews, to the overthrow of all natural equity;—to tell you that it suffices us, for instance, to look upon a man as our enemy, not to be able to render him justice any longer, so determined are we to censure and decry him, that from the moment when he attracted our indignation, or when, without any cause, he had the misfortune to incur our bad opinion, passion which prejudices us has the effect of blackening in our mind his most innocent actions, and of poisoning his very intentions, of hiding from us his virtues, and of magnifying his vices; that it would be in vain if he worked miracles, since his very miracles would only serve to render him more hateful to us: why? because we judge him, not by the qualities which are in him, but by the passion and hatred which are in us;—to tell you that, by an unworthy suspicion at which we ought to blush, and for which we cannot sufficiently reproach ourselves, we scarcely have the power of entertaining reasonable feelings towards those whom an unfortunate jealousy makes us regard as competitors, towards those who aspire to the same rank with ourselves, those who are in a condition to dispute it with us, still less towards those who obtain it, and are preferred to us;—to tell you that on that account, if we be not on our guard, we become enemies of all good, capable of all wickedness, that we therefore enter, without scruple or remorse, into intrigues which absolutely ruin Christian charity; that, therefore, using God to aid our injustice, as the prophet says, like the Pharisees, we call in religion to help our passion, and we regard our resentments and our vengeances as so many sacrifices; that thence spring slanders, deceits and impostures, thence a thousand other disorders so notorious and so hurtful to the society of men;—to tell you, in short, that, after the example of the Jews, because we are led by our passions, we are not merely blind but fickle, contradictory, hasty in our judgments: fickle, condemning to-day what we approved yesterday, depreciating to nothing in our contempt him whom we extolled to heaven, anathematizing him whom we had a few days ago applauded ; contradictory, only treating graciously those who please us, being obstinately capricious in favour of some, and exasperated unreasonably against others, indiscreetly or maliciously disparaging these to unjustly elevate those, and, since it is by passion we judge, preferring the most unworthy subjects to those whom true worth recommends in spite of us ; hasty, torturing our conscience to justify our severity, to persecute the just, and overwhelm the weak with more impunity :—it would, I say, open out too wide a field for me to dwell at length on this point, which is as healthful, as it is humiliating, for us. But I have something further to tell you, showing you Jesus Christ at the second tribunal.

The second tribunal, before which the Saviour of the world was brought, was that of Herod and his court : a tribunal of impiety, which, whilst pretending to judge the works of God, undertakes to judge the Person of God Himself. Let us not be afraid of explaining what we mean : speaking here before the most Christian of all kings, and the one who is most zealous for his religion, I can boldly, and without any risk, make use of the advantage my subject gives me, to represent to you in all its horror the disorder of a profane and impious court; and if, among my hearers, there still be to-day some reprobate courtiers, who make a boast of, and glory in, their libertinism, I know too well the disposition and the bent of the monarch who is listening to me not to encourage his piety, by declaring open war against such persons, and employing against them all the strength and all the freedom of the evangelic ministry. Herod, a man without religion, sees the Son of God subject not only to his power, but to his judgment. How does he act, impious man though he be? First, he receives Jesus Christ with honour and even with joy, in the hope of seeing Him work some miracles. Do not let any of these circumstances which I am pointing out escape you. Instead of the miracles that Herod seeks, Jesus Christ wrought others before him, still more convincing and more touching; but Herod does not understand them. Disappointed in his expectation, he despised that Man, of whom he had heard so many wonders. " Herod with His men of war set Him at nought," and in derision sent Him back clad in a white robe. We have here four marks of impiety, especially of such impiety as commonly reigns at court—namely, curiosity, ignorance, contempt for the things of God, and a mocking spirit. Can any example be brought forward more closely resembling what exists among us and more striking than this? For a long time, says the Evangelist, Herod had wished to see Jesus, "because he had heard many things of Him; and he hoped to have seen some miracle done by Him," and that is why he received Him so favourably. Such is the spirit of the world, and particularly the spirit of the court. The court wishes to see extraordinary men, men who are rare and singular, even men distinguished for the holiness of their lives. They are sought for, not that they may be heard nor believed, but that they may be examined and critically handled, to discover their weak points, so that they may be held in less esteem; for that is the end of the malignant curiosity on which the world prides itself. How smiling and pleasant are receptions at court, and how sad and melancholy the end of the connection with a court generally is! The Saviour Himself experienced this. He is received into Herod's court as a prophet and a worker of miracles, but soon afterwards He goes forth from it like an unfortunate and crazy man. And why? because the joy they showed at seeing Him there did not spring from a sincere desire of learning the eternal truths from His mouth, but from a vain and curious spirit which only sought to satisfy itself. But it is derogatory to God, S. Augustine aptly remarks, to serve as matter to foster vanity and curiosity of the mind of man; and therein consists man's impiety, that he insists on gratifying his reason at the expense of the majesty of God; or rather in his subjecting the majesty of God to the judgment of his reason, instead of following the contrary order, and by faith submitting his reason and his judgment to the mind of God.

Moreover, Herod hoped that Jesus Christ would perform some miracle in his presence, and he eagerly desired it. Another mark of the infidelity of the age—men wish to see miracles, and without their evidence will not believe anything: "Except ye see signs and wonders, ye will not believe." But Jesus Christ, far from yielding in this to the caprice and wish of impiety, leaves it in its hardness and confounds it, suspending the effects of that divine virtue of which He had on so many occasions given striking proofs, and not wishing to extend, so to say, His almighty power at the bidding and according to the caprices of a worldly mind. If He had wrought one miracle in Herod's presence, perhaps that prince might have been converted; but He prefers (O the profundity and depth of the counsels of God), He prefers that Herod should perish, rather than sanction in the person of that prince a curiosity directly opposed to the humility of true religion. He wrought, saith S. Chrysostom, miracles to aid the faith of peoples, He wrought them to alleviate the wretched, He wrought them at the prayers of sinners; but He will not perform any out of deference to the unbeliever and the libertine: and therein, O my God, Thy glory shows itself, as well as Thy wisdom; therein also Thy servants discover a well of consolation for themselves. He wrought miracles in the little towns of Judea and of Galilee, and He will not work any at court. Ah! my brethren, continues S. Chrysostom, is it not because the court does not deserve them, and because it was due to the honour and the holiness of Jesus Christ, seeing it in such entire corruption of morals and of belief, to despise it? Thus, even by declining to work miracles, that God-Man shows what He is, and rebukes the judgment of the world. But, again, you will say, Why did He refuse this remedy to impiety; and since impiety can only be convinced by miracles, why did He not condescend to its weakness? For two reasons, which are mentioned by S. Gregory: first, because impiety, independently of miracles, has otherwise so many reasons to convince it; and because it is

K

not just that God should be obliged to employ extraordinary means, whilst He furnishes us with others quite sufficient, but which we wilfully misuse : secondly, because every impious man and every libertine who asks for miracles that he may be converted, would be no less libertine and no less impious after having seen them ; and because, after he had smothered in his heart every spark of reason and of faith, he would, to continue his reckless course, still be able to evade the proof that miracles would form against him, by attributing them either to the illusion of the senses and magical art, or to some other power, which though hidden might be quite natural.

Such was Herod's state, such the attitude of his mind ; and such is the attitude of all the self-deceived strong minds that I oppose. For, once more, the Saviour, Himself practising what He taught, would not, as the Scripture says, give holy things to the dogs, and work miracles from which He could hope for no fruit. What do I say, Christians ? Jesus Christ did work miracles in Herod's presence, but miracles which Herod did not understand, and such as his ignorance, which is an inseparable companion of impiety, did not allow him to discern : for Herod's curiosity looked for miracles of power and grandeur, miracles of glory and splendour ; and Jesus Christ, in opposition to this worldly spirit—an opposition which He maintained to the uttermost, at the expense of His life—showed him miracles of humility, charity and meekness—miracles which the world ignores, and which it pretends to despise : wherein consists the depravity of its judgment. For if Herod had reasoned well, that modesty of a Man who had been rendered famous and respected on account of so many miracles, that constant silence, that refusal to justify Himself, that abandoning of His own cause and, consequently, of His life, that calmness and patience in the midst of outrages and insults, that firmness in suffering them without complaint; all that should have appeared to him more superhuman and more divine than even the miracles which he had desired to see. And, indeed, it was by this that one of the two criminals crucified with Jesus Christ was not merely touched, but persuaded and converted. The surprising and heroic strength with which he saw the Saviour on the cross receive and forgive insults, pray for His persecutors and commend them to His Father, made the malefactor conclude that there was in Him something more than man, and that He who died in that manner died, not as man, but as God. So he reasoned about it; and it could only be the Spirit of God, who, raising and strengthening his mind, gave him that sight, superior to all human sight. But the world judges in quite a different manner: these miracles of patience are neither recognized nor noticed by it. Far from considering them as miracles, it looks upon them as tokens of weakness; and in this, remarks S. Gregory, the world's ignorance is plainly shown, since it will not allow that there is more strength and virtue manifested in forgiving than in avenging; in self-sacrifice, than in self-preservation; in silence, than in self-justification. Be that as it may, Jesus Christ let Himself be condemned by this sentence of the perverse world, rather than deserve that sentence by doing miracles contrary to the plan of His Father. He chose rather, adds S. Jerome, to perish Himself, and to save the world by the miracles of His charity, than to gratify the world and glorify Himself by arbitrary miracles.

Herod, therefore, not finding in Jesus Christ any satisfaction for his curiosity, set Him at nought: a third mark of the reckless spirit of the world: " Herod, with his men of war, set Him at nought." Herod, with his court (note the word, with his court); for what cannot a king's example do in impressing a whole court with feelings of contempt or of respect, according as he is himself affected towards God? And, according to the custom of the world, what else can we look for from those who are attached to the court by their birth, their occupation, or some other engagement, but that they should be carried with the stream, and pride themselves on reflecting the impiety of the master they serve? Is not that the custom of the world? And when, in His mercy, God gives us a king who respects his religion, and who wishes that his religion should be respected, ought not you, my dear listeners, who, although you be courtiers, are Christians; you who, when it is a question about being Christians, ought to think little of the fact that you are courtiers—ought not you to esteem such a precious gift as a most singular mark of grace? Herod despised Jesus Christ, and would to God that Jesus Christ had never been despised except at the court of Herod! His was the court of an infidel king; and my grief is that from the court of an infidel king this impiety and contempt has passed into the courts of Christian princes.

Finally, as a last token of recklessness, Herod joins to his contempt the most outrageous mockery. The Word of God, the eternal wisdom of God, serves him as a plaything, and he makes Jesus Christ a gazing-stock for his whole court and for all the people, covering Him with a white robe and sending Him back as an insane person. Such is the most ordinary resource of the libertine, and his strongest defence, a mocking spirit. It is useless for you to bring forward the most convincing reasons to persuade one of these minds which are full of spiteful banter and raillery; a silly pleasantry is its only answer: and because the listeners are often no better instructed and no better disposed than the speaker, they will rather fasten on a witticism, a made-up tale, a taking sentence, than on the solid truths which you wish to make them understand. A spirit opposed to the Spirit of God, especially as to holy things. The wisest maxims of the Gospel are treated as foolish, and the most healthful practices of Christianity are regarded as frivolous. A spirit which is most difficult to heal, because it can only be healed by serious reflection, and it makes a jest and game of everything. The spirit of the court, where the conduct of a well-conducted man is frequently regarded only as superstitious, or visionary, as simplicity, weakness, cowardice. Now, therefore, since you have seen Jesus condemned at the tribunal of passion, and condemned at the tribunal of libertinage: there only remains for Him to be condemned at the tribunal of policy; that is, at the tribunal of Pilate.

Who else but Pilate ought, in so general a desertion, to declare himself the protector of innocence? Yet it was the unfortunate policy of Pilate which completed the sacrifice of the innocence of the Son of God, by pronouncing the sentence of His condemnation. A policy (mark this well, Christians), a policy weak and timid for God's interests; a policy eager and zealous for the world's interests; a policy subtle and artful, to make the interests of God agree with those of the world, a policy determined above all to further his own interest. Can I give you a more natural picture of it, and do not you recognize it by these features? I say a policy which was weak and timid for the interests of God, for Pilate ought to have made use of his absolute authority to uphold the rights of Jesus Christ, of which he was persuaded; he ought to have repressed with a high hand the violence of the Jews: but he wished to soothe them, he feared to irritate them, he dealt tenderly with their minds. He ought to have said to them, You are impostors and you are accusing that Man unjustly; but he wished to gain them by remonstrance; and to flatter them, he even consented that they should judge the Son of God according to their law, "Take ye Him, and judge Him according to your law." I say a policy zealous for the interests of the world: for as soon as he heard Cæsar mentioned, and the relation which this cause might have to the person of that prince, he re-entered the hall of judgment, and with eagerness and zeal, began his questions again, he no longer showed the same favourable disposition towards Jesus Christ;

on the contrary, he spoke to Him imperiously, threatened and menaced Him, to show how much he had Cæsar's interests at heart, how he bowed to that name alone. I say a subtle and artful policy to make the interests of God agree with those of the world : that was why he condemned Jesus Christ to a cruel and shameful scourging, hoping in that way, on the one hand, to save His life, and on the other to content the Jews; but little recking that, in his wish to content the Jews, he did the last outrage to Jesus Christ, and that in his wish to save Jesus Christ he would never content the Jews. I say a policy above all determined by his own interest ; for the Jews, continuing to press him, and declaring to him that, if he hesitated to pronounce the sentence of death, they would consider that refusal as a crime against the emperor, he granted all they asked for, preferring Jesus Christ's death to his own, and the preservation of his fortune to that of his conscience and his honour.

Once more, Christians, is there not in the person of that judge, that minister of injustice, a perfect picture of the policy of the age? For take heed that it was not Pilate's ignorance which led him to such an extremity ; it was not the pre-occupation of his mind nor the malice of his heart, but it was a false prudence; and he appeared on that occasion the most unjust and the most corrupt of men only because he was a shrewd worldling. He had the most upright intentions for Jesus Christ, he sought how to set Him free, more than once he protested that he found no fault in Him ; and, to declare it more openly, he washed his hands in the presence of the people, saying, I am innocent of the death of that Man. Nevertheless, it was he who sacrificed Him. Why? Because he had only good intentions for the Son of God, and nothing more. But with good intentions (mark this observation of S. Augustine, which is calculated either to edify you or to make you tremble), with good intentions men may and do commit every day the greatest evils: good intentions give rise to the worst acts of injustice; men are condemned and destroyed by good intentions. Such, my dear listeners, is the besetting sin, or, if you wish, the curse of the great. God having given them souls which are naturally noble and virtuous, they, as well as Pilate, have good intentions; and, if these intentions were seconded, what good might they not accomplish, and what evils might they not prevent? But, because they stop there—that is to say, because they are only intentions which a pitiable weakness renders vain and useless, and which, not being proof against the policy of the age, do not bear any fruit: with these good intentions they find themselves guilty before God of an infinite number of sins, which they commit from time to time without ever imputing them to themselves. And these people are so much the more guilty in that they are responsible, not merely for their own misdoings, but for those of another; and because, having intended to do good and resist the evil, and never having carried their intentions into effect, they are self-condemned, and have turned against themselves the integrity of their reason and the uprightness of their heart. It is well known that this is the rock on which they are wrecked, the point which they have most to bewail. We know that those to whom they listen, and who, abusing their confidence, act as obstacles to their just intentions, are more blameworthy than they; but does that justify them? And how can good intentions, which come to nothing either through bad advice or worldly wisdom, serve as a fitting redress to a neighbour who has suffered on that account? No, Christians, that is no excuse for them. It is useless for them to say, like Pilate: "I am innocent of the blood of this just person;" useless for them to wash their hands, as he did, from so many acts of injustice and violence. After having given the authority of their name, they must he held accountable for them; and whatever praise they may take to themselves for their good intentions, men will always say to them, his blood be on you. Yes, you were well disposed, but the blood of that poor man whom you allowed to be oppressed, the blood of that widow whom you abandoned, the blood of those wretched beings whose cause you took in hand, that blood, I say, will fall on you, and your good dispositions will make their voice the stronger to call down vengeance from God on your unfaithfulness.

Ah! Christians, do not draw down upon yourselves so frightful a curse. The advantage of your condition, if you will only see it, is that your honour, even according to the ideas of the world, is bound up in your conscience, and that your conscience is inseparable from your honour; that you cannot renounce the one without renouncing the other, and that even worldly considerations therefore, compel you to act as Christians. But however that may be, be zealous for God, and God will be zealous for you; interest yourselves for God, and He will interest Himself for you; expose yourselves, and, if it be necessary, hazard your life for God, and God will work miracles for you. That is what an Apostle calls pure and undefiled religion; and that is what you ought to establish as the groundwork of your conduct. Render to Cæsar the things which belong to Cæsar, that is to say, render to men what is due to men, to the great what is due to the great; but never separate what you owe them from what you owe God : and remember the excellent maxim of S. Jerome, that all the interests of Cæsar are also the interests of God, but that God's interests are not always those of Cæsar. My dear listener, if at the expense of your conscience you make yourself the slave of men, they will make you their tool and despise you; but, on the other hand, if, at the risk of displeasing them, you act like a Christian, and do your duty like an upright man, they will honour you, though they hate you. It is, however, much better to be honoured by them, though hated, whilst doing your duty, than to be liked and despised by them whilst not doing it. What do I say? If you do your duty constantly, and they be persuaded of it, they will both like and honour you, and your known uprightness will gain for you more esteem and confidence from them than would a cowardly and unlimited deference to their wishes. Be afraid of displeasing them, that is permissible, and you ought to be afraid of it; but never be afraid of so doing, when you are obliged to displease them, so as not to displease God. That is true piety: by that means you will keep yourself free from the corruption of worldly judgment, and by that means you will escape the severity of God's judgment, a judgment which began in the Passion and death of Jesus Christ, as you are going to see in the second part.

II. It was not without reason, Christians, but by a special dispensation of God's providence, that the same signs which are to precede the judgment of all men appeared plainly and distinctly at the death of Jesus Christ, since faith teaches us that the death of Jesus Christ was, as it were, the first scene of that general judgment of the world, or, to speak more simply, since the death of Jesus Christ was already the judgment of the world: " Now is the judgment of this world." There will be, said the Saviour, when instructing His apostles, and preparing them for that last day which must decide the lot of all men, there will be wonders in Nature: the sun will be darkened, the earth will quake, all the elements will be in confusion, the dead will come out of their tombs: and then men will see the Son of Man coming in clouds with great power and majesty. As for you, added this divine Master, speaking in the person of His disciples to all the faithful, when these things shall happen, be not afraid, but lift up your head, for your redemption draweth nigh. Now, without waiting for the end of the world, we see already that all these things have taken place, and none of these signs was lacking in the Passion of Jesus Christ. For at the moment when He

expired, by the most wonderful of miracles, and
contrary to all the laws of Nature, the sun appeared
eclipsed; the earth quaked with a marvellous trembling; the rocks were rent, the graves opened, and
the bodies of many saints, buried in the sleep of
death, arose. Was it not plain, then, that the judgment of the world was beginning? All that remains
is for us to see the Son of Man seated on the clouds
which were to serve Him as a throne; but, instead
of seeing Him on those clouds, we only saw Him
on His cross, and the cross was the first tribunal
where, as Judge of the universe, He was to pronounce the sentences of life and death : of life in
favour of the elect, of death against the reprobate.
"O adorable and mysterious Passion," exclaims the
learned S. Leo,* "which shows us beforehand, and
even makes us feel, the boundless severity of the
judgment for which we look, the holiness of the
Master before whom we must appear, and the
supreme power of that crucified God," who, dying
as He was, did not cease, according to S. Paul, to
be the living God into whose hands it is a terrible,
but yet certain fact, that we must fall.

That is why, says S. Augustine (and his remark
has a special bearing on my subject), that is why
Jesus Christ, in spite of the opposition of the Jews,
and by a very surprising destiny, was proclaimed
King on the cross, "And they set up over His
head His accusation written, this is Jesus the King
of the Jews." A rank which had hitherto been

---

* "O ineffabilis gloria passionis, in qua et tribunal Domini, et judicium mundi, et potestas est Crucifixi."

disputed, but which was judicially accorded to Him. Why? Because it was there that He began to exercise the function of Judge; for whoever says that He is King, says that he is absolutely Judge, Judge by birth, a Judge without appeal, whose decision is final. Hence it follows that in the description of the judgment—I mean that which will take place at the end of the world—the Evangelist gives the Son no other title than that of King: "Then shall the King say unto them on the left hand." Take heed, my brethren, continues S. Augustine, King on Calvary, and King on Tabor on His last coming, because it is on Calvary that He first made use of the power of Judge which His Heavenly Father had bestowed on Him; and it is on Tabor that He is to finish exercising that power. Let us try to fathom this important truth, for it will not be those outward signs of which the Evangelist gives us so striking a picture which will make the judgment of God so terrible; but the coming of a God-Saviour, transformed into an avenging God, a God burning with anger and armed with thunders to hurl them against sinners. Well it is the same with the terrible mystery of the Passion which we are celebrating. That the sun should be darkened, and that the stars should fall from heaven, S. Chrysostom eloquently said—that is not what troubles me when I think of the last judgment; but the subject of my fear and terror is the thought that the same God, who has saved me, will descend in person to judge me. Thus spake that holy doctor, and for my part, by the same reasoning, I say now, that the earth should quake and the rocks be rent, that is not what affects me; but what impresses me, in the sight of Jesus Christ dying, is the reflection not only that, the same God, who saves me and dies for me, is He who will judge and condemn me, but that He even now condemns and judges me, whilst He is dying for and saving me. If I have the gift of understanding, and can comprehend the works of God, that is what ought to make me shudder.

For it is true, my dear listeners, that this God, before whom you and I fear to answer, however severe and stern we may think Him, will not pronounce against men any other sentences of reprobation than those which He has pronounced and signed with His blood, when accomplishing the work of our redemption. The truth is, that if His judgment must be strict and severe, it is rightly so, on account of the relation it will have to His crucifixion and death. In short, it is true that His last curse on the sinners of the world, when He shall say to them, "Depart from Me, ye cursed," will only be a general ratification of all the special curses, which, in His death, He pronounced on all the enemies of His cross. What, indeed, will He do, when he shall judge the quick and the dead? Just what He did in preaching His Gospel, and in thundering against worldlings those famous anathemas, when He said: "Woe to you." Now it is from His cross, continues S. Jerome, that He solemnly and authoritatively thundered forth His sentences; it is on the cross that He had the right to say, and that He did say: Woe to the world. Woe to you, sensuous and pleasure-loving souls, which, although burdened with crimes, shake off the yoke of penitence, and breathe nothing but joy and pleasure! Woe to you, wealthy misers, who cling to your riches and never spend them, or who only make them serve your lusts, and are not touched by the miseries of the poor! Woe to you, slaves of ambition and of glory, who think everything permissible that tends to your elevation, and who sacrifice conscience and religion to your fortune! Woe to you, hard and unfeeling hearts, who treat the forgetting of an injury as a weakness, you who make of vengeance a false honour and a false triumph! Woe to you, murderers of souls, who, by your devices and causes of offence, make those perish, whom I came to redeem! It is on the cross, I say, that this God-Man, speaking with both reason and authority, or rather acting, not as a mere Lawgiver, but as a Judge, an irreproachable Judge, strikes with these curses all the bad Christians who draw them upon themselves. If He had not been raised upon the cross, these anathemas, although proceeding from His mouth, would have had less force; let me say rather, if He had not been raised upon the cross, these anathemas would never have proceeded from His mouth, since we know that He only received the power to judge because He was the Son of Man, and, as Son of Man, capable of suffering and dying: " The Father hath given Him authority to execute judgment also, because He is the Son of Man." So that the same cross which was the throne of His humility, of His patience and His charity, became, by a necessary consequence, at that very moment, the throne of His justice to condemn our pride, our self-love, the hardness of our heart, and the lusts of our flesh. He must needs be the Man of sorrows, and treated as the vilest of men, that He might be able to say to the ambitious and the shameless : " Woe unto you !" I am right, then, in representing Him to you in His crucifixion and death as judging and reproving the world, and in concluding with Jesus Christ Himself, "Now is the judgment of this world."

These are no vain speculations, nor merely pious opinions. Three essential tokens, specified in the Scripture to point out to us the judgment of God, will convince you of what I state. For, as a first token, faith teaches us that when all the nations of the earth shall be gathered together to undergo this divine judgment, the sign of the Son of Man will appear in heaven ; and, according to all the Fathers of the Church, that sign of the Son of Man, of which the Evangelist speaks, is the Saviour's cross. Why will it, then, appear in the heaven? asks S. Chrysostom, and after him, S. Hilary. To separate those whom the Saviour, then recognized and declared Judge, shall renounce and cast out of His kingdom, from those whom He shall crown and receive into the number of His elect ; that we may be confronted by it, if I may so say, so that it may be our justification or our condemnation, according to the conformity or the opposition which shall exist between us and it ; and therefore, that it may make known, and at the same time, by a secret and subjective action, execute the decisive sentence which shall reprove the impious. There is, then, no other sign of damnation more effectual and stronger against a soul perverted by the spirit of the world, than the cross of Jesus Christ ; and that cross, after having been the punishment of the God-Saviour, will for ever be the punishment of the reprobate and lost man. Yes, Christians, this is what the Gospel does not allow us to doubt ; that is the point in God's judgment, which all the saints, enlightened with the beams of grace, have contemplated with the greatest horror, when they have meditated on these words : " Then shall appear the sign of the Son of Man."

But, tell me, does not this true sign of the Son of Man appear to-day, and is it not to-day separating the proud from the humble, the vengeful from the merciful, the reckless from the penitent ? Does not the Church, by placing that sign upon our altars as an object of reverence, oblige us to look upon it as the symbol which even now divides the Christian world into two companies, as opposed as those which have been figuratively spoken of as sheep and goats ? To speak without a figure, doth not that cross, which we revere, even now suggest all that will fill us with consternation and despair, all that will overwhelm the souls of worldly men at the second coming of Jesus Christ ? And when it shall appear at the end of the ages, will it have anything more frightful, I mean more frightful for a lost soul, than it hath for a sinner in the mystery of to-day ? If, at the present time, this sinner of whom I am speaking, be not moved as he will be then, is not that the result of his hardness ? But draw near, I would say to him, if there be any one here of this character, and God grant there be only one ! draw near, and, however hardened thou mayest be, render out of thine own experience a sincere witness to the truth that I preach. Canst thou present thyself to-day before the cross of thy God? Possessed by a guilty passion, and addicted to an impure love, canst thou, according to the Church's custom, bow to the cross, and not feel ashamed of thyself in bowing to it? Will not that cross, whilst thou renderest to it this clearly religious duty, reproach thee for thy abominations and base proceedings? Will it not convict thee of the extravagances of thy pride, thine unprincipled love of gain, the injustice of thy plans and undertakings, and will it not overthrow all the pretexts wherewith thou seekest in vain to justify before God thy want of penitence and thy sin? Canst thou, whilst bowing before it, endure the home-thrusts which it will deal thee? Now this is what I call the judgment of the sinner: "Now is the judgment of this world:" Men of Galilee, said the angels to the Apostles, seeing them on the mountain, lost in the contemplation of Jesus Christ's glory in His blessed ascension; men of Galilee, why stand ye gazing up into heaven? Is not this triumph of your Master the thought which should now occupy your minds, yet think of what we tell you, and never forget it—namely, that "this same Jesus, which is taken up from you into heaven, shall so come in like manner as ye have seen Him go into heaven." Allow me, my dear listeners, to address to you the same words. Rest not to-day, Christians, in admiring meditation on the greatness and depth of the mysteries which have their consummation in the Passion of a dying God: do not content yourselves with looking at the cross of Jesus Christ as the source of His elevation and of your own; and if you have any feeling of piety, do not rest in an empty and barren compunction which the solemnity of this day commonly arouses in your hearts. What I have to announce to you is much more deserving of your reflection and of your tears; and what is that? It is that this same Jesus, whom you see lifted up on the cross, will not merely come, but will so come in like manner as you see Him, that is to say, armed against impiety, with that very cross on which He is dying. However languishing and dead your faith may be, ought not this prediction, which I make to you, to awake it? But there is another more forcible motive, which I add, it is that this Jesus, lifted up from the earth as He now appears to your eyes, will not only come, but is already come, since on the cross He has already done all which a God could do most like a judge, and most calculated to destroy impiety and to reprove the world. So that, says S. Augustine, this world will already find itself quite reproved, and impiety quite destroyed, when this Jesus, shining with glory, shall come for the second time. "This same Jesus, which is taken up from you into heaven, shall so come in like manner as ye have seen Him go into heaven." I repeat it, Christians, that is what ought to inspire fear and terror into our souls, if we know how to weigh matters in the balance of the sanctuary.

Indeed (and this second circumstance rests on the former), according to S. John, faith teaches us that the despair of the lost will come from beholding the God whom they have outraged, persecuted and crucified; and that one of the reasons why the Saviour of the world, after His resurrection, kept the scars and traces of His wounds, was that He might show them to the wicked when He shall judge them, as so many mouths opened to call for their condemnation. "They shall look upon Him whom they have pierced" by their deeds; and that sight, by the violent remorse which it will cause them, by the profound grief into which it will plunge them, by the secret madness against themselves wherewith it will inspire them, will serve as their conviction and punishment. The sight of the demons, who execute God's decree, will make but a slight impression on them: but that of a God sacrificed for them, that of a God still bearing the marks of His goodness and of their ingratitude, that of a God who, showing them His wounds, will seem to say to each of them, see what I have suffered for thee; it is for thee this side was opened, for thee that these feet and these hands were pierced; these wounds were never-failing founts, whence thou couldst draw the streams of My grace; I wished thereby to give thee access to My heart, but thy hardness hath rendered unavailing all the plans of My mercy: answer me then, foolish soul! What could I have done for thy salvation that I have not done? and what, that lay in thy power, hast not thou done, or wished to do, that might contribute to My loss? That sight, I say, accompanied by these reproaches, will be more unbearable than even the sight of hell. But, this very day, the reprobates of the age and the worldlings have to endure that sight; and when the Church, according to her ritual, shall unveil for them the figure of that Christ, which she hath so long kept covered, will not that of which S. John speaks take place? "They shall look on Him whom they have pierced." They shall see that God pierced with a lance and with nails, at least they shall see His image, and that will be enough to reproach them with their want of feeling, their abuse of divine graces, their forgetfulness of the state of salvation in which they have lived, and in which they would like to live. They will see Him, and little as remains to them of their religion, the sight of that Saviour, whose wounds cry for justice louder than the blood of Abel, will move all the springs of their conscience, and fill them with trouble and fright: "They shall look on Him whom they have pierced." Ah! Lord, exclaimed Job: "that Thou wouldest hide me in the grave, that Thou wouldest keep me secret, until Thy wrath be past!" As if the tomb, frightful as it is, were a shelter to be desired, when it is a question of hiding from a judge as angry as Jesus Christ will be. Thus spake that holy patriarch. And for my part, if I were so unfortunate as to be in the number of those Christians of this age whose lot I am now deploring, as I thought of Jesus Christ crucified more to be feared by me than Jesus Christ glorious, I would say to Him in the same spirit: Yes, Lord, hide me, if necessary, in the bottom of the pit, and let me be wrapped in gloomy darkness, rather than, sinner and impenitent as I am, see Thee on that cross to which my sins have nailed Thee, that cross which brings home to me all the depth of mine iniquity, and all the justice of Thy divine judgments: "They shall look on Him whom they have pierced." Why should not I say it, since it is the advice which He Himself gave to the daughters of Jerusalem, when, on His way to Calvary, He bade them weep and not weep—not weep for Him, who was going to be glorified by His death; but weep for themselves and for their children, because the time drew near when men should have cause to say: Mountains, fall on us: hills, cover us, and save us from that sad sight which is going to present itself to our eyes, the sight of a God dying for the world, and by His very death judging the world.

Let us continue and complete this thought. As a third and last circumstance: the prophets teach us that the Day of Judgment is to be specially and pre-eminently the day of the Lord's vengeance; the day fixed by God to punish all the sins of men, the day which He hath consecrated to His strictest justice, the day which He hath chosen amongst all others to exact satisfaction for all the insults He hath received. But it is, moreover, plain that God never, properly speaking, began to take vengeance, except in the Passion of Jesus Christ: why? because nothing but the sufferings of Jesus Christ could make sufficient amends for sin. The flood had swept over the earth; fire from heaven had consumed Sodom; but the fire from heaven, the flood, and so many other calamities wherewith God had scourged mankind, these reproofs which He had inflicted on sinners, had only been for Him trials of His vengeance: I say more, the eternity of punishment which the reprobate will suffer, however boundless in duration, will never be, in relation to God, a complete vengeance, and that is why it will never end. In the fulness of time a more perfect sacrifice was necessary, and one which, by its worth and dignity, should fully re-establish at man's expense what he owed to God. A God-Man must die, that it might once be true to say that God was satisfied. Now that is what is accomplished to-day. Here, then, is that day so clearly foreseen, and so distinctly pointed out by Isaiah, when, looking at the Saviour bloodstained and bruised on the cross, he put into His mouth these words: "The day of vengeance is in mine heart." And what is that day of vengeance, Lord? The day of the redemption. Mark, Christians, he does not separate these two days, and, far from separating them, He in some measure confounds them, and expresses the one by the other: why? because, indeed, says S. Augustine, God was first avenged in the moment when man was redeemed. Hence it follows that the day of redemption was that of vengeance, and consequently, that the day of the Passion of Jesus Christ was that of the judgment of the world. The judgment of the world, the vengeance of God, which took place then in the adorable heart of the Saviour, and of which we have only to look for the manifestation now: "The day of vengeance is in mine heart;" the vengeance of God, which began with the Just and the Innocent One, but which will end with the guilty; for, if the green wood be thus treated, said the Son of God to the women of Jerusalem, what will be done with the dry wood? That is to say, if the Only Begotten of the Father, the Saint of saints, because He had the likeness of sinful flesh, and was clothed with a body resembling a sinful body, underwent so much hardship, how will it fare with sin itself? How will it be with those who have all the malice of sin, those in whom sin reigns, and who by their shameless conduct allow sin to have the upper hand; those whose corrupt and unbridled flesh is a source of sin; those who seem only to use their reason and liberty to rebel against God and to be the slaves of their senses; those who, not content with being sinners, boast and glory that they are such? What can and ought they to expect, since the God of vengeance hath so little spared Him who, notwithstanding the likeness of sin, never once ceased to be the object of His tender love.

Would you still see some special results? I mean, some special results of the divine vengeance wherewith you are threatened, let us keep to the mystery, and, considering what took place at the Saviour's death, let us tremble. He died reproving the Jews, foretelling to them their future temporal and spiritual ruin. But, continues S. Augustine, if His death contrary to His own intention, served for the reprobation of the Jews, how much more will it serve for the reprobation of bad Christians? He died, reproving Judas and abandoning him first to his avarice, and then to his despair. He died, reproving a malefactor crucified with Him, and letting him die in his hardness and his impenitence. But what am I saying, my dear listeners, and, on this day of salvation, ought I to dismiss you without a word of consolation? God's judgment will not be terrible for all men : there will be some elect and some holy ones, for whom it will even be glorious ; and, whilst the reprobate will shrink with fear, the just will triumph with joy. Now it is relatively the same with this mystery. After all, Jesus Christ doth not appear on the cross so much to condemn men as to convert them, to touch them, to sanctify them, to bestow on them the gifts of His grace, and to assure them of heaven; and it is still to these men that I have the right to say: " Now is the judgment of this world." No longer a judgment of severity, but of favour. Attend to this concluding thought, Jesus Christ died, promising His glory to that penitent criminal who turned towards Him, and who asked to be received into His kingdom. But was not a sentence so favourable and so express as that—" To-day shalt thou be with me in Paradise"—something still more explicit than the invitation which He will address to His elect, when He shall say to them : " Come, ye blessed." He died, converting some Gentiles, that is to say, some infidels, opening their eyes, bestowing on them the gift of faith, calling them to His Church ; as for instance, the centurion and those of his band, who turned back glorifying God, and recognizing the Saviour, dead though He was, for the true Son of God. He died, saving those who had crucified Him, pardoning His enemies, pardoning them with a sincere and effectual pardon which prevailed to gain them, and even made them saints ; so that " their sin was blotted out," as S. Augustine* remarks, "by the very blood which they shed." This, then, is the day of salvation, of your salvation, sinners, if you will take advantage of it. God who dies on the cross hath here established the throne of His mercy. Draw near, you are invited. Go, catch that divine blood, it is for you that it flows; go, throw yourselves into the arms of this dying God, they are open to receive you. Ah, Lord, Thou wilt not disavow my words. Thou wilt ratify the promise which I make in Thy name. Thou wilt remember that on the cross Thou art Saviour rather than Judge. At the moment that the sinner comes to Thy feet to confess and bewail his sin, Thou regardest him tenderly again, Thou lavishest on him Thy merits; and by virtue of those infinite merits he will be purified, justified, restored to grace, he will re-enter into the rights of that eternal heritage, which Thou hast purchased for us. Lead us thither, we beseech Thee, Good Lord.

---

* "Iste sanguis sic fusus est, ut ipsum peccatum posset delere quo fusus est."

V.

THE PASSION OF JESUS CHRIST.

1 S. PETER ii. 24.—"Who His own self bare our sins in His own body on the tree, that we, being dead to sins, should live unto righteousness."

SIRE,—This is the sum of the whole mystery which to-day forms the subject of public devotion, and which causes in the Church so universal a mourning. We are celebrating the Passion of a God who died for us, a God who hath loved us so much as to make Himself the Victim of our salvation, as to render Himself accursed before heaven to draw down from it upon us the most abundant blessings, as to wish to be treated as a sinner, God though He was, and to take on Himself all the shame and all the suffering of our sins. For, even if Jesus Christ had been a sinner, even if He had been sin itself, would He have appeared in any other state than that in which we are going to consider Him? And why did He submit to so stern a chastisement, except, adds the sacred text, in order that we might be healed by His wounds, in order that we might be washed in His blood, in order that we might be justified by the sentence of His condemnation, and that we might find in His death the source of our life? Such, I say, was the excess of the charity of a God, and of a God-Saviour; but whilst the love of a God renders Him so concerned about what affects our welfare, how was it possible we should be indifferent to His sufferings? That, O Christians, is what I should regard as a mark of reprobation in you! And would not the threat which God made to the Israelites be accomplished in respect to you: "Whatsoever soul it be that shall not be afflicted in that same day, he shall be cut off from among his people?" God willed that on the solemn day intended for the expiations of His people, each one should assume feelings of sorrow; and if there were a soul so hardened as not to enter into the common affliction, He ordered that it should be cut off, and not reckoned any longer among His people. But this, my dear listeners, this is the great day of expiations, since it is the day on which Jesus Christ hath expiated by His blood all the sins o men; and therefore on this day God hath the right to say to us: "Whatsoever soul it be that shall not be afflicted in that same day, he shall be cut off from his people." However, my brethren, it is not now exactly a question of afflicting ourselves, and of weeping: it is for us to meditate on and to experience the important truths which are set before us; it is for us, so to speak, to open the book of the cross, which is the great book of our faith, and to understand, as far as we are able, what a horror God hath of sin, since He hath not spared His own Son; to recognize how God hath loved the world, since, to save the world, He hath sacrificed that very Son, the object of His eternal regard; to measure the degree of perfection and of holiness to which God calls us, since in the person of this dying Saviour He hath given us such splendid examples of all the virtues. That we may profit by these sound and necessary lessons, let us seek no other help than that of the cross; for the cross ought to be our refuge to-day, and the one mediation to which to have recourse. Let us pay homage to it, saluting it with the words of the Church:—

> "O Tree of glory, Tree most fair,
> Ordained those holy limbs to bear,
> How bright in purple robe it stood,
> The purple of a Saviour's blood!"

Of all the ideas of which the Holy Spirit has made use in Scripture to express the adorable mystery of the Passion and death of the Son of God, I cannot find one more noble than that of S. Paul in the Epistle to the Colossians, when he says that the Saviour of men, being fixed to the cross, fixed to it with Himself the written sentence of our condemnation, to blot it out with His blood, and at the same time disarmed powers and principalities, leading them in triumph, as it were, a spectacle for earth and for heaven, after He had conquered them in His own person: " Blotting out the handwriting of ordinances that was against us, which was contrary to us, He took it out of the way, nailing it to His cross; and, having spoiled principalities and powers, He made a show of them openly, triumphing over them in Himself."* Take note, if you please, Christians, how the Apostle represents to us Calvary as a battlefield on which the

---

* "In semetipso."—Coloss. ii. 15.

Son of God appeared to combat all the enemies of His Father's glory, but especially sin, which had shown itself the most intractable and rebellious. For a long time sin had been carrying on war against God; but the God-Man came to destroy it, and it is on the cross He gave it its death-blow. This is the great mystery about which I have to speak to you. However, what was the result? What often happens in private combats between man and man, when two adversaries chance to be equal, and each deals the other a mortal wound, so that both remain at once conquered and conquerors. Thus sin caused the death of Jesus Christ in His Passion, and Jesus Christ in that same Passion caused the death of sin. These two statements, to which I confine my attention, will make up the two parts of this sermon. In the first, I will picture to you sin acting against the Son of God, and causing His death; and in the second, I will show you the Son of God by His sufferings destroying and killing sin. That is what is indicated by these words of the prophet: "He was wounded for our transgressions, He was bruised for our iniquities." What covered that God-Man with so many stripes in His Passion? Our iniquities: "He was bruised for our iniquities." And why did He receive so many wounds? To blot out and make amends for our transgressions: "He was wounded for our transgressions."

(1.) The first point, then, is, sin as the essential cause of the Passion of the Son of God;
(2.) And the second is, sin finding its destruction in the Passion of the Son of God.

In all that follows of this sermon I shall keep faithfully to the history of the Saviour's sufferings, as related in the Gospel, both to satisfy your piety, which expects as much from me, and to gain your attention better.

I. That sin hath caused the death of the Saviour of the world is a truth, Christians, about which we cannot doubt, so evident is it in itself, according to the principles of our faith. For if there had been no sin, there would have been no Saviour; or at least He, whom we call Saviour, would never have been subject to sufferings and death, since He hath only suffered and died because man had sinned. I have no inclination to enlarge on this general proposition, of which you are already convinced; but, according to my plan, and to come to my subject, I apply it to certain special sins, which we may say were the nearest and immediate causes of the death of the Son of God. For, if I may so express myself, I see one which plotted the death of Jesus Christ, another which betrayed and sold Him, another which accused Him, another which forsook Him, another which condemned Him, and, lastly, one which carried out the sentence pronounced against Him. I draw up in order these different kinds of sins, and this will form the plan of this first part. The sin which plotted the death of the Son of God was the envy of the Scribes and Pharisees; the sin which betrayed and sold the Son of God was the covetousness of Judas; the sin which accused the Son of God was the slander of those who gave witness against Him; the sin which condemned the Son of God was the inconstancy and fickleness of the Jewish people; the sin which forsook the Son of God was the policy of Pilate; lastly, the sin which carried out the sentence of death pronounced against Him, was the cruelty of His executioners. Let us meditate on this, Christians, as the time allows us, and let us try to instruct ourselves with holy reflections, and try to conceive an eternal dread of sin. I begin, and I beg you to follow me.

It is through envy of the devil, says the Scripture, that death entered into the world, and it was through envy of men that the detestable crime of the death of the Son of God was undertaken. An envy, Christians, the various marks of which are so many lessons for us; an envy formed in a secret assembly, an envy, quickened by false zeal and hateful jealousy, coloured with a pretext of piety, and in reality violent and hasty, even to fury. That is what destroyed the Saint of saints, and aroused against Him the persecution by which His innocence was at last borne down. Pilate understood this from the very first, and, with no other proof than the conduct of Jesus Christ's enemies, he was persuaded that they were actuated by feelings of envy, "He knew that for envy they had delivered Him." Indeed, this Divine Saviour had no sooner appeared in Judea, than they rose against Him. It was a party made up of three sorts of persons, chief priests, who were appointed as ministers of the Temple, doctors of the synagogue, who were employed in interpreting the law, and Pharisees, that is devotees of Judaism, who, by profession, separated from other people, and affected an unusual austerity and strictness of life. For these were (O the depth of the counsels of God), these were the authors of the sacrilegious crime committed against the Son of God. These three factions, then, although their interests were divided in other matters, joined together against Jesus Christ, and, by means of a powerful and artful intrigue, undertook to crush Him. You ask me what urged them to this. I have already told you, Christians, a hateful jealousy. They saw with annoyance the success and the credit which the Saviour of the world had in Jerusalem: "What do we?" said they, "Behold, the world is gone after Him." What are we thinking about? All the talk is about that Man, every one runs after Him, the people hang on His lips as though He were a prophet, and, if we let Him alone, He will destroy us. But it is better to be beforehand with Him; and since His ruin is the only means of our defence, we must ruin and destroy Him. "Let us lie in wait for the righteous," they conspire in the book of Wisdom, so S. Jerome literally explains the words, "Let us lie in wait for the righteous, because He is not for our turn, and He is clean contrary to our doings." Let us lay snares for Him from which He cannot escape, "Let us condemn Him with a shameful death." Thus did they reason, and the Holy Spirit adds: "Such things did they imagine, and were deceived; for their own wickedness hath blinded them. As for the mysteries of God they knew them not." Such were the projects that these spirits of darkness formed; and yet they did not know the mysteries of God, and because they were blinded with envy, they did not perceive the adorable sacrament of the redemption of men which was taking place in their midst. The Son of God was too troublesome a rival; the Pharisees could not endure that, in spite of their hypocrisy, He should be esteemed holier than they; the wise men of the synagogue, that His teaching should be preferred to theirs; and the priests, that men had for Him alone more veneration than for all of them. And because it was difficult to obscure the fame of a reputation so well established as His, they attacked His person, and determined to put Him to death. But they must have a pretext. Ah, Christians, does envy ever fail to find a pretext? And if it should have no other, doth not the mask of piety always supply the specious veil with which envy hath been able to cover itself? They urge this conspiracy as a measure necessary for the glory of God and the welfare of the people, as a duty indispensable to maintain the law and the traditions of Moses: that is to say, they make the greatest of all sacrileges pass for an heroic act of religion. Thus, when their plans were laid, they began to declare themselves, but with a violence, or rather, with a fury which hath no equal, because passion hath gained the upper hand over their reason.

You see, my dear listeners, what are the evil effects of envy; and it is to you that this lesson is addressed, to you who are living in the midst of the court to which Providence hath called you, but where it is well enough known that envy is the ruling sin. It is for you to profit by this example. If I were to tell you that envy is a cowardly and shameful passion, perhaps you would be less touched by that motive; but when I tell you that it is the mortal enemy of your God, that it kills in your hearts the charity by which Jesus Christ ought to live there, need I say more to persuade you, however little faith you may have, to detest envy? Yet, it is not enough to detest that passion; the essential point is that you should guard yourself against being surprised by it, and that you should employ all the light of grace to discover in yourself its secret movements, because it is the most subtle of all temptations. A carnal passion easily makes itself known, and, however dangerous it may be to corrupt us, it is incapable of deceiving us. But envy hath a thousand disguises, a thousand false colours, under which it presents itself to our mind, and by means of which it insinuates itself into our hearts. But when it hath once found an entrance there, nothing less than a miracle is needed to drive it away, and you are aware how rare such a miracle is. The great rule, then, is to distrust its most specious pretexts, and chiefly the pretext of emulation; for, if there be virtuous emulations, there are also contentious and jealous emulations; and experience teaches us that, for one legitimate emulation, there are a hundred which are criminal. Above all, my brethren, said S. Augustine, let us never exercise our envy under the pretext of piety, or rather let us never make piety serve the most disgraceful of our passions, which is envy. This hypocrisy was the first motive of the conspiracy of the Jews against the Saviour. Envy alone would not have dared to attack Him, religion alone would only have had respect for Him; but envy, sanctioned by religion, religion corrupted by envy, that is what killed Him. And, Christians as we are, we have only too much cause to fear the same disorder. An envious passion of envy is enough of itself to annul in us all the effects of grace. Swayed by that, it is useless for us to pretend to be zealous, to no purpose that we work for God, in vain that we set ourselves to observe His law; that worm of envy will infect all: why? because, from the very good that we do on this principle, envy will make dissensions, animosities, quarrels, schisms, heresies arise; for such, my dear listeners, naturally follow in the train of envy; and are there not a thousand proofs to convince us of this?

The death of Jesus Christ being determined by the envy of His enemies, they only sought to make sure of His person. Judas met them half way, and prompted by an avarice the most infamous in its aim, the blindest in its bargain, the most hardened in its resolution, and the most desperate in its issue, he pledges himself, if they will treat with him, to deliver into their hands that God-Man. Is there anything which can teach us better than this example to what lengths the thirst of possession is capable of urging an interested soul? I say, prompted by an avarice the most infamous in its aim; for it is a disciple, and a disciple overwhelmed with favours, who betrays his Master. In a slave even, that infidelity would cause horror; what must be the case then in respect to a friend, a confidant, an apostle? An astonishing thing! says S. Chrysostom; Judas had just been consecrated priest, he had just received spiritual and all-divine power over the body and blood of Jesus Christ; but, instead of that supernatural power, he exercised another altogether sacrilegious and full of impiety. By the priesthood, with which he had just been invested, he was able to sacrifice on the altars the Lamb of God; and by the treason which he committed, he used a diabolic power over that adorable Victim, in sacrificing Him to the fury of the Jews. Can you fancy anything more monstrous or more enormous? But if the avarice of that apostle was so infamous in its aim, it was no less blind in his bargain. See what blindness! He sells for thirty pieces of silver the One who was to be the redemption of the whole world. If Judas had had a spark of prudence, and even of that reprobate prudence only, which belongs to the children of this world, he would have esteemed the Saviour, if not at His true value, at least at the price which might have been obtained for Him. Seeing the Jews determined to spare nothing to achieve His destruction, he might have taken advantage of their hatred, and, in making them pay dearly for their vengeance, he might himself have found the means of gratifying his insatiable cupidity: but his passion troubled him, and had extinguished all the light of his understanding. Listen to his words to the Jews: "What will ye give me, and I will deliver Him unto you?" He defers to their discretion, as S. Jerome* remarks, and he takes them as judges of the worth of Jesus Christ. The ordinary price of slaves was thirty pieces of silver, and he agrees to that. Ah! perfidious man, exclaims S. Augustine, what dost thou do? Jesus Christ wishes to save thee at the expense of His own person, and thou sellest Him, God though He is, for a paltry sum of money: He is going to give His life for thee, and thou givest Him for naught. But Judas closes his eyes to everything, and the blindness of his avarice leads him to hardness and obstinacy. In vain doth the Saviour of the world exert His grace to turn Judas from his purpose; in vain doth He in confidence declare that he will be the traitor; in vain doth He foretell the punishment of his reprobation; Judas is touched by nothing; he goes forth from the supper to seek the chief priests, he makes a covenant with them, marches at the head of the soldiers, shows himself in the garden, comes up to Jesus and salutes Him, thus making Him known, and betrays Him with a kiss. "Friend, wherefore art thou come?" "Betrayest thou the Son of Man with a kiss?" Such is the gentle rebuke of the Saviour of the world: but all the Saviour's rebukes and all His gentleness in bestowing them make no impression on that covetous and avaricious heart. Why? Because nothing tends to harden us more than avarice. When once it gets the upper hand there is no more friendship, no more fidelity, no more

---

* "Christum quasi vile mancipium in ementium ponens æstimatione."

humanity; men forget all their duties, and accustom themselves to the most shameful acts of cowardice, they make their souls like bronze, to resist the lively remorse of conscience and of honour.

This example of Judas terrifies you; but let us not expend so much indignation on that disciple as to reserve none for ourselves. For, behold, the effects which an insatiable covetousness daily produces in us: it renders us hard and insensible, not merely to the misery, but to the ruin of our neighbour; it casts us into a blindness the more criminal in that it is voluntary, and the more deadly in that we love it; it makes us commit shameful deeds which would for ever cover us with confusion, if, in prompting us to them, it did not also teach us not to blush at them. "What will ye give me?" people say in the world—in the world even where they appear most sensible of honour, in the houses, I mean, of the great, and even at the court; what will ye give me? and I will deliver you from this one, or I will sacrifice that one to you. Indeed, no enterprise is undertaken but with that hope and in that light of interest: with that in view there is no innocence which may not be oppressed, no wrong nor injustice which may not be perpetrated. As soon as a man has anything to give he can commit any crime with impunity, because he will always find people ready to serve him, and who say to him continually: "What will you give me?" How many friendships have been broken by the most sordid compacts! How many masters betrayed by the cupidity of a servant who has let himself be corrupted! How many acts of treason have been

executed by a scheming woman who was in want
of money, and who, without expressing herself,
nevertheless said but too plainly: "What will ye
give me?" For, however much the world may pride
itself on its uprightness, you know I am not exag-
gerating; and, since this iniquitous traffic is still
more abominable when sacred things are concerned,
and when carried on by people consecrated as Judas
was to minister at the altar, behold, said S. Bernard,
what to-day makes the abomination of desolation
in the Temple of God; this sin of simony whereof
Judas was the author, since he was the first in the
Christian Church who thought of selling, and taught
us to sell spiritual and even divine things. Hence
spring the countless abuses as to the positions of
honour and benefices in the Church, so many changes
and stipulations, so many mercenary resignations,
so many pensions purchased rather than granted.
A traffic, continues S. Bernard, which dishonours
religion, and draws a curse on kingdoms and on
states, which condemns alike those who make the
bargain, the agents, and those for whom they act.
For what is this, Christians, in the language of the
Fathers, what are these benefices? The blood of
Jesus Christ; and is not that blood of Jesus Christ
every day exposed, if I may make use of the
expression, to be put up to auction by so many
profane people who traffic in it? They do not
even disguise this from themselves: what propriety
at least used to oblige men to hide now passes for
an honest proposal: "What will ye give me?"
What will you give me in exchange? How will
you oblige me? What will you assure me of? A

traffic so much the more shameful to the Saviour of the world than that of Judas, since the Apostle at length repented that he had sold the blood of his Master, whereas those to whom I am now speaking do it without scruple and with the greatest impunity. But to what does this sin lead? Often to an absolute despair of salvation; to the despair of making amends for the disorders wherewith these hateful bargains embarrass us, or rather with which they overwhelm our conscience, to the despair of submitting in this respect to the strict laws of the Church; and thereby to the despair of ever obtaining pardon, and of finding grace with God. For such was the result of the avarice of Judas. Mark these words of S. Augustine, and consider if that great doctor ever doubted that Jesus Christ died for the reprobate.* Judas, moved by penitence, threw down the price for which he had sold his Master; but, in an excess of despair, he did not recognize the price of his salvation, whereby his Master had redeemed him. Such is the destiny of all the covetous of the earth, who, according to the reflection of S. Gregory, having made money their god, can no longer put their trust in another, but fall into entire forgetfulness of the providence and mercy of the true God, and despair of ever being reconciled to Him; and, to complete their reprobation, giving up at death in spite of themselves that which during their life hath made them renounce their Redeemer, they will not even then recognize the price He offered for them, and it

---

* "Infelix projecit pretium quo vendiderat Dominum, non agnovit pretium quo redempturus erat a Domino."

only remains for them to apply to their own case S. Augustine's words: "He did not recognize the price of his salvation whereby his Lord had redeemed him."

But calumny must needs second the treason of Judas, and we must now behold its working, or rather listen to it speaking against Jesus Christ. It was calumny which accused Him, calumny which bore so many false testimonies against that God-Man; the Jews acted as the instrument, but it was calumny which uttered itself by their mouth. Let us enter into Pilate's hall, and see with what boldness it advanced the grossest impostures, with what weakness it sustained them, what artifices it made use of to seduce and corrupt men's minds. Pilate, pressed by the Saviour's enemies, asks them what crime they have to impute to Him; and they content themselves with answering that if He were not guilty, they would not have brought Him to judgment. Mark, says S. Augustine, Jesus Christ passed in all Judea for a prophet sent from God; men spoke only of the holiness of His life and of the greatness of His miracles; and yet these men maintain that He is a Man already condemned by the voice of the people, a Man whose crimes are so well known that to doubt them is an insult to His accusers. The ordinary language of calumny, which never speaks out more boldly than when it speaks most falsely, and which, to give authority to the lie, never fails to bring it forward as evidence; whilst truth is always modest, and even when it is forced to speak evil, speaks always with reserve and fear, guarding all its statements with circumspection. Why? Because it only accuses and condemns as charity permits. But again, continues Pilate: "What evil hath He done?" What hath He done! He hath set Himself to pervert our nation: we found Him sowing dangerous doctrines among the people, doctrines tending to demoralize society. To believe the Jews, you would have thought that Jesus Christ was indeed a corrupter and seducer of the people; and nevertheless it was well known in Jerusalem that He had only preached obedience, humility, self-renunciation. Calumny shows itself as weak in supporting its impostures as it is bold in advancing them. For, when it comes to the verification of facts, it is then that iniquity belies itself; then nothing can be heard except the confused noise of a passionate multitude, but no positive nor probable charge; all declare themselves witnesses, but the evidence of one destroys that of another. Pilate is suprised to see at the same time so much eagerness, and so little proof; but that is the very reason, says S. Chrysostom, why there is so much eagerness, because there is so little proof. What then do they do? They have recourse to artifice, and, prejudicing the mind of the judge by state reasons, with a rashness deserving of punishment they allege that Jesus Christ had assumed the character of King, that He laid claim to the Jewish monarchy, that He often dissuaded them from paying tribute to Cæsar; accusations, the bare suspicion of which they saw would rest heavily on the Son of God. And in this way their groundless calumny had all the success of a truthful accusation.

I have no inclination, Christians, to dwell just now, and make long reflections on the horror of a sin which you yourselves detest, and which I know to be the lowest of all the irregularities into which passion might lead you. But if I had to bring a reproach against you, it would be that, detesting calumny as far as you yourselves are concerned, you do not cease every day to encourage it in others, by listening to it favourably, and believing it, taking a pleasure in detraction, and repeating what you hear. You would not like to be authors of the calumny; but how many times have you authorized the calumniators, by a criminal agreement with them, making them speak out, prompting and applauding them, and thereby rendering yourselves, not only aiders and abettors of them, but responsible for all their insinuations? Behold, I say, what I have to reproach you with; but a God inspires me to-day for your edification with a Christian exhortation based on that all-divine silence, which the Saviour of the world preserved in the midst of so many impostors. For, whilst they charged Him with calumnies, what did He answer them? Not a word; neither against His accusers nor for Himself: neither against His accusers, in the silence of submission to His Father's orders, and to the orders of charity towards His enemies; nor for Himself, in the silence of patience and humility, "Jesus held His peace." What mysteries, my dear listeners! Let us try to understand them. He is overwhelmed with false witness, that God-Man, and He does not complain of those who bear witness against Him, and does not appeal to heaven to be avenged of their injustice; and, although

He could easily do so, He does not attempt to confound them. A silence so heroic that the Holy Spirit specially praiseth it in the Scripture: "Who, when He was reviled, reviled not again." But why doth He keep silence in this way? Ah! Christians, it is that He may establish that maxim of His Gospel, so surprising and so opposed to the spirit of the world, "Blessed are ye, when men shall revile you, and persecute you, and shall say all manner of evil against you falsely." Human nature must set itself in opposition to this truth, and therefore the Saviour must needs justify it in His own person; for false accusation is the very thing which self-love finds most unbearable, to see calumny get the better of our innocence. That is what urges us to revolt, and sometimes throws us into violent fits of anger; but it is just these outbursts which the Son of God wishes us to repress; and how? by a means which His wisdom only was able to invent, and which is a miracle of His grace, namely, by making a beatitude of calumny itself, not thinking it enough to say to us, Calm yourself, control yourself, strengthen yourself, comfort yourself; but adding, Rejoice that you are calumniated and outraged: "Rejoice, and be exceeding glad." Our blind and presumptuous reason would treat that evangelic maxim, if not as foolish, at least as mistaken simplicity; but that God-Man, whose silence speaks to us, would show us to-day that such simplicity is true wisdom, and that our reason is thereby condemned by all the eternal reasons. He doth not complain in the least of His calumniators. Why? Because He looks at them, says S. Bernard, as executing the decrees of His

Father, and as instruments which God hath chosen to accomplish in His person the great work of redemption. In that character He cannot complain of them; and, far from opposing them, He feels Himself obliged even to honour them. He hates the calumny, but He is pleased at its effect; and because the fulfilment of God's decrees is connected with the calumny they inflict on Him, out of respect for those divine decrees He answers nothing. That calumny is the most outrageous of all injustices; but He knows that God's greatest glory and the holiest act of justice must be the result of that act of injustice; and that is why He maintains a deep silence, adoring the justice of God in the injustice of men. In a word, He distinguishes, in the sin of the Jews who accuse Him, what God wills and what man does; He holds in execration the deeds of men, and He regards with reverence the will of God; but since God's will happens to be the result of the deeds of men, He doth not find fault with men, so as not to murmur against God; He suffers the one because He submits to the other, and thus He teaches us the admirable rule of silence, submission and charity.

You see, my dear listeners, what it was which obliged the Son of God to remain dumb before those who oppressed Him; and you see what it is which obliges us also to say nothing in a thousand cases when we suffer calumny, nay, which obliges us even to pray for our calumniators. "Being reviled, we bless," said S. Paul, "being defamed, we entreat;" men slander us, and we bless; men overwhelm us with blasphemies, and we reply by praying for them. Such was, in the time of the Apostle, the mark of a Christian; that was the badge which distinguished the faithful; and any one who did not constantly observe that practice, and curb his tongue, imposing on himself silence in respect to his enemies, whatever perfection he might have reached in other matters, was thought to be only half a Christian. Why? Because faith and true religion teach us that those who, in God's Providence, assail us with calumny or slander are to form our merit and our crown in God's sight; but he who doth not curb his tongue shows by his conduct that he is not convinced of this. Hence, S. James concludes, speaking of one who was not persuaded of this principle, that, whatever appearance of religion he had, it was only an imaginary religion, calculated rather to deceive than to sanctify him: "If any man among you seem to be religious, and bridleth not his tongue, but deceiveth his own heart, this man's religion is vain."

But, do you ask me, why did not Jesus Christ at least speak to justify Himself, however determined He might be to spare His false accusers? Ah! Christians, that is a marvel which pagan morality with all its pretended wisdom never knew. To that silence of submission and of charity, the Son of God adds another, which I call the silence of patience and humility. Pilate urgeth Him to reply to the accusations of the Jews: "Hearest Thou not how many things they witness against Thee." Speak, then, and if Thou art innocent, prove it. But Jesus "answered him to never a word." It was, it seems, for God's glory that calumny should be confounded. True, replies S.

Bernard, but it pertained still more to His glory that One who was falsely accused should remain silent, and that is why "Jesus held His peace." It concerned the honour of His ministry that He who had preached the truths of salvation should not pass for a corrupter of the people. I admit it; but the honour of His ministry obliged Him still more to practise what He taught, namely, to give up His own cause, and that is why He did not utter a single word: "Jesus held His peace." The interests of religion demanded that He who was its head and its author, should not be regarded as a criminal, I agree; but it was no less the interest of religion that He who was to be the example and pattern should teach men to make the greatest of all sacrifices—that of their reputation: for that reason He did not open His mouth: "Jesus held His peace." He ought to spare His disciples the shame and reproach of having had a seditious Master, I allow; but He preferred rather to leave them that noble lesson of having had a Master patient even to such a degree as to be entirely forgetful of Himself; that is why He continued dumb: "Jesus held His peace." He owed to Himself the justification of His life and conduct, especially in the presence of Pilate, who, being a stranger, could not be acquainted with it; and who, as judge, had to draw up a report of it and forward it to Rome—to Rome, I say, where it was so important to Jesus Christ not to be spoken against, since His Gospel was soon to be preached there, and He wished to establish His Church there. I admit it; but His Gospel was to be a gospel of humility, and

His Church was not to have any other foundation than that. He considered His life justified by His silence rather than by His words, therefore He did not speak: "Jesus held His peace."

How much that silence says to us if we knew rightly how to understand it! The Fathers of the Church ask why the Saviour of the world was so constant in not wishing to defend Himself, and they allege various reasons. S. Ambrose maintains that He so acted, because He was quite assured that His enemies had already resolved on His destruction, and that, whatever He might plead in behalf of Himself, He would not be believed. But if He were not believed by His enemies, at least Pilate, who was well disposed towards Him, and who sought to save Him, would have exercised his authority against the Saviour's enemies. The opinion of S. Jerome is that the Son of God did not justify Himself, for fear that Pilate, whom He perceived to be well disposed, should acquit and dismiss Him, and thus the redemption of men should be disturbed and interrupted; and because, according to the eternal decrees of God, that redemption depended on His condemnation. But it seems to me that such a thought attaches God's decrees and the whole plan of the salvation of men to too trifling a circumstance. The conjecture of Theophylact appears to me more natural, that Jesus Christ would not say anything, because by speaking He would only have irritated His accusers still more, and they, to support their first calumnies, would have invented fresh accusations, which would only have served to make them yet more guilty.

Others believe, with S. Chrysostom (and this opinion is the most probable), that Jesus Christ did not undertake any apology, because He needed none, since His innocence was manifest, and Pilate His judge was himself convinced of it. But of all the reasons suggested, that which commends itself most to me is one calculated to instruct us. For the Saviour of the world did not justify Himself before Pilate, that He might teach us not to justify ourselves, but be silent on a thousand occasions when we could not explain our conduct without troubling the public peace, that He might condemn a thousand restless and impatient emotions which we are apt to feel concerning things of which we believe ourselves to be innocent, when in reality we are not; to check them even when we are indeed innocent; to make us resign our cause to God, saying to Him in the words of His prophet, " Unto Thee have I opened my cause ;" and moderate our eagerness in defence of our rights on several occasions when it is more reasonable to waive them; in short, to correct in us that passion which is so general, the determination at all costs to maintain our innocence, a passion which is the source of so many quarrels; for we always think that we are right; and by a most fatal mistake, we persuade ourselves that since we are in the right, we must make a stir and resist. But, from this feeling the most shocking occurrences of the world spring : hence arise a thousand faults contrary to Christian humility, a thousand bursts of passion prejudicial to true obedience, revolts against our betters, estrangement from our equals, and I know not how many other scandals; because, says S. Bernard, we have not well understood the truth, that there are times and circumstances when we ought to sacrifice to God even our innocence. It is a noble lesson which the Saviour gives us! For, however good a right I may have, and whatever reasons I can allege, if I am governed by faith, how can I have so much boldness as to justify myself when I see that a God doth not justify Himself? Can I help yielding to the force of that example? I am not more holy nor more just than Jesus Christ was; the things of which I am accused are not more atrocious than those which were laid to the charge of Jesus Christ; they have not yet treated me as a traitor or an outcast, as they did Jesus Christ; my reputation is not of more consequence than that of Jesus Christ, and it is not of more importance to God that my innocence should be acknowledged than that Jesus Christ's should. Whether I be in the wrong or not, why should not I be ready to give up all my rights when God wills, when it is a question of suffering for Him, when necessity or His will compels me? And why should I not have the courage to say like S. Paul, "With me it is a very small thing that I should be judged of you, or of man's judgment?" Accuse me, blacken my character, calumniate me, think what you like about me; what matter to me how you judge me, if only I be favourably judged by God? for it is not my concern to justify myself except before Him, who ought to judge me. But men are not to be my judges, it is God who is to be my Judge "He that judgeth me is the Lord."

But to continue : if, for the accomplishment of His adorable purpose, God had not permitted the faithlessness of men to go to excess in the Passion of Jesus Christ, the divine Saviour might have promised Himself everything from the attachment of the people when He was thus abused and calumniated, for they had always been devoted to Him, and, according to the Gospel, had often made His enemies tremble by declaring themselves for Him. Above all, since Pilate had, by his final decision, given the Jews the choice of the criminal who should be set free to them at the feast of the Passover; there can be no doubt that, notwithstanding the rage of the Pharisees, the people would have saved the Son of God. And yet, Christians, it was that very people who forsook Him, impelled by a fickleness as violent in the lengths to which it carried them, as it was sudden in the change it wrought in them. A fickleness very sudden in its change, for it was just six days after the inhabitants of Jerusalem had solemnly received Jesus Christ, six days after they had proclaimed Him King of Israel, six days after they had showered praises on Him, calling Him Son of David, blessing Him repeatedly, and saying, " Hosanna to the Son of David : Blessed is He that cometh in the name of the Lord ;" it was then I say that they declared themselves most bitterly against Him, and compassed His death with the greatest eagerness. A fickleness very violent in the lengths to which it carried them, since suddenly they prefer Barabbas to the Saviour, that is to say, prefer an ignoble robber to Him, and insist that He, whom they had just acknowledged as their Messiah, should be crucified, "Let Him be crucified." Behold what the world is, Christians; behold the faithlessness and perfidy of the world; and yet it is this world, this world so changeable and so perfidious that we love, and on which we rest our faith; those very persons who pass among you as being best acquainted with it being the first to let themselves be deceived by it; they have had a thousand proofs of its infidelity, and, after so many proofs, they still adore it; they give others advice about it, they are eloquent in speaking about it, but there is always a certain charm which attaches them to this world which they despise; and it seems that the more inconstant it is towards them, so much the more obstinate are they in their constancy towards it. But let us turn from the partisans of the world to consider ourselves. Behold, my dear listeners, what happens to us, when, by acts of guilty unfaithfulness in respect to our God, we are now for Him, now against Him; to-day full of zeal, and to-morrow cowardice itself; to-day Christians and religious, and to-morrow reckless and irreverent, renouncing God in circumstances similar to those in which the Jewish people renounced Jesus Christ, that is to say, immediately after having received Him into ourselves, as our God, in the Holy Communion, preferring to Him an object as unworthy as Barabbas, some vile interest or shameful pleasure, and, for that pleasure or that interest, consenting that He should die, and, according to the expression of the Apostle, that He should be crucified afresh. If S. Paul had not told us so, should we ever have believed that our unfaithfulness could go to such lengths as that?

However, Christians, when all were so unjustly setting themselves against the Saviour, whose business was it to take His cause in hand and defend Him? Pilate's. But, on the contrary, it was the policy of this judge which made him sacrifice the Innocent One, and decree His condemnation. Who would have thought it? After having so openly protested that he found no fault in Jesus Christ, and nothing worthy of death; after having made so many attempts to rescue Him from the hands of His enemies, Pilate at length delivers Him to the Jews. Why? Because he is afraid of Cæsar, with whom they threaten him, and instead of listening to the reproaches of his conscience, he is only attentive to the interests of his fortune. If he had followed the spirit and rules of an inflexible and straightforward justice, he would have opposed the Jews, he would have declared himself against the accusers of the Son of God; he would himself have appealed to the Emperor on His behalf; and, risking the loss of that prince's favour, he would have upheld the right and the innocence of the Just One. But where do we find men so disinterested as to act in this way? And how many courtiers would still sell all that is most sacred to advance or maintain their position near their master! Let them pay him all the homage due to his rank, attach themselves to his person, respect his orders, hasten to do his behests; I should wish them to do so; it is their duty as far as conscience and the law of God permit; but if they must betray both of these, if, not to offend man, they must offend God; if, not to draw down on themselves disgrace from man, they must expose themselves to the hatred of God. Ah! it is then that every Christian ought to arm himself with a holy boldness, and trample under foot all human considerations; it is then that he ought to make up his mind to lose all and become the object of public indignation, rather than fail towards God in what the welfare of his soul and equity alike demand.

Nevertheless, that is not the spirit of the policy of the world, that unfortunate policy which makes us have so blind a desire to please the great that we do indiscriminately all that they wish, often more than they wish; and that at the expense of our most essential duties. A fatal reef on which all the firmness and uprightness of Pilate were wrecked. Up to that point he had behaved like a fair and prudent judge; but at the mere mention of Cæsar's name, he is troubled, terrified, makes calculations; he is shaken, disconcerted, overcome; and the consequence is that he shamelessly abandons Jesus Christ to the soldiers, and that he allows the Jews full liberty to wreak on Him all their fury—"he delivered Jesus to their will."

They do not lose a moment; and it is here, Christians, that you are about to see the humility of a God, His modesty, His holiness outraged and profaned by the insolence of men; for the insolence of recklessness added in no small degree to the sufferings of Jesus Christ. "Then," says the Evangelist, "the soldiers of the governor took Jesus into the prætorium," that is to say, into the audience chamber; and there, having assembled all their company, they treat Him in a manner equally brutal and impious; brutal, without any feeling of humanity; impious, without any respect for religion. Barbarous and brutal, I say; for if Jesus Christ had been guilty, seeing Him condemned to death, they ought to have had compassion on Him; that is a feeling with which Nature inspires us, even for the greatest wretches. But their hearts became harder than stone and bronze: they were to carry out His punishment, and they wish to recompense themselves beforehand for their trouble at the expense of His Person; this Victim hath been given them to sacrifice, but they wish to prepare Him for the sacrifice of the cross by ceremonies which only their brutality was capable of devising. What do they do? Condemned as He is, they set about insulting Him with cutting raillery; they heap upon Him insults and blasphemies; and bandaging His eyes, they strike Him with the palms of their hands, asking Him who struck Him. Was there ever more cruel treatment? Was there ever a deed more impious than to profane, as they did, two of the most august and holy characters of that Divine Saviour, His character as Christ, and His character as King? They treat Him as Christ in derision, bidding Him prophesy. "Prophesy unto us, Thou Christ." They make Him a King in appearance, giving Him a reed as a sceptre, clothing Him with purple, bending the knee before Him, and saying, "Hail, King of the Jews." O my Saviour, must Thy royalty, adored in Heaven, be thus profaned on earth? Must that sacred unction of King, of High Priest and of Prophet, which is expressed in Thy name of Christ, and which is the source of all grace and blessing, serve as a jest for impiety and irreligion?

But I venture to say that is nothing in comparison with what followed : behold the preparation of a new torture, of which we have no previous record, and of which the strictest laws furnish no example. They try it first on the Son of God. They get ready for Him a crown of thorns, and place it violently on His head. Blood spurts forth everywhere, each sharp point makes a wound. Behold how the synagogue treated its King! behold how it treated your King and mine! behold how it treated the Master and King of all Nature! An indignity which we detest! But whilst we detest it in others, why do we not detest it in ourselves? For, are not we guilty, Christians, we who have a hundred times acted in this way towards Jesus Christ? Let us compare ourselves with the soldiers who insulted that King of Glory; let us recognize what we are, and what we do every day ; for the spirit of the sinners of this age is just like that of sinners then. S. Paul, writing to the Philippians, called them his crown. According to the same rule, cannot we say that we are the crown of Jesus Christ, but a crown of suffering? He expected that our good works should make for Him a crown of honour, and by our misdeeds we make for Him a crown of shame. He looked for fruits of grace, truth and virtue from us; but He only gathers briers and thorns. It is thus, saith S. Bernard, that He is crowned with our sins; but at least, adds the same Father, let us present to Him in that state the homage of a sincere grief and of a lively compunction. " Go forth, O ye daughters of Zion, and behold the King with the crown;" go forth, ye souls redeemed with the blood of a God; go forth, recognize and bewail your infidelities; go forth to make reparation with tears and with the holy severity of penitence for what you have made Him suffer by your crimes; and after learning how sin caused the death of Jesus Christ, learn how Jesus Christ caused the death of sin, and how you ought to kill it in yourselves: that is the second part.

II. It is a principle and a truth of the faith, that, as the grace of innocence and of original righteousness sanctified the entire man, so the entire man hath felt the hurtful effects of the disorder and corruption of sin. He hath felt them in his body, in his spirit, in his will, and in his passions: in his body, by the revolt of his feelings and their love of ease; in his spirit, by pride; in his will, by the love of independence; and in his passions, by their blind and unrestrained longings. The Son of God, then, dying to destroy sin, must kill it in every part of man. But, indeed, I say that He hath killed it in the body of man, by inspiring us with a desire to copy His example in mortifying the body so as to root out sensuality and the love of ease. I say that He hath killed it in the spirit of man, by inspiring us, after His example, with submission as a remedy against our love of independence. Lastly, I say that He hath killed it in the passions of man, particularly in the most violent of all—that is, resentment, by teaching us, after His example, to forgive insults, and to return good for evil. This will give me the opportunity of presenting Him to you in these four conditions, which are calculated alike to affect and teach you. Give me your attention, I beg you.

First, I picture to myself a sensual Christian, one who is a slave to that concupiscence of the flesh which is the deadly source of sin; or rather, one who is the slave of sin itself, for that is the infallible consequence of the concupiscence of the flesh, when it is encouraged by an easy and voluptuous life; and to destroy in such a person that body of sin, of which S. Paul so often speaks, I confront him with the Saviour of the world in the condition in which Pilate presented Him to the Jews, when he said to them, "Behold the Man:" that is to say, I confront him with that God-Man all covered with wounds and lacerated with blows, just as He appeared after being scourged. The Evangelists do not tell us what was the limit or the extent of that infliction: they leave us to imagine it; and perhaps our imagination of it surpasses any description they could have given us; for Pilate, when he could not content the hatred of the people, at length devised a means of satisfying them, namely, by condemning Jesus to be scourged. Behold how we ought to judge of what the Son of God suffered. The people were beside themselves with rage; there was nothing but the blood of that Victim which could appease them; they repeatedly demanded His blood, and Pilate wished to gratify them. Hence you may infer the severity with which He was treated. When the meditations of certain pious souls on this point are reported to us, they sometimes seem exaggerations, and scarcely make any impression upon us. But when I say that, by the orders of Pilate, the

Saviour of the world was subjected to such treatment that the cruelty of His enemies, pitiless as it was, could be satisfied with that treatment, do I not say all, nay, more than is necessary? Why have not the Evangelists entered upon this point more in detail? Ah! replies S. Augustine, because the Evangelist of the Old Testament, Isaiah, had already sufficiently expressed it for them. What, then, hath that prophet said? He hath said things, Christians, which surpass all description—namely, that Jesus Christ, after that cruel scourging, had no longer the features of a man:* "We beheld Him, and it was no countenance of man." He was a terrible sight to behold. "We did esteem Him a leper, smitten of God."† For it is not by adaptation or figuratively, but in the literal sense of the prophecy, that this text of Isaiah refers to Jesus Christ.

It is in that condition I set Him before the sinners of this generation, with those words which are so touching and calculated to soften even the most hardened hearts. "Behold the Man;" behold Him, Christians, that Man whom you adore as your God, and who is indeed your God: do you recognize Him? It is you who have thus disfigured Him, you who have thus bruised and wounded Him. Do not try to justify yourselves; for He bears witness Himself, and He ought to be believed. "Sinners have marked My back."‡ He gives us to understand that

---

* "Vidimus eum, et non erat aspectus."—Isa. liii. 2.

† "Putavimus eum quasi leprosum, et percussum a Deo."—Isa. liii. 4.

‡ "Supra dorsum meum fabricaverunt peccatores."—Ps. cxxix. (Vulg. cxxviii.) verse 3.

they are sinners who have dealt Him blows, and are not you of that number? It is to you, then, that this reproach is addressed. Yes, it is by you and for you that His innocent and virginal flesh hath been immolated in that sacrifice of pain. Without mentioning a million irregularities, the remembrance of which I do not desire now to renew, it is for your ease, for those unworthy pleasures with which you fatten and pamper up your body, giving it all that it asks, and even more than it asks for; it is for those excessive cares for your health at the expense of the chief duties of your religion, for those dispensations from the laws of God and of His Church which you grant yourselves, for that criminal laziness, for your immoderate diversions, for that horror of true penitence, for that life of sensuality, so opposed to sound reason, that life which holds you under the dominion of sin; it is, I say, for all these that Jesus Christ became a Man of sorrows. For if your flesh had been submissive to God, His would never have been given up to the executioners. "Behold the Man," the Man ordained by God as our Head, and to whom we must of necessity be united as living members. But between the members and the Head there must be something in common; and it is, saith S. Bernard, a monstrous thing to see the members living at ease under a Head crowned with thorns. When the Head suffers, all the members suffer by sympathy; and if any of them do not suffer, it is a corrupt member. "Behold the Man, the Man to whose image God hath predestined us, and to whose image you must therefore strive to conform yourselves, lest you be rejected of God. For whatever your condition may be, there is no mean between these two, conformity with Jesus Christ suffering, or eternal reprobation; and with whatever hope you may flatter yourselves, you must make your choice of one of these alternatives, since it is certain that God will allow no relaxation from the strictness of that law, " whom He did foreknow, He also did predestinate to be conformed to the image of His Son." " Behold the Man ;" the Man whose life S. Paul wishes you to shadow forth in your own persons. He is not content that you should reflect it before angels and before God Himself in the secrecy of your souls; He wishes that you should reflect it outwardly, and that your bodies should bear visible traces of it. But that can only be by the mortification of the flesh ; and therefore the great Apostle desired that our bodies should always be clothed with that holy mortification, " Always bearing about in the body the dying of the Lord Jesus ;" so that, said he, the life of Jesus, which was a continual mortification, may appear in us, as in so many subjects which it ought to animate and quicken : " that the life also of Jesus might be made manifest in our bodies." For it is somewhat inconsistent that a body nourished in ease, and which hath never made trial of Christian penitence, should represent that Jesus, who, bound to the column, underwent so stern a punishment. " Behold the Man" whose flesh, mortified as it hath been by the cruelties to which it was subjected, still wants, as the complement of its sufferings, something which is lacking, something without which all that it hath suffered is of no account before God. But that which is lacking is that which we have to accomplish in ourselves. But where have we to accomplish it? In our heart, in our will, in the restraint of our desires? Perhaps we should like to stop there; but that is not enough; for S. Paul, who understood it better than we, and who no longer had need of penitence, makes it an indispensable duty to accomplish it in his flesh: "I fill up that which is behind of the afflictions of Christ in my flesh." An admirable reason this to make us love the mortification of the senses, if we regard it as the supplement, or, I would rather say, as the accomplishment of the Saviour's sufferings. A forcible reason also to sustain us in the practice of that virtue, if we consider the mortification of our bodies, as being not so much our mortification, as the mortification of Jesus Christ Himself. "Always bearing about in the body the dying of the Lord Jesus." For if it were mine own mortification, said S. Chrysostom, necessary as I believe it to be, I should regard it with something of contempt; but since it is that of Jesus, how can I help loving and honouring it?

Such, Christians, is the first enemy of the salvation of man which the Son of God hath destroyed by His Passion—namely, carnal love of ease. There was also another yet more dangerous, pride of the spirit, the ambition of making one's self great; the obstinate pursuit, if I may so speak, of a worldly glory, to which we think we not only can but ought to sacrifice everything else. This monster, which set itself in opposition to God, had to be overthrown; and what did the God-man do to accomplish that? Ah! Christians, follow Him in His walk from the prætorium to the place of His sufferings, and behold Him in the depth of humiliation in which He appeared that day in the sight of heaven and earth—that is to say, laden with His cross, led to Calvary like a criminal, accompanied by two robbers, escorted by soldiers, guards, executioners, and dragged through the streets of Jerusalem in that shameful plight. Remember, above all, that it is He before whom the angels tremble, and who thought it no usurpation to claim to be equal to God, His Father. Behold, said S. Chrysostom, the lowest depth to which a God could be reduced; and as for me, I add, behold the sovereign remedy which ought to cure the pride of man. Mark, well, the Saviour of men, what astonishing steps He took in abasing Himself in the eyes of the world; and the Holy Spirit, to give us a just conception of them, compares them to the stride of a giant—" He rejoiced as a giant to run his course." The first of these steps, His Incarnation, consisted in the emptying Himself of His glory—" He emptied Himself;" but in that state, He still found it possible to descend some steps lower; for, besides being made man, He willed to be born an infant, He took the form of a servant and of a slave. Besides taking the form of a slave, He was clothed in the likeness of a sinner—a sinner, a slave, an infant; all those stages, says Zeno of Verona, were infinite supererogations of humility in the adorable mystery of an incarnate God. The lesson all this teaches is very remarkable. But His humility, or rather His zeal to destroy our pride, carries Him yet further on this day. He wills to be numbered among the transgressors, even among the transgressors condemned by the law of man; He wills, in that character, to sustain all the scorn attached to the most shameful punishment, and that in the very midst of His nation, in the capital of His country, on the day of their greatest festival, in the most conspicuous part of the town; He wills to be led thither in a procession, and to fulfil the words of Jeremiah, " He is filled full with reproach." What surprises me is that He did all this without being shaken in His purpose by the thought that He would be a stumbling-block to the Jews, and to the Greeks an object of contempt; foreseeing that the former would never acknowledge a crucified Messiah, and that the latter would regard Him as foolish and beside Himself, "to the Jews a stumbling-block, to the Greeks foolishness." No matter, let the Jew take offence, let the Greek mock, that God, so grand in Himself, wills to be given as a spectacle to angels and to men: as a spectacle of confusion, I say: for what confusion must it have been for Him, when they laid on Him that shameful piece of wood, an object of execration to all the people! what confusion, when He had to come forth in that state, and to show Himself in public!

Ah! Christians, we now feel a reverence for all these mysteries, and faith, which teaches us that they are the mysteries of a God-Saviour, hides from us the awful ideas with which we ought to regard them. When to-day we see princes and monarchs bend the knee before that wood which hath been the instrument of our salvation, instead of finding it difficult to honour it, we feel ourselves obliged to render it the reverence which religion commands. But on that sad day on which we picture to ourselves a God suffering, what did men think of the cross and of Him who bare it? I blush to tell you, and leave you to imagine for yourselves. At least I know that Jesus Christ regarded the shame of that punishment with such a feeling of horror, that, if His mind had yielded to that feeling, He would have given up His purpose of redeeming us, rather than redeem us at that cost. He even made the proposal to His Father, when He prayed, "O My Father, if it be possible, let this cup pass from Me." But the decree had been pronounced; and He pronounced it to Himself at the same time that He uttered that prayer, submitting His will and accepting all the shame of the cross. It was thus that He was to stifle the pride of men. That is what the Saviour's humiliation accomplished in a most pre-eminent, efficacious, and striking manner. For, saith S. Bernard, it seemeth to me impossible that a Christian should adore a humiliated God, and, according to the expression of S. Paul, a God emptied of His glory; and that he should at the same time be obstinately in pursuit of the vain honours of the world; that he should be striving to raise himself, to distinguish himself, and to take a prominent position; that all his study, all his aims, all his plans should only tend to the content-ment of his ambition, and that without setting any bounds or limits to it; without setting any bounds to it, I say, wishing always to increase his fortune, always to reach a higher rank, always to attain new honours; without any regard for straightforwardness and good faith, for equity or justice, for his conscience or his salvation; sacrificing everything to his passion, the interests of God, the interests of his neighbour, the interests of his soul; jealously exacting what is due, or what he believes to be due to himself, and constantly refusing to relax the least of his rights, or to pardon the slightest insult. That a Christian should have his heart filled with these sentiments; and that he should make these maxims the rules of his conduct; that, my brethren, is what seems to me impossible. Feeling that he is proud, he can no longer invoke God, nor trust in God; and if he do, he must be all the while feeling within himself, " I am a hypocrite, for I am calling upon God who hath only saved me by abasing Himself beneath all men; and, nevertheless, I only seek greatness and honour before men: I am placing my trust in His humiliations, and in my practice I detest and shun those very humiliations: what is that but hypocrisy and contradiction? But to acknowledge that contradiction, that hypocrisy, and to admit the necessity of condemning myself, that is what I call the destruction of pride in a Christian. Let us proceed.

When the Saviour of the World arrived at Calvary, they made ready the cross and stretched Him on it; and it is here you are about to see a third enemy of the salvation of man, the licence of the will, overcome by the heroic obedience of that God-man. Which, asks S. Augustine, was the most haughty and proud of those principalities and powers over which, according to S. Paul's words, Jesus Christ triumphed by His cross? It was, replies that holy doctor, the will of man: that will which is an enemy of subjection, that will which desires always to be its own mistress, which follows its impulses in everything, and is ever striving to gain more liberty, and with that end in view is ever in revolt against law and duty. That is the power which might rightly be named the principality of the world, since it reigns there to the prejudice of God Himself. But learn, Christians, how it hath been vanquished by Jesus Christ in the mystery of His crucifixion. That divine Saviour is nailed to the cross, and submits to death on it. It is not merely, remarks S. Chrysostom, through a motive of charity, it is not merely through zeal for the glory of His Father, it is not through a simple desire to save men, but it is through obedience, " He became obedient," and through the strictest obedience, "obedient unto death, even the death of the cross." But when I say, through obedience, I mean submission to an express command from Heaven, to duty, to necessity, to the sacrifice of a will which is no longer its own, and which hath no longer any right over its actions: for obedience includes all that. I know that the theologians and Fathers teach us that the obedience of the Son of God was voluntary in its source, that the order to die was only given Him because He willed to accept it; that it was He Himself who prayed His Father to impose it on Him, and that He was free to demand a dispensation from it. I admit all these truths; but what I find still more wonderful is that, He being able to choose or not to choose the punishment of the cross, He willed that it should be appointed and ordained for Himself; I wonder that, since He was able to obtain a dispensation from that decree, He willed to fulfil it in all its extent. That is not all, not merely was He crucified in obedience to His Father, but in obedience to men, even the most unworthy men, who were His executioners and persecutors. These servants of iniquity dispose of Him as pleaseth them: if they speak, He does their bidding; their cruelty devises a novel mode of attaching Him to the instrument of His death, and He offers them His hands and His feet to be pierced by the nails. There is only one point on which He refuses to listen to them. For, if they reproach Him that, after saving others, He cannot save Himself; if they defy Him to come down from the cross; if they ask for that proof of His Divinity, and promise, after that proof, to believe in Him, He prefers the merit of obedience to such enticing hopes. Instead of coming down from the cross because He is the Son of God, that is the very reason why He doth not come down, saith S. Bernard; since, being the Son of God, He ought to obey God. He prefers to be accounted weak, and not to give any token of His Almighty power, rather than to show it by miracles of His own will. He prefers to stay in that state of dependence to which He was reduced, and to let the faithless perish, rather than to come forth from that state to convince and soften them.

But what do we learn from this, and what ought we to learn? Two things chiefly, which tend to the destruction of our own will—namely, the necessity of obedience, and the measure of obedience. The necessity of obedience, since that is what accomplished our salvation to-day: no, Christians, is was not exactly the cross, but the obedience of the cross which effected that. The cross by itself would not have saved us; obedience must give it the worth which gained our salvation. It is useless then for us to pretend that we can save ourselves by any other means. Work miracles, practise all the austerities of Christian penitence, convert the whole world; but if this be not done in entire submission to God and to His Church, all your zeal, all your miracles, all your austerities and your penitences count as nothing. For, as the prophet Samuel said, obedience is better than sacrifice, and all sacrifices without obedience are worthless in the sight of God. There must be obedience, Christians, not merely to God, but to men endued with authority from God, be they ever so imperfect, ever so vicious, "not only to the good and gentle, but also to the froward." Is there any one, Lord, whom I ought not to obey for Thy sake, when I see Thee for my sake obey even profane men who were about to murder their God? There must be obedience "unto death, even the death of the cross," that is to say, without exception and without restriction. For such is the measure of the obedience of a Christian; and if there be any point not included in our obedience, and in which we are not prepared to obey, ours is an obedience rejected by God. That perfect obedience is heroic;

but, after all, it is not more than is required for our salvation, and God deserves and desires nothing less from us. Let us but understand what God is, and what is meant by eternal salvation; then we shall no longer be surprised at anything which God demands from us.

There remained still another enemy which Jesus Christ had to overcome—that is, the thirst for revenge. Nothing is more natural to man than that passion, and nothing more contrary to the feelings of man than the forgiveness of injuries. In everything else, saith S. Augustine,* our religion prescribes nothing in what concerns our everyday life that is not plainly reasonable and just; but when it bids us love our persecutors, religion seems then to encroach upon our reason; and, all submissive as we are to its law, we can scarcely refrain from condemning it. It is, nevertheless, this love of our enemies which makes us Christians indeed; and, according to Tertullian,† this is the token of our holiness. Therefore, in order that Christianity may be firmly established, all desire for vengeance must be suppressed. But, it was only a God—a God dying in the most unjust persecution—who could accomplish that; and that is what He wrought upon the cross, which was, as it were, the theatre of His charity. We might say, that He was lifted up on the cross only that He might triumph over

---

* "Quum vero legitur, Diligite inimicos vestros, et benefacite his qui oderunt vos, tunc ipsa pene accusatur religio."

† "Ita jubemur inimicos diligere, ut haec sit perfecta et propria bonitas nostra."

that demon. The first word that He utters is on behalf of those who are crucifying Him: "Father, forgive them." He does not think of His Apostles; He does not think of the faithful in Jerusalem ; He does not even yet think of His holy mother, nor of the beloved disciple, but He thinks of His executioners, of His calumniators; and as if He owed them the first place in His heart, He bequeaths them the preference in His will : "Father, forgive them." Is He content merely with pardoning them? No. Doth He only forget the outrages He hath received? Ah! replies S. Chrysostom, that was too little for Him, because He doth not wish that to be enough for us. He loves them, He prays for them, He tries to justify them in His Father's sight, He showers on them His most special graces and His most abundant mercies, He converts them, makes them predestinated, and that, even whilst they are enraged against Him, and at the very moment they are heaping curses on Him. See what was the charity of that God-man. Yes, my brethren, He loved His executioners; it was indeed to love them, saith S. Gregory, when He wished to reconcile them with His Father; for He could not reconcile them with His Father without reconciling them with Himself. He prayed for them; and what is more astonishing, He made use of the wounds which they had inflicted on Him to plead their cause with God. "O marvellous love!" exclaims the great Hildebert, Archbishop of Tours, "whilst the Jews pierced the Saviour's hands with nails, whilst they opened His sacred side with a spear, whilst they slaked His parched mouth with gall; mouth and hands and side were crying for pardon for His enemies!"* He excused their crime: "Father, forgive them, for they know not what they do;" and although strictly their ignorance was without excuse, He made use of it to lessen the greatness and the enormity of the guilt of the action they were committing. What would He not have done, Christians, if that ignorance had been entirely involuntary? He lavished on them His most special graces and His most abundant mercies, not considering, saith S. Augustine,† that it was by them, but that it was for them, He was suffering.

After that, my dear listeners, He claims the right to address you in these words: "I say unto you, love your enemies." I say it, and not content with saying it, I teach you to do so by My example, which ought to be a most convincing and touching example. You wish to have your revenge? But have I been avenged? Have I asked to be? You have been offended: but have you been more offended than I? Have you been as much offended? Behold My cross, that will teach you. In your position you cannot help feeling an insult; but ought you to be more sensitive, or as sensitive as I? For what are you, and what am I? That man has turned against you out of pure malice and with the premeditated intention of injuring you; but with what intention did My persecutors turn against Me,

---

* "O caritas admiranda, dum clavis manibus, dum lancea lateri, dum fel ori admoveretur; et manus, et latus, et os agebat pro inimicis."

† "Non enim attendebat quod ab ipsis patiebatur, sed quia pro ipsis moriebatur."

and with what fury did they execute their intention!
It is an outrage which you cannot forgive, and
which is never forgiven by the world: but I for-
gave it. He who inflicted the outrage on you
doth not deserve forgiveness: but am I unworthy,
I, who interest Myself in his behalf; and ought you
to behold him or Me in the pardon you grant him?
So, Christians, under whatever cloak your revenge
may hide itself, this God-Saviour can always confound it, repress it, and stifle all these feelings.

In conclusion. You see then sin destroyed by
the cross; but, alas! my dear listeners, how many
times are we going to give it new life? It is the
enemy of God, and His principal enemy; it has
caused the death of Jesus Christ: ought not that
alone to make you understand this abominable
monster? is not that enough to make you hate it
above all else? Go, sinners, go to the foot of the
cross; contemplate there the sorrowful mystery of
our Saviour's Passion; count, if you can, all the
blows which He hath received, all the wounds with
which He is covered, all the thorns which pierce
His head, all the drops of blood which He
hath shed, and ask Him, with the Prophet, who
hath struck Him in that manner, and treated Him
so. You will hear Him reply that it is sin, that it
is your sin, that it is you yourselves. I, Lord, I the
author of Thy cruel Passion! And I am not pierced
to the heart by it, thrilled with grief! I the
author, and yet with a calm and indifferent eye I
can still love sin which dealt Thee Thy death-blow!
Moreover, my brethren, if sin is the principal enemy
of God, God is no less its enemy; if it caused the

death of Jesus Christ, Jesus Christ caused its death. But what did all that cost this Divine Redeemer? Can you be ignorant of what it cost Him? And if you be, are not the open wounds on His body so many mouths which cry aloud to tell you? But, will you raise up against Him again the enemy He hath overthrown? Will you engage yourselves again in a slavery from which He hath set you free at so great expense? Will you stir up against Him new stripes, expose Him to new sufferings, crucify Him afresh? Have you no other feelings to adopt on this day of penitence and conversion? Ah, Lord, penitence and conversion, that is what I long for: but a sound, sincere, effectual conversion, a lasting and enduring penitence. Thou hast conquered sin; like Thee and by Thee I too will triumph over it. Thou hast conquered it by the punishment of the cross; I will triumph over it by the healthful discipline of an austere and mortified life. In that struggle, Thy cross shall be my pattern, my support, as it is my hope for all eternity.

VI.

THE RESURRECTION OF JESUS CHRIST.

Rom. iv. 25.—"Who was delivered for our offences, and was raised again for our justification."

SIRE,—It is on this testimony of S. Paul that S. Bernard relied when he said that the Resurrection of the Son of God, which is properly the mystery of His glory, had been at the same time the fulfilment of His charity towards men. No other proof of this is needed than the words of my text, since they teach us that it is for our sake, for our wealth, for our justification, that this adorable Saviour has entered into possession of His glorious life, and has risen again. According to our way of looking at matters, we might at first think these things ought to be separated, and that Jesus Christ, having completed on the cross the work of our redemption, ought only to think of His own greatness, that is to say, that having died for us, He ought only to rise again for Himself. But no, Christians, His love for us has not been able to agree to that separation. He is a God, says S. Bernard, but a God-Saviour, who wills to belong to us entirely, and whose glory and blessedness must for that reason pertain to us, as well as His humiliations and His sufferings,* all that He underwent was for our sake : since His humiliations were beneficial and necessary to us, He humbled and abased Himself; since for our redemption He must needs suffer, He gave Himself up to torments and death. From the moment that God's decree demanded the glorification of His humanity, He wills that we should profit by His same glory; for if He rises, continues S. Bernard, it is to establish our faith, to confirm our hope, to quicken our charity : it is to raise Himself in us, and to enable us to rise spiritually with Him : in a word, as He died for our sins, He " was raised again for our justification" and for our sanctification. That is the mystery that we are now celebrating, and which the universal Church makes the subject of its joy to-day ; a majestic and venerable mystery, on which rests not merely the whole of the Christian religion, since it is the key-stone of our faith, but the whole of Christian piety, since it ought to be the rule of our conduct. This is what I undertake to show you.

To enter into my subject, I presuppose here, Christians, what faith teaches us, and what we ought to regard as an essential point of our religion—namely, that in dying Jesus Christ has perfectly justified us, and that the merits of His death lacked nothing to place us again in a state of grace with God. But, besides these merits, said S. Chrysostom, we needed an example and a model after which we might form ourselves, and which we

---

* " Totus in usus nostros expensus."

might ever have before our eyes, so that we might ourselves work for the accomplishment of our justification, or, if you wish, of our conversion, in which, according to the dispensation of God, we ought to co-operate; and it is to this end the Saviour has divinely appointed His glorious Resurrection.

You know, Christians, and you cannot be ignorant, since it is an article of the faith which you profess, that the sin of the first man was a rash presumption which urged him to exalt himself above himself, and to wish to measure himself with God, to have the knowledge of God, to be like God, "Ye shall be as gods." But you know also the wise way in which God dealt with man, when, by a surprising secret of His Providence, He appointed for man's remedy that which seemed to have been the cause of His evil, and He obliged him to sanctify himself by that which had made him guilty. I mean, when that God of glory became incarnate and was made man, and brought Himself into positions in which it was not only allowable to man to wish to be like his God, but in which his greatest fault would have been not to wish to be like, and, indeed, not to be like, Him. But what state specially do the Scriptures point out to us as that in which the Son of God has insisted we ought to be like Him, and in which it is not a crime, but a merit and duty to fashion ourselves after His likeness? The state of His Resurrection.

For it is for that, as the great Apostle expressly states, that He has risen from the dead, in order that, sanctified by His example, we may take a new life, "that like as Christ was raised up from the dead by the glory of the Father, even so we also should walk in newness of life." Moreover, my brethren, S. Chrysostom adds, the words are not simply an instruction of the Apostle, but the advice of the Holy Spirit, who reveals to us God's purpose, and enables us to understand it: whence it follows that not only has the Saviour's Resurrection of itself all the necessary qualities to serve as a pattern in our conversion, but that God has set it before us as a pattern, and it is particularly with that end in view that He willed that Jesus Christ should rise again, "that like as Christ was raised, so we also should walk." This made Tertullian say, that sinners converted and reconciled by grace are in some sort a sequel to, and copies of, the Resurrection of Jesus Christ.* For so he named them, and why? Because every sinner, who is converted and who changes his life, ought to show in himself a perfect imitation of that character which belonged to the humility of Jesus Christ in His Resurrection. Let us observe, then, what the features of that character have been; and, by the comparison of them which we are about to make, let us recognize to-day what we ought to be before God. "The Lord is risen indeed, and hath appeared to Simon," said the two disciples, speaking of their Master. There are the two rules we ought to follow, and in which that conformity between Jesus Christ and ourselves ought to consist. He is risen indeed, to give us the idea of a true conver-

---

* "Appendices resurrectionis."

sion; and He hath appeared in His risen state, to give us the idea of a pattern conversion. He is risen indeed, so that we may be truly and thoroughly converted; that is the first part: and He hath appeared in His risen state, so that, if we be converted, we may freely and openly appear so to the glory of our God; that is the second part. Either without the other, says S. Augustine, is defective; for to appear converted and not to be so, is imposture and hypocrisy; and not to appear so, or rather to fear to appear so, is weakness and consideration for the world. We must then both be converted and show it. He is risen, and hath appeared. We must be converted in spirit and in truth, by a conversion of our manners such as holds good before God, "He is risen indeed:" we must show it with an holy freedom, so that our conversion may also be, according to the Gospel, a light which shineth before men, "He hath appeared to Simon." Shall I be successful, Christians, in persuading you of these two important obligations? They will form the divisions of this sermon. Let us proceed to consider them.

I. It is S. Paul who has said it, and in the first proposition that I have advanced I have aimed at nothing less than to establish a principle of religion, about which we are not permitted to doubt. Jesus Christ is truly risen, and it is after that pattern that God wishes us to be truly converted. But I add, as following naturally from this starting-point, that Jesus Christ, after coming forth from the tomb, hath no longer lived as a mortal man, but as an heavenly, a risen man, and that it is a law for us, that after our conversion we should no longer live like carnal and worldly men, but live a life quite spiritual, and agreeable to the blessed state into which men sincerely and thoroughly converted find themselves raised by grace. Two thoughts to which I reduce these admirable words of the Epistle to the Romans, which I consider as completely proving the truths that I am preaching to you, "Buried with Him by baptism into death: that like as Christ was raised up from the dead by the glory of the Father, even so we also should walk in newness of life." We are, my brethren, buried with Jesus Christ by baptism, to die unto sin, so that, as this God-Saviour hath risen again by His almighty power, we may be quickened by the same spirit, and raised inwardly to lead that new life which is the result of a true conversion. Give your attention, Christians, and do not lose anything of so necessary an instruction. "The Lord is risen indeed;" a starting-point, I repeat, to which you and I ought to attach ourselves at first to form a just idea of the conversion of the sinner. Do not be astonished, my dear listeners, that Jesus Christ, according to the account of the Evangelists, interested Himself so to prove, and to prove by Himself, His resurrection. The Apostles were seized with fear at beholding Him, because they thought they saw a spirit; and He could not allow them to remain in that uncertainty and distress. No, said He to them to assure them, it is not a spirit, it is I Myself. Look at My feet and My hands, touch My wounds, and you will learn that I am not an apparition, but a substantial and real

P

body. Why, asks S. Chrysostom, why such exact care to show them the truth of His resurrection? Ah! my brethren, replies that holy Doctor, it was because, besides the reasons which He had for acting thus, He well knew the law henceforth imposed on us, and the engagement by which we were bound, as sinners, to rise to the life of grace, as He had Himself risen to the life of glory, "that like as Christ was raised up, even so we also should walk in newness of life." But it was to be feared that that spiritual resurrection of our souls, instead of being a truth, should only be an unreality, and that, whilst we passed for converted men, we should be very far from what we outwardly seemed to be. For that reason He omitted nothing to convince His disciples that He had not merely risen in appearance, but in fact, wishing that true resurrection to serve us as a pattern and example.

Do you understand, Christians, and have you ever fathomed the consequence of those words, "He is risen, indeed?" See, however, to what they lead—condemnation of so many imaginary conversions, which have only the shell and mask of a true conversion, without having its inner part and its merits. For, allow me to make to you here an observation exactly like that which S. Paul made when he was instructing the Corinthians about the resurrection of the body,* "Behold, I tell you a mystery: we shall indeed all rise again, but we

---

* 1 Cor. xv. 51.—"Ecce mysterium vobis dico: Omnes quidem resurgemus, sed non omnes immutabimur."

shall not all be changed." He wished thereby to teach them that, although the reprobate would have a share in the future resurrection as well as the elect, their bodies would not be changed in it like the bodies of the elect, nor made like the glorious body of Jesus Christ; a terrible difference, on which the Apostle insisted, to give the faithful a healthy fear of the judgment of God. But, terrible as in the judgment of God must be the difference between the reprobate and the elect, there is yet another difference which, though less striking, is not less fatal to the sinner, and which, without waiting for the end of the ages, shows itself in Christianity to-day according to the different dispositions of Christians on this festival. We have all celebrated the Resurrection of Jesus Christ; but I do not know if we have all experienced that happy change which that holy celebration, by a grace peculiar to itself, ought to work in our souls. In the reception of the adorable Sacrament of our Saviour, we have all seemed to be spiritually raised again; but perhaps we were very far from being all renewed, and from being able on this great day all alike to bear witness before God, that we are no longer the same men. That is the mystery, but the dreadful mystery that I proclaim to you, and in respect of which every one ought to examine himself. "We shall indeed all rise again, but we shall not all be changed."

For let us honestly acknowledge it, and since unhappy experience compels us to admit it, let us not spare ourselves the confusion of doing so. The chief irregularity, which you cannot bewail enough, and for which you cannot reproach yourselves too much, is that, in that solemn celebration of Easter, by an abuse of penitence, which according to the Fathers, is the sacrament of the resurrection of sinners, we often lie to the Holy Spirit, and by that very penitence impose upon the world, and deceive ourselves. Yes, my brethren, even in the tribunal of penitence we lie to the Holy Spirit, and abjure with the mouth what we love in the heart; saying that we renounce the world, and never renouncing that which cherishes in us the love of the world; giving God pledges which we do not intend to keep, and which we have not made up our mind to fulfil, having less good faith towards God than we have towards men, even the very lowest man. We impose upon the world by a wondrous punctiliousness in acquitting ourselves of the public duties of religion at this holy season; by the fame of some good works soon accomplished; by a display of zeal in matters in which such a display is possible without our being any the better for it; by the reformation of a few points, of which we make a show, without trying to advance any further, and making no effort to overcome our besetting sins and the passions by which we are enslaved. We deceive ourselves by confusing the resolutions of amendment and the graces of conversion with conversion itself, imagining to ourselves that we are changed, because we are touched with a desire to be changed; and without it having cost us the least struggle, we flatter ourselves that we have gained great victories, and since, as far as penitence is concerned, all this is only an illusion and a lie, the Gospel opposes to it to-day this single test, "He is risen indeed;" and by that single test enables us to judge how far we have strayed from God's paths, since between our new life and the glorious life of Jesus Christ there is an opposition as enormous as that which exists between nothingness and reality, appearance and fact, falsehood and truth. Ah! my beloved hearers, how many shadows of conversion, or, to use the expression of S. Bernard, how many a chimera of conversion I could bring forward as a proof, if I were permitted to enter into the secret of your hearts and disclose to you their inmost recesses! How many conversions from worldly motives, how many the result of worldly calculation, how many of interest, how many which were prompted and inspired by another spirit than that which ought to influence us in the question of returning to God! conversions, if you like, fruitful in good resolutions, but fruitless in deeds; grand in words, but miserable in practice; calculated to dazzle, but not to convert us. How many consciences have presented themselves before the altar as whited sepulchres, and under that deceitful surface still hide decay and corruption! Are these living copies of that God-man, who is born again from the bosom of death to be, as S. Paul says, "the Firstborn among many brethren?" No, no, Christians, it is not in that way we can have the happiness and glory of being like Him. But, what is a true conversion? Please to understand that it is a conversion of the heart, an unfeigned and supernatural conversion of which God is the source, the object and the end. Would that

I might unfold these two important articles in all the fulness of their extent!

A sincere and unfeigned conversion; for, says S. Bernard, why should we dissimulate before God, who, having made us what we are, sees better than we ourselves what is in us, and what is not in us? And why should we act a false part before men, whose esteem will never justify us, and whose false estimate of us will one day be our confusion? Is not this the reason why S. Paul, representing to Christians as so many obligations the consequences they ought to draw from this mystery, returned always to this law; that Jesus Christ, our Pascal Lamb, had been sacrificed for us, and that we ought to "keep the feast, not with the old leaven," that leaven of dissimulation and malice with which our hearts had perhaps hitherto been infected, but in a spirit of sincerity and truth. Why? Because the Saviour Himself had said that such sincerity of conversion was the essential condition which should endue us with a holy resemblance to Jesus Christ risen again.

In truth it is generally a leaven of sin, which we foment within ourselves, and of which we do not strive to get rid, which causes our condemnation before God, and hinders us from rising again in spirit, as Jesus Christ rose again according to the flesh. Let me explain what I mean. A man is reconciled to his brother, and forgives his enemy; but yet there always remains a leaven of bitterness and of vexation which differs but little from enmity and hatred: we break off a criminal inclination, but we do not break it off so completely as not to reserve, so to say, certain rights which we pretend God's law does not strictly oblige us to give up, certain dealings which honesty and custom seem to permit, certain liberties which we allow ourselves, persuading ourselves that we shall not go beyond them: this is what S. Paul calls "the leaven of malice and wickedness." But, my brethren, the Apostle adds, that you must purify yourselves from that leaven, if you would celebrate the new passover. You must remember that, as a little leaven, when it is corrupt, suffices to spoil the whole lump, so what remains of a passion imperfectly extinguished, though dead in appearance, can destroy and make of no effect all the merit of our conversion, " Purge out, therefore, the old leaven, that ye may be a new lump." A supernatural conversion, a conversion in the sight of God: for of what use are all the opinions of men and the considerations of the world when it is a question of making ourselves live again unto God, and of making spring up afresh in us the spirit of grace after having lost it? We are told that the irregularity of our life may be a hindrance to our fortune, that such a propensity makes us contemptible, that this offence makes us hateful, and thereupon we straightway correct ourselves: what, after all, is such a conversion, even though it had all the show of the most exact and most sincere regularity? We estrange ourselves from the world for some private vexation, from an inability to succeed in it, or from despair of reaching a certain position which our ambition covets; we part company from a certain person, because we are tired of him, or because we have discovered his faithlessness and infidelity; we leave off sinning, because the opportunity for sin forsakes us, and not because we forsake the opportunity for sin: all this is only a shadow of a conversion. We must be quickened by a supernatural principle, as Jesus Christ was raised by a divine virtue. As in the Resurrection of Jesus Christ He appeared entirely God, because in virtue of that mystery the Humanity was completely absorbed in the Divinity; so, after His pattern, there must not be in our conversion anything which speaks of man, anything which belongs to man's imperfection, anything which partakes of man's corruption; interest must not be taken into consideration, nor must worldly prudence have anything to do with it; and if the creature be the moving cause, the Creator must be the end kept in view in our conversion. In this way the Apostle guided himself, when he said, Far from me be that false righteousness which I might find in myself, and which would be of myself, because God would be henceforth neither the object nor the source of it! It is not enough even for me to have that imperfect righteousness which comes from the law, but I must have that which comes from God by faith; that which makes me know Jesus Christ and the power of His Resurrection, that I may attain, if it be possible, to that blessed resurrection which distinguishes the living from the dead—that is to say, sinners who are justified from those who are not. So, according to the Apostle, all true penitents have made use of these expressions in turning to God. They have closed their eyes to everything else, they have not consulted flesh and blood, they have trampled the world under their feet, they have raised themselves above themselves; and why? because, says S. Paul, they seek a more substantial and more advantageous resurrection than that which is typified in the pretended conversion of worldlings, "that they might obtain a better resurrection." For, I repeat, there is a diversity of conversions now, as at the end of the world there will be a diversity of resurrections; and as, according to the Gospel, some will come out of their tombs to rise again unto life, the others to rise again unto condemnation and death, " They that have done good shall come forth unto the resurrrection of life; and they that have done evil, unto the resurrection of damnation;" just as we now see sinners come out of the tribunal of penitence, some quickened by grace and reconciled to God, others, by abuse of the sacrament, yet more hardened in sin and at greater enmity with God. Blessed, concludes the Holy Spirit in the Revelation, " blessed and holy is he that hath part in the first resurrection." He is speaking of the resurrection of the just: by the same rule I say, Blessed and holy is he that hath part in the first conversion! Blessed and holy is he who, rising again with Jesus Christ, according to the Apostle's rule, only sees in his conversion heavenly things, turns aside his sight from earthly objects, does not seek prosperity, rises above adversity, is content to possess God, and attaches himself to God for the sake of God Himself! But that is the conversion, Christians, which God demands from you to-day, and the pattern of which He sets before you in the Person of his Son.

Let us not, however, stop there: I have said that the Saviour of the world, after coming forth from the tomb, no longer lived like a mortal man but like an heavenly and risen man, and that it is a law that we should lead after our conversion a new life and one agreeable to the blessed state of men truly converted, to which we are raised by grace, "that like as Christ was raised up from the dead, by the glory of the Father, even so we also should walk in newness of life." But wherein does that newness of life consist? Let us return to our pattern. Behold Him, Jesus Christ, in His character of man, as a Being composed of body and soul; but His body, in the moment of His resurrection, by a wonderful change of all that was material and earthly in its substance, became a completely spiritual body in its attributes; and His soul, by virtue of the same resurrection, was by another miracle perfectly separated from the world, though it was still in the midst of the world: two points of resemblance which Jesus Christ risen ought to imprint on us, to work in us this renewing which is the necessary but unmistakable proof of our conversion. He had a body, and that body, clothed in glory, seemed to be of the nature and of the condition of spirits; a truth so admitted that S. Paul, having in mind the mystery which we are celebrating, feared not to say to the Corinthians, "Yea, though we have known Christ after the flesh, yet now henceforth know we Him no more." This is why, my brethren, although formerly we have known Jesus Christ according to the flesh, now that He is risen from the dead, we know Him no more in the same manner, nor according to that same flesh. What do you say, great Apostle? S. Chrysostom thereupon exclaims. What, you no longer know your God according to that adorable flesh in which He has accomplished your salvation? that flesh formed by the Holy Spirit, conceived of a Virgin, united and joined to the Divine Word; that flesh which He has offered for you on Calvary, which He has left for your nourishment in His sacrament, and which ought to be one of the objects of your blessedness in Heaven, you know it no more? No, replies the Apostle without hesitating, since that God-man, freed from the bonds of death, has entered upon His glorious life, I know Him no longer according to the flesh. "Yea, though we have known Christ after the flesh, yet now henceforth know we Him no more." So spoke the Master of the Gentiles, and cannot you at once apply his words? That is to say, that if you be truly converted, men must no longer know you, or rather, you must no longer know yourselves according to the flesh; you must no longer seek to satisfy the unrestrained desires of the flesh; you must no longer be slaves of that flesh which has hitherto governed you; that flesh, purified by penitence, must not henceforth be subject to the corruption of sin; and that we, ministers of the Saviour, who groaned formerly at only being able to look upon you as sensual and carnal men, may now have the consolation, not merely of knowing you such as you were, but moreover of knowing you divinely changed and transformed; so that we can say of you in a measure, Yea, though we have known you after the flesh, yet now henceforth know we you no more.

That is how, according to the doctrine of S. Paul, our bodies, beginning from that life, partake of the glory of Jesus Christ risen; this, my dear listeners, is how they become spiritual, incorruptible, full of strength, of force, of honour: but let us bear in mind, that they are only such in proportion as we co-operate for that end, and as, by a perfect correspondence, we strive, according to the rule of the Holy Spirit, to make of our bodies pure and agreeable offerings in the eyes of God. Glorified bodies possess all these attributes by a kind of necessity; but they only belong to our bodies according as we use our liberty: that is what makes our merit on earth; but it is also what ought to double our fear, and what demands all our watchfulness. For, however we may be established in good, we are liable to be shaken: the graces which have strengthened us in our conversion are not graces to encourage our laziness, still less to authorize our presumption. Whatever trust we ought to have in the mercy and help of God, it is always true that we may belie our firm resolutions, and that our fickleness may make us fall from that state of purity to which we have been restored by penitence. What, then, must we do, and how ought we to live henceforth in the world? Like Jesus Christ, after His resurrection. He was in the world without being of the world—that is to say, without taking part in the affairs, the interests, the assemblies and conversations of the world; holding communion only with His disciples, and speaking to them only of the Kingdom of God. You, then, my brethren, concludes S. Paul, and I conclude after him, "If ye then be risen with Christ," only have a longing for the things of heaven, "seek those things which are above." Separate yourselves from the world, live apart from the world, not by always going out of the world, since your condition keeps you in it, but let not your heart and mind be engrossed by it; above all, when you show yourselves in the world, let it be to edify it by your change. To be converted, that is the first duty, and it has been the subject of the first part of the sermon. To show yourselves converted, that is the other duty, of which I must speak to you in the second part.

II. It is a mystery, Christians, but it is not an obscure mystery, nor one difficult to unravel, to know why Jesus Christ willed after His resurrection to live among men for the space of forty days. In the natural order of things, from the moment when He rose again, the Heaven ought to have been His abode, and the earth was nothing for Him but a strange habitation. Why, then, did He put off that triumphant ascension which should put Him in possession of a kingdom due to His merits? and why did He in some measure defer the accomplishment of that happiness which He had fairly earned, and to which He had so many claims? Why? A higher reason made Him consent to this delay: a reason, my dear listeners, taken from the Gospel itself. It was that He wished to maintain throughout His character of Saviour, and to connect the mysteries of His glory with our justification, as the mysteries of His sufferings were connected with it, that it might be true in all points to say, "He was delivered for our offences, and was raised again for our justification." But for that, says S. Chrysostom, He was not contented with being raised, but He wished to show Himself raised; He wished that the world should see Him in the state of that new life into which He had entered; He wished by His appearances to shed abroad the rays of that Divine light wherewith He was endued. That, I say, is why He employed forty days in showing Himself, now to all His disciples assembled, now to a few in private, now in a wonderful draught of fishes, now in a mysterious repast, now under the form of a gardener, now under that of a traveller, acting, speaking, communicating Himself, and diffusing everywhere tokens which made themselves felt, of the miracle which had taken place in His person, and giving proof of His return from the dead. An excellent lesson for us Christians, if we know how to profit by it. All this concerns us, and teaches us that, as it is not enough to appear converted, if we be not so in reality, so it is not enough to be converted and not appear to be so. For, my dear listeners, this important lesson contains two different obligations, to be converted, and to appear converted; and our mistake is not to distinguish them properly. As they are two kinds of disorders to be impious, and to appear impious (for to be impious, said Tertullian, is a crime; and to appear so is a scandal); so we ought to be well persuaded that there are two precepts in the divine law, one of which obliges us to be converted, and the other to give outward tokens of our conversion; so that to obey one of these two precepts, without setting about the accomplishment of the other, is only an imperfect righteousness. Indeed, if Jesus Christ, after coming forth from the tomb, had kept Himself in concealment in the world, and had not appeared in His risen state, He would, if I may venture to say it, have but half accomplished the purpose of His adorable mission, He would have left our faith in trouble, and, in relation to ourselves, the religion which He wished to establish would have had no solid foundation. In like manner, if after our conversion we neglect to appear converted, or if we be afraid of doing so, we only perform imperfectly the work of God; and, far from pleasing Him, we incur the curse pronounced by the Apostle S. James, when he says, "Whosoever shall .... offend in one point, he is guilty of all." I say more, that to be and to appear converted, are two different obligations, which are nevertheless so inseparable, that in strictness it is impossible for a man to acquit himself of the first without satisfying the second, because it is an established fact, as the angelic Doctor, Thomas Aquinas, has justly observed, that to appear converted is a part of conversion itself. Let me explain. You have at length, you say, made up your mind to change your life and to renounce your sin; but you have, besides, you add, a certain appearance to keep up, and you do not wish men to perceive your change. But I maintain that there is a contradiction in your proposal, because one of the most essential circumstances in that change of life, which your conversion ought to bring about is, that it should be apparent, so that men may perceive it. I say that as long as it shall not appear and men shall not perceive it, whatever idea you may have of it, it is a doubtful and untrustworthy change, or even a fancied and imaginary change: why? Because a conversion, to be complete, ought to embrace without exception all the duties of the Christian man. But one of the duties of the Christian man is to seem to be what he is; and if he has been a sinner and rebellious against God, one of his most indispensable duties is to appear obedient and submissive to God. I say that duty rests upon the interest of the God you have offended, on the interest of the neighbour you have shocked, on your own interest, I mean the interest of your soul and of your salvation which you have openly abandoned; three unanswerable proofs of the truth which I preach to you, and with which I can promise myself you will be touched.

The obligation to appear converted is based on the interest of God whom you have offended; otherwise, Christians, what reparation will you make to God for so many crimes, and how will you give back to Him the glory of which you have robbed Him in committing them? What, sinner, who are listening to me, you have a thousand times outraged this God of majesty, and you blush now to appear humbled before Him? You have highly despised His law, and you believe to have made amends by a secret repentance? Your wantonness, which displeased Him, has been public, and shall your penitence, which ought to appease Him, be hidden. Is that dealing with God as God? "No, no, my brethren," says S. Chrysostom, "to treat Him thus is not properly to be converted. If we had never sinned, and had always preserved our baptismal innocence, God would have had us confess ourselves; and in vain do we protest to Him in our heart that He is our God, if we be not ready to make a free and generous confession to this effect before men, and even before tyrants." "Whosoever shall confess Me before men," such is the condition which He proposes to us, and without which He reproaches us as unworthy of Him. "But if the just man even, although just," continues S. Chrysostom, "be subject to this condition, how much more the sinner who is converted, since it is a matter not only of confessing the God he serves and adores, but of doing justice to the God whom he has dishonoured! And how shall he do Him that justice except by a conversion which edifies, a conversion of which we can see the fruits, a conversion as exemplary as it ought to be genuine and sincere? The life of a sinner in his state of penitence," concludes S. Chrysostom, "must therefore be henceforth an honourable amends which he makes to his God." His reverence in the sanctuary, his regard for the Holy Communion, his frequent attendance at the altar, his faithful observance of the rules of the Church, his modest and religious demeanour, his regular conduct, must all speak for him and witness to God of the contrition of his soul: why? in order that God may be recompensed; and that those who, when they formerly saw that man in the irregularities of an impure and careless life, asked where his God was, and almost doubted if he had one, not merely may no longer doubt, but may glorify God for such a plain and notable conversion: "Lest the heathen say, where is now their God?" That is what I call the interest of God.

And forsooth, when S. Peter, after the Saviour's Resurrection, appeared in the synagogues and public places, preaching the name of Jesus Christ with an holy liberty, whence did he specially get that zeal? From the thought and remembrance of his sin. "I have betrayed my Master," said he in the bitterness of his heart, "and my faithlessness has been to Him keener than the cruelty of the executioners who have crucified Him: I must now at the expense of everything show what I now am to Him, and must sacrifice myself to wipe out with my blood so shameful a stain." This is what stimulated and determined him to undertake all, and to suffer all for that God-man whom he had renounced. But it is into that thought, my dear listeners, that you ought to-day to enter. Like the prince of Apostles, you recognize, and you are obliged to recognize, that on a thousand occasions into which the torrent of the world dragged you, you have renounced your God; you confess that your life, if I may so say, has been a continual subject of confusion for Jesus Christ: is it not, then, just that you should put yourselves in a state to do Him honour, and that, by a Christian life, you should at least efface the impressions against His law to which your impiety may have given rise? Is it not just—another very touching thought—is it not just, that you should honour the very grace of your conversion? For do you know, Christians, with what feelings the grace of penitence ought to inspire you? Do you know what you ought to be in the world by reason of that grace, if you have responded to it? I say you ought to be in the world what the Apostles and the first disciples were after the Resurrection of the Son of God. Scripture teaches us that their chief, or rather their only employment, was to serve Him as witnesses in Judea, in Samaria, and to the ends of the earth, "Ye shall be witnesses unto Me both in Jerusalem, and in all Judea, and in Samaria." Thus, my brethren, you ought to be persuaded that God expects from you, as converted sinners who are reconciled with Him by sacramental grace, a special witness, a witness which you can render Him, a witness which ought to be glorious to Him. As though He said to you to-day, "Yes, it is you whom I choose to be my blameless witnesses, no longer in Samaria and Judea, but in a place where it is still more important for Me to have disciples who maintain My glory—namely, at the Court, where this witness, that I ask from you, is still more advantageous to Me—ye shall be My witnesses. You, men of the world, you who are given up to carnal passions, but in whom I have created a new heart, you on whom I have made a perceptible impresssion by My grace, you whom I have drawn out of the abyss of sin, it is you who will serve Me for witnesses; and where? In the midst of the world, and of the greatest world? for it is there especially that I need faithful witness,

Ye shall be My witnesses." It is true that you have hitherto lived in irregularities; but far from the irregularities of your life weakening your testimony, they are the very things which will strengthen it and render it more convincing; for, on comparing you with your former selves, and seeing such public irregularities followed by so edifying a conversion, the world, impious as it is, can draw no other conclusion than that this change is the work of grace, and a miracle of the right hand of the Most High, "Ye shall be My witnesses." And indeed, Christians, if you had always led a regular life, whatever glory God might gain from that in other respects, He would not gain from it the witness of which I speak to you. You would be less guilty before Him, but you would also be less fitted to make known the power of His grace. To serve Him at court as witnesses, such sinners as you were needed; and it is thus that He unfolds to you in your very sin something by which you may honour Him.

There is an obligation to appear converted, resting upon the welfare of your neighbour, whom you have shocked; for as S. Jerome said:* " I owe to myself purity of manners, but I owe to others the purity of my reputation." But this thought is still more suitable for a converted sinner: I owe to myself my conversion, but I owe to others the appearance and tokens of my conversion: and why the appearance? To make amends by a proportionate remedy for the offences of my life; for

---

* " Mihi debeo meam vitam, aliis debeo meam famam."

what has offended my brother, he may add, is not exactly my sin, but as much of my sin as showed itself. I accomplish nothing, then, if I do not oppose holy appearances to these criminal appearances ; and I flatter myself if I content myself with hating sin inwardly, and yet impose on myself no outward restraint. This neighbour, whom you have caused to stumble, must, my dear listener, profit by your return, and must be entirely undeceived of the opinion which he had of you ; he must see that you are no longer that man whose example has been so hurtful to him ; that you no longer keep up that connection, that you no longer frequent that house, that you no longer see that person, that you no longer assist at those profane spectacles, that you no longer indulge in those immodest conversations —in a word, that it is no longer you : for it is a presumption in you to suppose that, whilst he shall see you in the same society, in the same engagements, in the same habits, he will believe, on your word, that you are a changed and converted man ; and it would be simplicity in him to think so. Let us keep to our mystery. The Resurrection of the Son of God, which we have before our eyes, will be for you and for me a manifest proof of what I say. Why did Jesus Christ appear risen ? or, rather, to whom did He appear risen ? This deserves your attention. " He appeared risen," said S. Augustine, "to some to console them in their sadness, to others to bring them back from their wanderings ; to those, to overcome their unbelief, to these, to reproach them for their hardness of heart." The Magdalene and the other women who had followed Him wept near His tomb, pierced with the lively grief which the remembrance and image of His recent death caused them; He appeared to them, says the Gospel, to fill them with an holy joy, and to assuage their tears. The weak and cowardly disciples had forsaken Him and taken flight, seeing Him in the hands of His enemies; He appeared to them to gather them like scattered sheep, and to make them come into His flock again. S. Thomas persisted in being unbelieving, and would not yield to the testimony of those who had seen Him; He appeared to that Apostle to convince him, and to quicken his faith, which was well nigh extinct. The others, though persuaded of the truth, were still cold and indifferent. He appeared to find fault with them for their indifference, and to re-awaken their zeal. He is, I repeat, the Divine pattern after which we ought to mould ourselves; for it is thus that we ought to appear converted for the consolation of the just, for the conversion of sinners, for the conviction of libertines. Let me enlarge this thought.

For the consolation of the just.—For in your state of sin, my dear listener, you were dead; and how many holy souls wept over you! What grief the charity which moved them, made them feel at the sight of your irregularities! With what anguish, or, if you will, with what sorrow of heart have they not groaned before God! By how many secret acts of penitence have they not tried to expiate your sins! And for how long a time, might we not say, they have been in pain, asking God to give you His grace, and sighing after your conversion! At length God has heard them, and, according to their longing, you are spiritually raised; but you are told that being spiritually raised, they have a right to ask that you should appear to them to be so, that they may rejoice at it on earth as the blessed angels glory at it in heaven; you are told that it is an act of justice which you owe them, that as your sin has afflicted them, so your return to God must console them. Ought not that alone to pledge you to give them tokens, but unmistakeable tokens, which on the one hand fill their cup with joy, and on the other put, as it were, the seal to the work of your salvation?

For the conversion of sinners.—There are some of your brethren in the world who are earning their own condemnation; having gone out of the way from God, they are living, dragged hither and thither by their passions, and no longer following any other path than that of iniquity. The question is how to save them, and to bring them back in a gentle, yet effectual manner, to the true Shepherd of their souls—that is, Jesus Christ; and it is you, you I say, converted sinner, who ought to serve for this purpose. Why you? I repeat it, because after your wanderings, you have a particular fitness for succeeding in this respect, which the just, who have always remained just, have not. So remarks Origen, S. Peter was singled out to bring back to the Son of God the disciples who had been scattered by temptation, "When thou art converted, strengthen thy brethren." He did not give that commission to S. John, who had always been attached to His person, nor to S. Mary, who accompanied Him to the cross, but to S. Peter, who had denied Him. Why so? A master-stroke of Providence! "Because," said Origen, "to draw other sinners, a disciple who had been a sinner was needed, and because the greatest sinner of all was best suited to draw all!" Ah! Christians, how many conversions might not your example alone produce, if you were to look upon yourselves as, like S. Peter, charged with the honourable duty of gaining your brothers to God! "When thou art converted, strengthen thy brethren." What a wonderful success might not that example, freed from all ostentation, and supported by a zeal equally humble and prudent—what a wonderful success might it not produce, and what could the preachers of the Gospel accomplish in comparison to it! What an attraction would it be, above all, for certain sinners, who were discouraged and tempted to despair, when they could say to themselves, There is a man whom we have seen in the same low life as ourselves; there he is converted and submitting to God! Could there be a more powerful charm to convert them? And when, to accomplish that, it is only a question of showing what you really are; are you not afraid, when you abstain from doing so, of falling under the curse with which God, by His prophet, has threatened you: "His blood will I require at thine hand?"

For the persuasion of reckless and unbelieving minds.—The Apostle S. Thomas, when he had become faithful, had a special grace for diffusing the gift of the faith; and if he had never been unbelieving, it is the reflection of S. Gregory, his preaching would then have been less touching. But the wonder was to see a man not only believe what he had obstinately striven against, but go the length of publishing it before judges, and not shrinking from death that he might establish the truth. It was this that persuaded the world. His unbelief by itself, says S. Chrysostom, would have been our destruction, his faith by itself would not have been enough for us; but his unbelief followed by his faith, or rather his faith preceded by his unbelief, has made us what we are. In like manner, I say, Christians—applying that thought to you—if you, to whom I am speaking, had never gone astray, the world might perhaps respect you; but the world, which in the present day is overwhelmed with license in matters of belief, would scarcely draw from your case a certain conviction of which it specially stands in need. That which affects impious people is to hear an impious person like themselves, one, moreover, whom the world counts wise, prompted by nothing else than the truth which he has learnt, say: I am persuaded I can no longer resist the grace which urges me, I wish to live as a Christian, and I pledge myself to do so. For that declaration is a weighty argument, which stops the mouth of impiety, and against which the most abandoned souls cannot make any reply.

Lastly, an obligation to appear converted founded upon self-interest.—For that worldly prudence which supplies us with so many pretexts not to declare ourselves, is a clumsy trick, of which the enemy of our salvation makes use to keep us always in his bonds, at the very moment that we flatter ourselves we have come back into the liberty of the children of God. In fact, we do not wish it to appear outwardly that we have changed our conduct. Why? Because we are assured that if this change were once to make itself seen, we should be obliged to act up to it, we could no longer get rid of it, and honour itself coming to the help of duty and religion, we should take upon ourselves the most difficult virtue—namely, perseverance—not as a simple engagement, but as an absolute necessity. But however well disposed we may be, we wish nevertheless to reserve to ourselves the power of doing as we like in the future. Although we actually renounce our sin, we do not wish to bind ourselves, nor to shut out the hope of ever turning back to it. That necessity of persevering appears frightful, and we fear the consequences of it; that is to say, we do not wish to be inconstant, but we wish to reserve to ourselves, in case of necessity, the power to be inconstant: and since, after giving tokens of our conversion, we could be so no longer, or we could only be so at the expense of a certain reputation of which we are jealous, we prefer to dissemble, and thus to run the risk of inconstancy, rather than make sure of ourselves by taking away a hurtful liberty. Such, my dear listeners, are the illusions of man's heart. But I reason in quite a different way, and I say that we ought to look upon it as an advantage to appear converted since, by our own admission, to appear converted is a reason which necessarily pledges us to be so, and to be so always. I say that we ought to reckon it as a grace to have discovered in this the means whereby we may make our conversion fixed and unchangeable. But if I fall, through unfortunate weakness, into my former irregularities, my conversion, instead of edifying others, will become a fresh cause of offence. That is an abuse of reason, Christians, a point on which the grace of Jesus Christ forbids us to speak, except inasmuch as that thought may be healthful to us, to give us strength, and to rouse us. I ought to fear my weaknesses and anticipate the danger, but I ought not to go too far in that anticipation and fear; it ought to make me watchful, but it ought not to make me weak; it ought to take away from me occasions of sin by a holy mistrust of self, but it ought not to take away from me my trust in God so as to hinder me from taking steps towards mine own salvation, without which, the resolution I have made to work for it will always be wavering. If I declare myself, men will judge and talk about me; ah well, that will be an aid against the natural inclination that I shall have to belie myself, to consider that I shall have to endure the judgments and censure of the world. I shall be accused of simplicity, vanity, hypocrisy, interested motives; I will try to do away with all these suspicions—that of simplicity, by my prudence; that of pride, by my humility; that of hypocrisy by the sincerity of my penitence; that of interested motives, by a perfect disregard of all things. "Besides," said S. Augustine, "the world will speak according to its maxims, and I shall live according to mine: if the world be just, if the world be Christian, it will approve of my change, and it will profit by it; if it be not, I ought to despise and abhor it."

However it may be, the great moral which Jesus Christ risen preaches to us, is to be and to appear converted, to be and to appear faithful, to be and seem to be, my dear listeners, what you are. Happy shall I be, if at the end of this discourse I leave you, not merely instructed, but persuaded and touched by these two important obligations. After that, however unworthy my ministry may be, perhaps I may be able to say, as S. Paul said when he parted from the Christians at Ephesus, that I am pure before God and innocent of the loss of souls, if among those who have listened to me, there be some who must perish, "Wherefore I take you to record this day, that I am pure from the blood of all men." And why? Because Thou knowest, O my God, that I have not hidden Thy truth from them, but that I have taken care to represent it to them with all freedom, yet in a seemly way, as becometh a minister of Thy Word. When in time past Thou didst send Thy prophets to preach in king's courts, Thou didst wish them to appear there like pillars of iron and walls of brass; that is to say, as disinterested, brave, and fearless ministers, "for, behold, I have made thee this day . . . . an iron pillar and brazen wall . . . . . against the kings of Judah." But I am bold to say, O Lord, that I needed not this character of fearlessness to announce Thy Gospel in this place, because I have had the advantage to announce it to a Christian king, a king who honours his religion, honours it in the court, and who makes an outward profession of honouring it; in a word, a king who loves truth. Thou didst forbid Jeremiah to tremble in the presence of the kings of Judah—"be not dismayed at their faces:" and I have rather to console myself that the presence of the greatest of kings, far from inspiring me with fear, has increased my confidence; far from weakening my ministry, has strengthened and confirmed it; for the truth, which I have preached at the court, has never met with anything in the heart of this monarch but an edifying submission and a powerful protection.

You see, Sire, what has sustained me: but behold what ennobles Your Majesty, and what ought to be for you a fund of merit that nothing will ever destroy, the love and zeal you have for the truth. Scripture teaches us, that what saves kings is neither strength nor power, nor the number of conquests, nor the conduct of affairs, nor the art of governing and reigning, nor so many other royal virtues which make heroes, and which men canonize. "There is no king that is saved by the multitude of an host:" wisdom and greatness of soul have caused Your Majesty not to stop there, but to set before yourself something yet more substantial. What saves kings is the truth; and Your Majesty seeks it, takes pleasure in hearing it, loves those who make it known, and would only feel contempt for whoever would veil it from you; and, instead of resisting it, Your Majesty makes a glory of being overcome by it: for," says S. Augustine, "nothing is more glorious than to allow yourself to be overcome by the truth." This, Sire, is what I call the greatness of your soul, and at the same time your salvation. "We esteem our princes happy," added the same S.

Augustine, "if, being able to do everything, they only wish for what they ought; if, being raised by their dignity above all, they hold themselves by their goodness indebted to all; if they only look upon themselves as the Lord's servants upon earth; if, in the honours that men pay them, they do not forget that they themselves are men; if they take a pride in doing good; if they use their power for the correction of vice; if they be masters of their passions as well as of their actions; if, when it is easy for them to avenge themselves they be always disposed to forgive; if they place religion before politics; if, divesting themselves of their majesty, they every day offer to God in prayer the sacrifice of their humility." An admirable portrait of a truly Christian king, which I have no fear in presenting to Your Majesty's eyes, since it only represents you to your own feelings and ought to be the subject of your consolation. It is Thou, O my God, who dost give to Thy people men of this character to govern them, Thou who holdest in Thine hands the hearts of kings, Thou who watchest over their salvation, and dost glorify Thyself in Scripture as being specially the author of it: "who givest salvation to kings." Show, O Lord, show that Thou art indeed the God of the salvation of kings, by shedding on our invincible monarch the abundant dew of Thy blessing and Thy grace, but chiefly the grace of graces, that of eternal salvation. When we pray to Thee for the preservation of his sacred person, for the prosperity of his arms, for the success and glory of his undertakings, although these prayers be right and a necessary duty, they are none the less somewhat interested, for our fortunes, our lives being attached to the person of that great king, his glory being ours, his prosperities ours, we cannot interest ourselves on his behalf without doing as much for ourselves. But, when we beseech Thee to pour upon him those special graces which constitute the salvation of kings, it is for him alone that we are then making supplication unto Thee; since there is no private benefit, nor any which pertains to him specially, nor to any king in the world, except the benefit of salvation. Such, Sire, is the feeling wherewith God inspires the lowest of your subjects concerning your august person; such is the desire which I daily express, my most sincere, most hearty desire. God will hear it; and after having made you reign so splendidly upon earth, He will make you reign yet more happily and gloriously in Heaven, whither may He bring us all at the last!

VII.

THE RESURRECTION OF JESUS CHRIST.

S. MARK xvi. 6.—"He saith unto them, Be not affrighted : Ye seek Jesus of Nazareth, which was crucified : He is risen : He is not here. Behold the place where they laid Him."

SIRE,—These words are very different from those that we generally see engraven upon men's tombs. However powerful they may have been, to what are the magnificent praises bestowed upon them reduced—those praises that we read on the superb monuments which man's vanity rears? To this sad inscription, " Here lies :" that great man, that conqueror, that hero so esteemed in the world, rests beneath this stone, buried in the dust, and all his power and greatness is not able to raise him out of it. But it was very different with respect to Jesus Christ. Hardly has He been shut in the bosom of the earth, when He comes forth on the third day, victorious and resplendent with light; so that the devout women who come to look for Him, and who, since they do not find Him, wish to learn what had happened to Him, can get no information except that He lives again, and that He is not there. This is how, according to the expression of Isaiah, His tomb was made glorious : " His rest shall be glorious." Instead, then, of the glory of the great which finishes at the tomb, it is in the tomb that the glory of this God-man begins. It is there, so to speak, in the midst of His weakness, that He puts forth all His strength; and that even within the arms of death He recovers, by His own virtue, a happy and immortal life. A wonderful change, Christians, which ought to strengthen His Church, which ought to console and re-assure His disciples, and which ought to serve as a ground of faith and of Christian hope: for such are, or ought to be, the effects of the Saviour's Resurrection, as I intend to show you in this sermon. Yes, Christians, the glorious Resurrection of Jesus Christ is one of the most substantial foundations both of our faith and of our hope. I am following S. Augustine: and, in so doing, I find that Father gives us in two short sentences a complete and an accurate division of the intent of the Resurrection. For, according to that holy Doctor, the Son of God therein presents to us at the same time a great miracle and a great example: a great miracle to confirm our faith, and a great example to stimulate our hope.* It is, in fact, on the Resurrection of Jesus Christ that the two most important truths of Christianity are established; of which the one, namely, that Jesus Christ is God, is the basis of all religion; and the other, namely, that as Jesus Christ rose, we, too, shall also one day rise again, is the underlying principle of the whole system of Gospel ethics.

---

* "In hac resurrectione et miraculum et exemplum; miraculum, ut credas; exemplum, ut speres."

So, my brethren, without any further introduction, this is what I want to set before you to-day :—

(i.) The miracle of the Resurrection of Jesus Christ as an indisputable proof of His Divinity : it is by that means He confirms our faith. That will be the first section.

(ii.) The example of the Resurrection of Jesus Christ as a pledge to assure us of our resurrection hereafter : it is by that means He stimulates our hope. That will be the second section.

Two points, these, of great importance. In the first, Jesus Christ will teach us by His Resurrection what He is : in the second, Jesus Christ will teach us by that same Resurrection what we shall be. Both together comprise all that is most sublime and lofty in Christianity. Heaven grant that they may serve equally for your instruction and your edification!

I. It is a grand sentence, and one which deserves to be listened to with all the sentiments of respect with which religion can inspire us, that sentence in which S. Paul tells us that the august mystery of the Resurrection has established in the world the belief in the Divinity of Jesus Christ : "Who was predestined to be the Son of God in power . . . . by the resurrection from the dead." Thus spoke the Apostle, persuaded of, filled with, penetrated by, that truth : We adore, my brethren, a Saviour who has been predestinated Son of God by virtue of His glorious Resurrection. Instead of "predestinated," the Greek and Syriac texts have "manifested" and "declared;" but S. Ambrose* reconciles these two versions, by saying that Jesus Christ, who was a God hidden in His Incarnation, was, according to His eternal predestination, to be a God revealed and known by His Resurrection. I do not know if you have ever reflected on the other very remarkable statement of that same Apostle, which he made in that striking sermon of his to the people of Antioch, as related in the book of Acts. It is thus the teacher of the Gentiles expressed himself: "We declare unto you glad tidings, how that the promise which was made unto the fathers God hath fulfilled the same unto us their children, in that He hath raised up Jesus again; as it is also written in the second Psalm; 'Thou art My Son; this day have I begotten Thee.'" What is the meaning of this, Christians? Of what day was S. Paul speaking? If he meant the day when Jesus Christ, as Son of God and the uncreated Word, was begotten by His Father, why did he apply it to the mystery of His Resurrection? And if he meant the day when Jesus Christ, as the God-man, was raised according to the flesh, why did he mention His eternal generation? "He hath raised up Jesus again, as it is written, This day have I begotten Thee." What connection is there between the two? Ah, replies S. Ambrose, it is admirable, and never did the Apostle's thoughts follow each other more naturally. How so? Because in reality

---

* "Christus latens in incarnatione prædestinatus erat ut declararetur Filius Dei in resurrectione."

the Resurrection of Jesus Christ had been for Him a second birth, but much more fortunate and more advantageous than the first; because in being born again, so to say, from the tomb, he had strikingly revealed in His own Person that character of Son of God with which He was endued. And that is the reason why the eternal Father particularly acknowledged Him in that mystery, addressing these words to Him with a special meaning, "Thou art My Son, this day have I begotten Thee." Yes, My Son, it is on this day that I beget Thee for the second time, but in a way which will perfectly establish the greatness of Thy origin, and the truth of that divine being that Thou hast received from Me: to-day hast Thou proved Thyself My Son. As if he said unto Him: Whilst Thou wert upon earth, although Thou wert indisputably Son of God, Thou wert only regarded in the character of Son of Man; but now, that Thou triumphest over death, and Thou art born again to the life of glory, Thou givest so unmistakable a token of the divinity that dwells in Thee, that henceforth it can no longer be disputed or denied Thee; and although I have always been Thy Father in time and in eternity, I none the less make a special honour of it to Myself to-day, distinguishing this happy day from among the other days which make up Thy destiny, and choose it to declare to the whole universe that, "Thou art My Son: this day have I begotten Thee."

Now, that we may better understand such an essential truth as this, let us consider in what sense and how far it is true that our faith in the Divinity of Jesus Christ rests mainly on His Resurrection; for, you will say to me, Did not the Saviour of the world, during the course of His mortal life, work miracles such as proved that He was indeed what He claimed to be? Were not demons cast out, men blind from their birth healed, the restoration to life of him who had been four days dead, so many plain and evident proofs of the Divine power which resided in Him? What more remarkable power could His Resurrection have to confirm that belief? That is the difficult point in the mystery to which I am directing your attention. I say that the revelation of the Divinity of Jesus Christ was particularly connected with His Resurrection, " He was predestined to be the Son of God . . . . by the resurrection from the dead." How so? For four reasons, or rather for a single reason stated in four propositions.

(a) Because His Resurrection was the proof which the God-man expressly promised to give the Jews in order to convince them of His Divinity.

(β) Because it was in reality the most natural and most convincing proof that could be given.

(γ) Because of all the miracles that Jesus Christ wrought by virtue of His Divinity none was better attested; of no other was there such indisputable evidence as of the Resurrection of His body.

(δ) And because of all His miracles this is the

one which has had most to do with the propagation of the faith and the establishment of the Gospel, the sum and substance of which is to believe in Jesus Christ, and to confess His Divinity.

For this reason the Christians of the first centuries, when they wished to express in a single word the idea they attached to the Resurrection of the Saviour, were wont by a custom which had grown up amongst them, to call it simply "The Witness;" so that when the Emperor Constantine built in Jerusalem a handsome church dedicated to Jesus Christ raised from the dead, he gave it the name of "Martyrium," that is, "The Witness." And S. Cyril, the patriarch of that same town, gives this reason of the name, that the church was consecrated to a mystery which God had Himself chosen to be the solemn witness of His Son's Divinity. This is what I hope to show you in expanding these four propositions.

For, is it not a true remark, that as often as Jesus Christ was pressed by the Jews in the Gospel, on the subject of His Divinity, and they asked Him for a proof it, He never referred them to any other proof than His Resurrection, to convince their minds of His claims or to confound their incredulity? That faithless nation, said He, wishes to be assured by a miracle of what I am; and it shall have no other miracle than that of the Prophet Jonah, or rather that of which Jonah was the type— namely, that after I have been shut up for three days in the bosom of the earth, I will come out of it, as Jonah came out of the whale's belly. You ask Me, He added, speaking to the Pharisees, by what miracle I show you that I have the right to make use of the absolute power and independent authority to which I lay claim, "What sign shewest Thou unto us, seeing that Thou doest these things?" But, this is how I mean you to judge them: after you have, by a cruel and violent death destroyed this visible temple, that is, My body, I will rear it up in three days in the same state. "Destroy this temple, and in three days I will raise it up." Mark this fact, I beg you. He might have referred to a hundred other miracles which He had wrought amongst them; but He passed by them all in silence, so that it would appear that it was not His intention in working them to convince men of His Divinity. For if He changed the water into wine at the marriage of Cana at Galilee, He was as it were constrained to do so out of deference to His mother's wishes; if He freed the daughter of the Canaanite woman, it was that He might free Himself from the importunity of that woman; if He restored to life the widow's son, it was a pure act of compassion. In the majority of these superhuman deeds, after allowing His Almighty power to go forth, He enjoins secrecy on those who had felt its virtue. And when He discovers to the three disciples His glory in His transfiguration, in which the heavenly Father, speaking in Person, recognizes Him for His well-beloved Son, He forbids them to make it public until after His Resurrection from the dead. "Tell the vision to no man, until the Son of Man be risen again from the dead."

Why not? For the reason mentioned by S. Chrysostom, that the Resurrection of Jesus Christ, as in God's purpose ordained to be the sign of His Divine Sonship, might put the seal on all His other miracles and complete their proof. Faith in all the other miracles rested on that one; for, as the Saviour of men had said, I am equal to God, God is My Father, and, to shew you that this is true, I will rise again three days after My death. If He had not been what He claimed to be, it was impossible that He should rise again, since God then, by aiding the miracle of His Resurrection, would have given His sanction to an imposture and a lie. If then, after that declaration, He rose again, we must conclude from it that He was God; and being God, all His miracles stand unquestioned, since it is natural to God to work miracles. And on the other hand, if He did not rise again, the belief in His Divinity would be destroyed by His own mouth; and His Divinity destroyed, His miracles could no longer stand, His words were only falsehoods, His life an artifice and illusion, the whole Christian faith a phantom. Such is the literal meaning of S. Paul's words, " If Christ be not risen, then is our preaching vain, and your faith is also vain." All that, let me repeat, is because Jesus Christ had fixed upon the Resurrection of His body as the distinctive token of His Divinity.

But why did He choose that miracle in preference to all the others? Ah, Christians, could He have chosen one more striking or which should make itself more felt than the Resurrection of Himself?

"Miracles," says S. Augustine, "are to intelligent creatures the language and voice of God, and the greatest of all miracles is the resurrection of a dead man; but amongst all instances of resurrection, which is the most miraculous? Is it not," continues the holy Doctor, "that in which a Person restores life to Himself, and quickens Himself by His own power?" It was not without good reason, then, that Jesus Christ fixed specially on this sign to prove that He was God, and Son of God. In fact, it is only God Who can say, "I have power to lay down my life, and I have power to take it again:" the one is as easy to Me as the other; and as I shall only lay it down when I will, so shall I take it again when it shall be My pleasure to do so; it is only God, I say, Who can express Himself in this manner. Before Jesus Christ (mark this observation of S. Ambrose, which is alike well-founded and ingenious), before Jesus Christ the world had seen men quickened, but quickened by means of other men. Elisha by the breath of his mouth had re-animated the corpse of the Shunamite's son: Elijah by his prayers had restored to his desolate mother, the widow of Sarepta, her child, who had wasted away: he restored him to her full of health and vigour. But, as S. Ambrose remarks, those who were then quickened, only received life through the power of another; and those who performed these miracles only worked them on others, not on themselves. It was an unheard-of wonder that the same man should at the same time perform the double miracle of quickening, and of quickening himself. For "since the world began was it not heard:" and this is the miracle that God reserved for His Son,* so as to declare to the world that He was both God and man; man, since He was quickened, and God since He quickened Himself. An adorable mystery, to which S. Jerome, by that deep understanding of the Scriptures which he had, applied the words from the Psalms, words which to the letter suit Jesus Christ, and can only refer to Him, " I am counted as one of them that go down into the pit: and I have been even as a man aided by none, free among the dead."† They put Me among the dead, and they thought that My lot would be like that of all men: but there were nevertheless between Me and them two great differences, the one that I was " free amongst the dead," and the other that among the dead I needed not the help of anybody, " a man aided by none." What does that mean, Christians? It means that Jesus Christ entered the kingdom of death, not as its subject, but as its sovereign; not as a slave, but as a conqueror; not dependent on its laws, but enjoying a perfect liberty: " free among the dead." So that to come forth out of it by resurrection, He needed the assistance of none but Himself: no prophet to pray for Him, to command Him to rise, to draw Him forth from the tomb by force, because, since He was God, He ought only to be helped by the virtue of His Own almighty power: " I have been even as a man aided by none,

---

* " Ut ostenderet quoniam erat in ipso, et resuscitatus homo, et resuscitans Deus" (S. Ambrose).

† Psalm lxxxviii. (Vulg. lxxxvii.) 3, " factus sum sicut homo sine adjutorio."

free among the dead." Words, adds S. Jerome, which seem to have been dictated by the Holy Spirit to form the epitaph of Jesus Christ, Who was to quicken Himself. It is, then, true that the Resurrection of the God-man was the most unmistakable proof which He could give of His Divinity: and that is why the whole synagogue, which had conspired against Him, made powerful efforts to hinder the belief in that Resurrection from being received in the world. The Jews were all persuaded that if men once believed, and it became an admitted fact, that Jesus Christ had risen, He would henceforth be fully invested with the character of Messiah, and that of Son of God. But what did happen?

By the wonderful overruling of Providence, of all the miracles on which our religion is founded, there is none so well attested, none of which the evidence is so indisputable; so that, says S. Augustine, even a heathen and an infidel, if he examine without bias all the circumstances of this miracle, is obliged to recognize its truth. And what is more astonishing, continues that holy Doctor, is that the two things which would naturally have been obstacles to faith in the Resurrection—namely, the hatred of the Pharisees and the incredulity of the Apostles—are just the two means of which God made use to support and strengthen it. Yes, the most inveterate enemies of Jesus Christ have in spite of themselves contributed by their very hatred to prove the truth of the miracle of the Resurrection of His body, and consequently to establish our faith. For mark, Christians, Jesus Christ has no sooner expired than they address Pilate; and what representation do they make to him? "We remember that deceiver said, when He was still alive, I shall rise again three days after My death: He publicly pledged himself to do so, and challenged us to test by that if He were faithful and truthful in His words. All the people are in expectation of the fulfilment of that prediction: and if His body were now to disappear, nothing more would be needed to confirm such a pernicious error. It is, then, important to provide against it, and we come to you that we may do so with more authority."

"Go," says Pilate to them, "you have a guard, employ it as seemeth best to you; I give you all power." And immediately the sepulchre is invested with soldiers; the stone which closes the mouth of the tomb is sealed; no precaution is omitted to make it perfectly sure. What is the result of all that forethought? Nothing, except to do away with the least doubt and slightest mistrust of the Resurrection of Jesus Christ. For when, notwithstanding all their precautions and all their care, the body of our Saviour, after being buried three days, was no longer to be found in the tomb, what could the Pharisees say? That His disciples, under cover of the night, had snatched it away whilst the guard slept. But, replies S. Augustine, how could they approach the sepulchre, move the stone, and carry off the body without waking any of the soldiers? Besides, if the guard were asleep, how could they know that some men had taken the body away, and who had taken it away? And if they were not asleep, why did they let men take it away? What likelihood was there that the disciples, who were weakness and timidity itself, should suddenly have become so bold, and passing through the guards with manifest personal danger, should have dared to seize a body placed for safe keeping under the public seal? Further, when they had dared to do this, by what artifice could they make others believe a thing, the falsehood of which was well known by them? What could they hope to gain by that? For if they had snatched away the body, it was plain to them that Jesus Christ was not risen, and that He had deceived them; and as they had for His sake exposed themselves to the hatred of the whole of their nation, it was natural that, when they saw themselves abused in that manner, they should, instead of upholding His interests, renounce Him, and make known to the magistrates that He was an impostor; this being evidence which all the synagogue would have received with united applause, and which would have gained for them the affection of all the people; whilst, on the contrary, in publishing His Resurrection, they could only expect the most stern treatment, persecutions, prisons, stripes, and even death. However, the only subterfuge of the Jews in order to evade the miracle of Jesus Christ's Resurrection was to say, His disciples took away the body. It is not from the Evangelists alone that we learn this, but from S. Justin Martyr also, who was better acquainted than any one else with their traditions, because he had himself been a Jew. They spread the report in the world, he says, that the sepulchre had been forced open. But the lie was so manifest that the Resurrection of the Saviour did not cease to pass unquestioned among the people. Josephus, interested though he was in casting a shade on the glory of the Son of God, has not been able to deny it; and in order that Gentiles as well as Jews might render homage to that risen Deity. Pilate, who was well acquainted with the truth, and already a Christian at heart, according to the statement of Tertullian,* wrote to Tiberius about it. Whereupon that Father has not shrunk from remarking that the Emperors would forthwith have believed in Jesus Christ, had they not been obliged as emperors to adopt the opinions of the age in which they lived; or if it had been possible for Christians, who renounced the age in which they lived, to be emperors.† But what surprises me above everything else, and what we cannot too much wonder at, is to see the Apostles, who, during the life of their Master, could not even understand what He said to them about His Resurrection; who, at the time of His Passion, had become absolutely hopeless on that account; and who after His death rejected as tales and dreams what they were told about His appearances; to see, I say, men so ill-disposed to believe, or rather so determined not to believe, become preachers of, and martyrs for, a mystery which had hitherto been the usual subject of their incredulity—to see them go before the courts and judges of the earth to confess a Resurrection which

---

* "Ea omnia super Christo Pilatus, et ipse pro conscientia sua jam Christianus, Tiberio renuntiavit."

† "Si aut Cæsares non fuissent sæculo necessarii, aut Christiani potuissent esse Cæsares."

had always been a cause of offence to them—to see them not fear to die for the confirmation of this truth, and count themselves happy, if in dying they served as faithful witnesses to Jesus Christ in His glory and His triumph! What occasioned this change in them, and what was capable of causing it, except the assurance of, and belief in, His Resurrection? But was not so firm a faith, after such an obstinate incredulity, the work of the hand of the Most High? "This change is of the right hand of the Most High."*

It is also in virtue of this faith in so miraculous a Resurrection, that Christianity has spread, that the Gospel has made such astonishing progress in the world, and that the Divinity of the Saviour, notwithstanding Hell and all its powers, has been believed even to the ends of it. We have only to consider the origin and infancy of the Church. Never did the Apostles preach Jesus Christ in the synagogues but they brought forward His Resurrection as an unanswerable proof: "Him God raised up the third day." It is He, they were ever saying, He who was raised on the third day; He whom the God of our fathers hath glorified by delivering him from death; He whom you have crucified, but who has since shown Himself in a state of new life. We might say that it was the one article which made their preaching effectual and irresistible. For wherein did they display the strength of that apostolic zeal with which they

---

* Psalm lxxvii. (Vulg. lxxvi.) 10, "Hæc mutatio dexteræ Excelsi."

were filled? By bearing witness to the Resurrection of Jesus Christ, "With great power gave the Apostles witness of the Resurrection of the Lord Jesus." Therein lay all the care and all the fruit of their ministry; so that when they had to elect a new disciple in the place of the perfidious Judas, the main condition on which they laid stress was that he should have seen what they had seen; and that, being related, as they were, to the Saviour of the world, they ought to ally with themselves some one to be "witness with them of the Resurrection;" as if their Apostleship had been reduced to this single point. And, in fact, S. Luke adds, the whole world surrendered to the force of that evidence. The Jews could not withstand it, the Gentiles were persuaded of it, the number of Christians increased daily; and we learn from S. Chrysostom, that immediately after the profession of faith made by the catechumens, in which they acknowledged that Jesus Christ had risen, baptism was bestowed on them. And why? Because to confess the Resurrection of Jesus Christ was to confess that He is God; and to confess He is God is to embrace His religion, since it is certain that the whole of the Christian religion rests on the Divinity of Jesus Christ, and that the Divinity of Jesus Christ has been unmistakably revealed to us only by the miracle of His Resurrection.

Let us dwell on this point, and that we may respond to God's purpose in this mystery, let us raise ourselves by feelings of faith above our grovelling thoughts. Let us enter, if I may venture to use the expression, into the sanctuary of the Divinity of Jesus Christ which is open to us; and, taking advantage of the festival we are celebrating, let us say with the elders of the Revelation, prostrate before the throne of the Lamb: "Worthy is the Lamb that was slain to receive power, and riches, and wisdom, and strength, and honour, and glory, and blessing." Yes, the Lamb who was sacrificed for us is worthy to receive the homage which the whole Church renders Him to-day. Adoring His Divinity, let us make to this Saviour the same confession which S. Peter made, "Thou art the Christ, the Son of the living God." Or to express it in words as forcible and energetic, as they are simple and natural, let us make use of the declaration of S. Thomas, "My Lord and my God;" a declaration which formerly confounded the impiety of Arianism, and will for ever shut the mouth of libertines in respect to infidelity. Whereas before the Resurrection of the Son of God, S. Thomas and the other Apostles were contented to say to Him, Master, Lord; now, since He has risen, let us make it a duty to say to Him again and again a hundred times, "My Lord and my God." Thou art my Lord and my God, and Thou showest it to me so plainly in Thy resurrection, that I almost fear it detracts from the merit of my faith. For I feel my soul penetrated through and through with the clear rays of light which gleam forth from thy Holy Humanity, and which are like rays of the Divinity therein enshrined. I did not understand what S. Paul wished to prove to the Hebrews, when he told them that the eternal Father had commanded the angels to adore

His Son in the moment that He rose again and made a second entrance into the world, "and again, when He bringeth in the First-begotten into the world, He saith, and let all the angels of God worship Him;" but I now see the meaning of these words: they mean that Jesus Christ, by rising again, proved to the whole universe that He was God, and that worship is the prerogative of God, and belongs to Him alone. This is why the eternal Father willed that these blessed spirits should solemnly render such worship to Jesus Christ, "Let all the angels of God worship Him." Would you know why He addressed that order to the angels and not to men? Ah! my brethren, says S. Jerome, explaining that passage, it is partly our instruction, but partly our confusion. For He only addressed the angels in the foreknowledge that He had of the ingratitude, the hardness, the deadness of men. He only addressed angels because He foresaw that men would be of worldly minds, and that, far from adoring Jesus Christ, they would outrage Him, blaspheme Him, and by the irregularity of their life cover Him with shame and disgrace. It is true that men, still more than the angels, ought to adore this God new-born from the tomb, since He was their Saviour, and not the Saviour of the angels; but the irregularities of men, the libertinage of some, the hypocrisy of others, the pride of these, the cowardice of those, all this determined the heavenly Father to appeal to the angels as to His most faithful creatures, when He wished to procure for His Son the special tribute of honour which was due to Him in consequence of His Resurrection. "And again, when He bringeth in the First-begotten into the world, He saith, And let all the angels of God worship Him;" as if He had said, Let the angels be His worshippers, since men are impious creatures who shock Him by their conduct. For such is the reproach that each one of us ought to apply to himself in the bitterness of his soul: a reproach which ought to suffice to arouse us from the drowsiness into which we are fallen, and to quicken our faith; a reproach which, as a necessary consequence, ought to bring about our conversion and a change in our mode of living.

In reality, this faith in the Divinity of Jesus Christ has sanctified the world. And is it not by the same faith that the world, which enchants us, and which corrupts us by its maxims, ought to be sanctified in us? If I have that faith, I am either justified, or I am on the way to be justified: if I have it not, there is nothing in me but sin and iniquity. "Who is he that overcometh the world," asks the beloved disciple S. John, "but he that believeth in the Son of God?" That is to say, who is he that, being master of his passions, is regular in his behaviour, temperate in his desires, restrained, patient, charitable, but he that allows himself to be guided and ruled by faith in this God Saviour? On the other hand, who is he that remains always a slave of the world and of his lusts, a slave of ambition, of interest, of sensuality, but he that has renounced this faith, or in whom this faith is languishing? "Who is he that overcometh the world, but he that believeth that Jesus is the Son of God?" Consult experience, and you will see with what reason the Apostle spoke. Human prudence believed that it could maintain itself independently of this faith, and has sought to shake off its yoke, but we know how it has succeeded, and the sad results of that guilty independence. We have seen Christians set themselves up for philosophers, and abandoning Jesus Christ, retain only faith in a God ; but, by a secret over-ruling of Providence, their philosophy has only served to bring out more vividly the error of their minds and the corruption of their hearts. They think that having the knowledge of God, they must of course, be wise and virtuous; but since men cannot be naturally wise and virtuous except by grace, since grace comes from Jesus Christ, since Jesus Christ is nothing to us without faith, and since the faith which unites us to Him is that which shows us His Divinity, it follows that with all these fine ideas about wisdom, they have been foolish and headstrong. They have allowed themselves to be dragged on by the torrent of vice ; they have yielded to the most shameful passions ; they are, as S. Paul describes them, dazzled by their own thoughts, and pretending to be philosophers, they have ceased to be men. On the other hand, where do we find innocence and purity of life ? In that holy and divine faith which teaches us that Jesus Christ is the true Son of God : " Who is he that overcometh the world, but he that believeth that Jesus is the Son of God ?" That is what justifies us ; that is what opens to us the store of grace and of virtues ; that is what gives us access to God, so that we may one day share in that happy resurrection which is promised us. The Resurrection of Jesus Christ as an indisputable proof of His Divinity: it is by that He confirms our faith. The Resurrection of Jesus Christ as a pledge to assure us of our future resurrection: it is thus that He stimulates our hope, as you will see in the second part.

II. Of all the articles of our religion, there is not one, says S. Augustine,* which has been more contradicted than the resurrection of men, because there is not one more calculated to retain them in their duty, and to make them more subject to the divine laws. For if men must rise again, there is then another life besides this; all our hopes do not end at death; we have to look forward to a good or a bad lot in eternity; God reserves for us other rewards or other punishments than those we see. Our chief business is, then, to strive here to deserve the rewards and to escape the punishments hereafter; we must regulate all our actions to this end, and everything else ought then to be indifferent. We are, then, very much to be blamed for allowing ourselves to be troubled by the miseries of this life, and for allowing ourselves to be attracted by the glitter of human prosperity. Virtue is our only reliable blessing upon earth, and even our solitary blessing. For all these consequences necessarily follow from the principle of the resurrection of the dead. That is why Tertullian began the excellent work which

---

* "In nulla re tam vehementer contradicitur fidei Christianæ quam in resurrectione carnis."

he composed on this subject, with these beautiful words:* "The confidence of Christians is the resurrection of the dead." On the other hand, S. Paul says, if we are fated not to rise again, and if our hopes be limited to the happiness of this world, we are the most miserable of men : for all that we do is useless. It is in vain that we expose ourselves to so many dangers, in vain that I sustained so many combats for the faith at Ephesus : there is no more any rule or habit of life to keep, and we may gratify our senses in all their demands; duty and piety are imaginary benefits, and present interest is the only interest which ought to govern us ; guard carefully, Christians, against that error that men will not rise again. The Apostle drew all these conclusions as a theologian ; and there are but few persons in the present day who understand the full force of his argument, but S. Chrysostom has aptly expanded it, remarking against whom S. Paul was then disputing. It was not, says that Father, against heretics who admitted the immortality of the soul, and would not admit the resurrection of the body; if so, his argument would have been pointless ; but he was opposing libertines and atheists, who deny the resurrection of the body, because they do not wish to believe in the immortality of the soul or in a future life. For although these two errors have not any necessary connection, they are nevertheless inseparably united in the opinion of wicked men, who, trying to shut out from their mind all thought of eternal things, so as to enable them-

---

* "Fiducia Christianorum, resurrectio mortuorum."

selves to sin with more impunity, wish to do away with, first, the faith in the resurrection of the body, and, by the almost inevitable progress of infidelity, afterwards blind themselves even so far as to persuade themselves that souls are not immortal. And that is why S. Paul makes use of the same weapons to attack both these impieties. However that may be, Christians, to keep exactly to my subject, I say that in the Resurrection of Jesus Christ we have a palpable and trustworthy pledge of our resurrection. How so? Because in that Resurrection of the Saviour we see at the same time the principle, the motive, and the model of our resurrection; the principle by which God can raise us, the motive which pledges God to raise us, and the model after which God wills to raise us. This demands all your attention.

I maintain, first, that we see in the Resurrection of the Son of God the underlying principle of our own. How? Because that miraculous Resurrection is, on the part of Jesus Christ, the effect of a sovereign and almighty power. For, if He was able by that almighty power to quicken Himself, why could He not accomplish in others what He has accomplished in His own Person? Such is the unanswerable argument of S. Augustine. There are some, says that Father, who believe in the Saviour's Resurrection, and who in that respect yield to the indisputable evidence of the Scriptures. But, though faithful on this point, they corrupt their belief in other respects, and lean towards a grosser error, not understanding, or not wishing to understand, how it follows from our

Saviour's Resurrection that we ourselves can one day rise again. But, continues that holy Doctor, is not Jesus Christ, raised with flesh like mine, and raised by His own virtue, an evident proof that I shall one day, not raise myself as He did, but be raised by Him? If, according to the erroneous notions of the Manichæans, continues S. Augustine, He had only taken, when He came upon the earth, a shadowy and unreal body; if He had left in the corruption of the tomb that flesh formed in S. Mary's womb, that flesh with which He was endued to live amongst men; if, on taking up again a glorious life, He had taken a body differing from mine, a body of a finer substance or composed of more perfect qualities, I might perhaps doubt of my resurrection. But to-day He is born again with the same flesh, with the same blood, with which He was conceived in the chaste loins of a Virgin; and what reason can I have to doubt but that what I see accomplished in Him may be accomplished in me? For is He less powerful in me and for me, than He was in Himself and for Himself? and if it be always the same virtue, will it not be always in the condition to work the same miracles?

It is, therefore, by that supreme power that He will go into the depths of the sea, into the bowels of the earth, into the furthermost recesses of dens and caves, into the most out-of-the-way and most secret places of the world, to gather these remains of ourselves that death had dissolved, to collect these scattered ashes, and, lifeless as they will be, to make them hear His voice and to quicken them.

S. Paul thus understood it when he spoke to the early Christians. Jesus Christ is risen, my brethren, that teacher of the Gentiles said to them; this news is proclaimed to you, and you believe it: but what astonishes me, added the great Apostle, is that, this God-man being risen again, there are some among you who dare to dispute the resurrection of men. "Now, if Christ be preached that He rose from the dead, how say some among you that there is no resurrection of the dead?" For is not the one a consequence of the other? and will it not be this risen God Who will repair the ruins caused by death, and Who will restore our bodies in their first form and first state? "Who shall change our vile body?" But again, How will He work this miracle? Will it be merely by having His intercession granted? Will it be merely by virtue of His merits? No, remarks S. Chrysostom, for the Apostle shows us that it will be by the absolute dominion that the God-man has over the whole of Nature, "According to the working whereby He is able even to subdue all things unto Himself."

So also had the patriarch Job, that man by whom God spoke, understood it 3,000 years before Jesus Christ, so that he was able to express in forcible and exact words, and to predict clearly our Saviour's Resurrection and our own. Yes, I believe, he exclaimed, to encourage himself and sustain himself in his sufferings, I believe and "I know that my Redeemer liveth," and that I must, after the pains of this life, and after having paid my tribute to death, rise again in my own flesh: "I know that my Redeemer liveth," these words are admirable,* "and in the last day I shall rise again from the earth." You see the connection which he makes between these two resurrections, that of Jesus Christ his Redeemer and his own. What would he have said if he had lived in our days, and had been witness as we are of that glorious Resurrection of the Son of God, in which we find not merely the principle of our own but also the motive?

For it is natural that the members should be united to the Head; and when the Head raises Himself, does it not naturally follow that He should raise His members with Him? But our Head is Jesus Christ, and we are all members of Jesus Christ. I can then fitly apply to this mystery that which S. Leo said of the triumphant Ascension of the Saviour into Heaven, that there where the Head enters, His members must follow Him: and in like manner, as Jesus Christ, according to the thoughts of this Father, has not only entered into the abode of glory for Himself, but for us, that is to say, to open to us its gates and to call us thither after Him, by the same rule and in the same sense, am I not right in concluding that it is for us that He hath broken the gates of death, for us that He hath come forth from the tomb and is risen? And indeed if as Head He wills that His members should act as He

---

* Job xix. 25. "In novissimo die de terra surrecturus sum." (Vulg.)

acted, suffer as He suffered, live as He lived, why should He not will that they shall rise as He rose? Is it not just that, as we are partakers of His burdens, He should make us partakers of His reward; and since one part of His reward is the glory of His body, since His adorable body has entered into participation in merit with His soul, is He not pledged on that account to recompense in us both body and soul? That is the beautiful and consoling theology of S. Paul; and that is why this great Apostle calls Him "the First-fruits of them that slept," "the First-born from the dead." First-fruits supposes others to follow; and to be the First-born, or if you will, the First-raised from the dead, the dead at the end of the ages must in like manner be born again and take up a new life. This was so unquestionable a truth in the teaching of the teacher of the Gentiles, that he found no difficulty in saying, If the dead are not to rise after the Resurrection of Jesus Christ, and by virtue of that blessed Resurrection, it follows that that was only an imaginary and unreal resurrection. "If there be no resurrection of the dead, then is Christ not risen."

It is true, then, my dear hearers, that we shall rise again by Jesus Christ, or rather, by the almighty power of Jesus Christ; it is true that we shall rise again, because Jesus Christ has risen; and to crown our hope, I add that we shall rise again like Jesus Christ, and that His resurrection is the model of ours. For, asks S. Augustine, why has God willed that the resurrection of His Son should be so evident? And why has the only

Son of God Himself sought so earnestly to make it public? Ah, replies that holy Doctor, it is so that He might evidently unveil to us in His Person the vast extent of our claims; it is in order to show us by what He is, what we are to be, or what we shall become. I have only, then, to picture to myself the most brilliant moments in my Saviour's triumph; I have only to contemplate that glorified humanity, that body, material and corporeal though it be, yet endued with all the attributes of a spirit, radiant with light, crowned with an eternal brightness; such is the blissful state to which I am myself to be raised, and which faith promises me. This hope is founded on the very word of God, since it is upon the word of His Apostle. For, says the Apostle, when God shall come to raise our bodies from the dust, and to quicken them by His breath, that will be to conform them to the divine pattern which is set before us in the Resurrection of Jesus Christ, "Who shall change our vile body, that it may be fashioned-like unto His glorious body." Now they are bodies subject to corruption and decay; now they are bodies subject to pain and suffering; now they are frail bodies and subject to death; now they are only clumsy, vile and contemptible flesh; but then, by the most sudden and most wonderful change, they will have, if I may so express myself, the same incorruptibility as the body of a Divine Being, the same impassibility, the same immortality, the same refinement, the same transparency, "fashioned like unto His glorious body." But yet, my brethren, there is a condition attached to all that, namely, that we strive in the present life to sanctify them. And how? By Christian mortification and penitence: for if they be bodies which we have pampered and made idols of, bodies of which we have gratified every fleshly lust, and of which we have made by that means bodies of sin, they will rise again; but how? As objects of horror to serve for the confusion of the soul and share its torment, after having served and had a share in its crimes. Ah! Christians, these are great truths. Woe to him who does not believe them; woe to him who believes, and lives as though he believed them not! But a thousand times blessed be the faithful one who, not content merely to believe them, makes them the rule of his life, and draws from them powerful motives to stimulate his earnestness! Be good enough to consider with me this important moral truth.

Woe, I say, to him who does not believe this fundamental point of Christianity and of that future resurrection! If there be among my hearers one of these libertines, this is what I would say to him with all the sincerity and all the warmth of my zeal: My dear brother, irregularity must be very deeply rooted in you, and you must be steeped in vice to be brought so low as not to believe one of the first principles of religion. Your heart must have sadly corrupted your mind to blind and pervert it in this manner. For, tell me, I beg you, if you be still capable of following this reasoning, which of us two has the more trustworthy foundation for his belief—you who do not believe what you are told in respect to a life other than this, and in respect to the resurrection of the dead; or I who believe it with a firm faith, and with an entire submission? On what do you ground your unbelief of it, or at least doubt of it? On your judgment, on your prudence, or more likely on your presumption. You do not believe these mysteries because you do not understand them; because you wish to measure everything by your senses; because you will not defer nor submit to anything except your own eyesight; because, like the doubting Apostle, you say, "Except I shall see, I will not believe," which is a faulty and ignorant line of conduct; that is the root of your unbelief. But I, in my belief and the faith which I have embraced and for which I am ready to pour forth my blood, I rest on the witness of God Himself, on the principles of His Providence and His wisdom, on the truth of a thousand prophecies, on a countless number of miracles, on the authority of the greatest men of every age, of the most intelligent and most enlightened men, the most blameless and the holiest of men. I find that I am in possession of a faith which has worked so many wonders in the universe, which has triumphed over so many kings and peoples, which has destroyed and abolished so many superstitions, which has given birth to so many virtues, and caused them to be practised, which has had so many witnesses, which has been sealed by the blood of so many martyrs, which has been advanced even by the persecutions to which it has been subjected, a faith against which all the powers of earth and of hell have never been able, and never will be able, to prevail; such are the reasons which bind me to it. But of these reasons and of yours, judge once again, which are the better founded and the more calculated to lead a heart right and establish it.

But, will you say to me, how can we understand that resurrection of the dead? It is not, my dear hearer, a question of understanding it in order to believe it, but of believing it, even though it appear to you utterly beyond your powers of understanding. For whether you understand it or not, that cannot make it more or less true, or more or less certain, or, it follows, more or less easy of belief. However, I am well justified in my surprise, my dear brother, that you, who make so much of your pretended strength of mind, should find so many difficulties about that. As though that resurrection were not clearly possible with God our Creator; for, says S. Augustine, if He has been able to create out of nothing our bodies, will He not be able to fashion them a second time out of the matter of which they were composed? and who shall hinder Him from restoring what already once existed, since He has been able to call into being that which had never existed? As though that resurrection were not easy to God, since He is all powerful, and nothing can resist a boundless power. As though all created things did not make that resurrection impress us the more. A grain of corn dies in the bosom of the earth—this is S. Paul's illustration—and indeed that little grain must rot and die; but afterwards do we not see it spring up again? And is it not strange that what makes you doubt of your resurrection should be the very thing whereby Providence has willed to make it the more easily understood by you? As though that resurrection were not quite agreeable to the laws of Nature, which, by the inclination of the soul and body towards each other, and by the close connection which exists between the two, demand that they should be united again for ever. As though belief in that resurrection were not one of the most widely spread and common notions in the world. The very people, said Tertullian, who deny the resurrection, recognize it in spite of themselves, by their sacrifices and their ceremonies for the dead; that care with which they adorn their graves and preserve their ashes, is a proof so much the more divine as it is the more natural. It is not only, he added, among the Christians and the Jews that the belief that men will rise again exists, but also among the Pagans and idolaters; and it is not only a popular opinion, but also that of the wise and learned. As though God, in short, had not made faith in that resurrection easy by other resurrections which had been seen and testified to by trustworthy witnesses; resurrections which we cannot regard with suspicion without denying the sacred Scriptures and the most reliable histories. Ah! my dear hearer, let us go to the root of the evil, and learn just this once more to know yourself. You have a difficulty to persuade yourself that there is another life, a resurrection, a judgment at the end of the ages, because with that persuasion you must adopt quite a new line of conduct, and because you fear the consequences of being persuaded; but are the consequences of your dissoluteness less to be feared for you and less frightful? God has created you unaided by your will or your efforts, and He can easily, without your aid, and in spite of your will, quicken you again. " Not because thou willest, shalt thou not rise again ; nor if thou dost not believe, shalt thou on that account not rise again ;"* such are S. Augustine's words. Your resurrection will not depend on your belief; but the good or evil of your resurrection will depend on your belief and on your life. But what a shock at that last day, and what despair, if you must rise again to hear the formal sentence of your doom ; if you must rise from the shadow of death to go into the darkness of hell; if you must rise to complete your damnation by the reunion of your body and soul, because in a matter of so much importance you would not take so wise and sure a precaution as to believe and regulate your life !

I say to regulate your life ; and here is the fatal mistake, not of the libertine, who does not believe, but of the sinner, who believes, and who lives as though he did not believe. What is the use of believing and of not acting in conformity with your faith ? What do I say ? acting even in a manner totally opposed to your faith ? believing in a resurrection which shall make us appear before the sovereign Judge of the quick and the dead, and not striving to conciliate this awful Judge, and to incline Him to forbearance? believing in a resurrection which shall place us before the eyes of the whole

---

* "Non quia vis, non resurges; aut si resurrecturum te non credideris, propterea non resurges."—S. AUGUSTINE.

world to be known such as we shall be, or such as we shall have been, and yet cherishing habits and evil ways of life, now hidden and secret, but which, when they shall then be revealed and made public, will overwhelm us with shame and disgrace? believing in a resurrection by which we shall pass to a life, either of never-ending happiness, or of never-ending misery, according to the good which we have practised in this present life, or according to the evil which we have committed in it, and yet doing nothing in this present life of all the good which might procure us a happy immortality, and committing in this present life all the evil which might draw on us the most terrible condemnation, and lead us to a wretched eternity? Once more, I ask, what is the use of believing like that? or rather, is not believing like that to render us still more deserving of punishment and to condemn ourselves? It is for you, women of the world, to meditate well on this point of your religion, and to profit by it. Little troubled about the future, you think only of the present; and refusing your soul all care, you busy yourselves only about your body. Alas! whilst striving to preserve it, you destroy it. You never think about that, and you will think about it too late, when at the sound of the last trumpet that body shall arise again from its own ashes, and you will hear coming from the mouth of God these fearful words: "How much she hath glorified herself, and lived deliciously, so much torment and sorrow give her." After you have made an idol of your body, after you have so pampered and fondled it, death will make of it food for worms; and the new life that God gives it will make of it food for flames, to feel which will be so much the more painful in proportion as it has tasted the vain delicacies with which you have nourished it: "How much she hath glorified herself and lived deliciously, so much torment and sorrow give her."

In conclusion, my dear hearers, happy is the faithful one who believes and looks for a glorious resurrection, because he places himself, by the practice of all Christian works and by the holiness of his life, in a state to deserve it! That is what inspirited S. Paul, that is what consoled the infant church in persecution, that is what in the course of ages has sustained so many martyrs, so many hermits, so many monks; for, said they, we suffer, we mortify our bodies, we deprive ourselves of the pleasures which the world offers us, but it is not in vain: and since we are assured that the soul outlives the body, and that at the end of the world the body must again be united with the soul that they may begin together a never-ending life, we may well rejoice in the thought that we shall then be abundantly recompensed by a sovereign happiness, for all that we shall have forsaken upon earth, and for all the sacrifices that we shall have made to God. That is what ought to inspire the same zeal and the same earnestness in every pious soul which is listening to me; I say more, that is what ought to sanctify every Christian to whom I am speaking. It is on this that they ought to rest their resolutions; they will never rest them on a more trustworthy foundation. If they have not yet done their duty as to that solemn act, you see how it ought to pledge them to acquit themselves of it sincerely, promptly, completely. If they have fulfilled the command of the Church, and have thus returned to God's ways, that ought to keep them in them, and to make them continually walk therein; for everything depends on that continuance, and to rise in glory we must, by holy perseverance, die in grace. But, alas! who will persevere? Permit me, my beloved hearers, to dwell on this point as a conclusion to this sermon. Who, I say, will persevere? Where are those souls faithful to their promises and unshaken in their resolutions? It is only Thou, O my God, Who knowest them, since there is none but Thee Who can know both the heart of man and the future; two things which are ever present to Thee, but which are equally hidden from us, and to which our weak light can never reach. Yet, Lord, I may console myself by the conjectures I may form of a secret the full knowledge of which Thou has kept to Thyself; and specially do I know—the whole universe knows it with me—that there is here a heart which Thy hand hath formed, a heart which is an enemy of all fickleness and inconstancy, faithful in its words, equal in its conduct, unchangeably attached to the laws which it has seen good to prescribe to itself; which, after having set before itself great plans, could not be turned aside from them by any obstacle; which has performed marvellous feats of bravery to carry them out; and, what is not the least wonderful, a heart which has renounced for that, not merely its rest and its pleasures, but even its advantages and its interests. To what height cannot the perfection of Thy law, O my God! lead this resolute and fearless heart? and who in that sense has been better fitted than it for the kingdom of heaven?

It is your Majesty, then, Sire, that makes all my consolation here. But what am I, to speak of myself? Let us say rather, the guardian angels of your kingdom have this as their consolation, the saints who day and night redouble their prayers for your sacred person. Will not God Himself, if I may venture to say it, find in your firmness of character something wherewith to console Himself for the fickleness of the majority of Christians? Sire, it is God Who hath stamped on your soul this character of firmness; and as your Majesty, stopping in the midst of his conquests, hath not taken an ambitious obstinacy for an heroic firmness, so he cannot mistake what use he ought to make of that virtue. The example that he has just given to all Europe is a proof that posterity will never forget. More steadfast in religion than in military enterprises, your Majesty has made his military enterprises yield to the common interest of religion. At the mere report of enemies to the Christian name, your Majesty has interrupted the course of his arms, your royal piety not being able to endure that your arms, once so gloriously employed, and perhaps still at the present time singled out by Providence to repulse the infidels, should in any way further their schemes. Unable, then, to think of yourself, and to take advantage at that crisis of the weakness of those whose strength your arm had so often subdued, ready to sacrifice everything from the moment you understood the cause of God was at stake, you have forgotten your most just claims, when it was necessary to give tokens of your zeal and your faith. That is what I call firmness, pure firmness, since neither ambition nor interest was mixed up with it.

But, after all, Sire, your Majesty knows well that the firmness of a Christian king ought not to stop there : that it ought to be occupied in himself with something more worthy of it : that he ought himself to be the subject of it, and that, as all the attributes that we admire in a hero would be little esteemed by men if firmness were wanting, so firmness itself is little esteemed by God if it be not joined with grace, which alone makes our merit in His eyes. Yes, it is to preserve grace that your Majesty has received from God this character of firmness and constancy, and never has war, that sphere wherein royalty may display itself, afforded instances of more noble triumphs that those of a monarch who makes the grace of God triumph in his own person. If in all states of life Christian perseverance is the utmost effect of grace, we may say that it is a kind of miracle in a king, and, above all, in the most absolute of kings, since he finds in his very greatness the most dangerous enemy against which he has to struggle. For what ought he whom everything obeys not to fear about his salvation, he to whom everything yields, whom nothing can resist, whom every one strives to please, and whom every one fears exceedingly to displease ? and what firmness of soul ought he not to oppose to all that, if he wish, as says S. Bernard, that all that do not destroy him whilst it exalts him? But what merit also before God ought the perseverance of a prince to have, one who, seeing himself above everything, and master of everything, studies to be still more above himself; one who receiving every minute men's homage, never forgets what he owes to God; one who unites the majesty of the throne with the humility of religion, the charity of a Christian with the independence of a sovereign, the strictest equity and all the feelings of the most exact probity with the right of impunity? Such, Sire, are the victories which the almighty grace of Jesus Christ ought to gain in you. Continuing steadfast in that grace, you will confound the libertines who fear your perseverance; you will console good people, who make it the subject of their supplications; and being constant for a God who is Himself so constant for you, in governing an earthly kingdom, you will earn possession of a heavenly kingdom. God grant that it may be so with you.

VIII.

THE RESURRECTION OF JESUS CHRIST.

S. LUKE, xxiv. 15, 16. "And it came to pass that, while they communed together and reasoned, Jesus Himself drew near, and went with them. But their eyes were holden that they should not know Him."

WHEN I consider, Christians, the disposition of these two disciples spoken of in the Gospel, it appears to me that the Saviour of the world had two great diseases to heal in their persons, and for that purpose He must needs employ all the might of His grace. For in the first place, they had not that faith in Him which they ought to have had; and moreover, although they had hitherto been of the number of His disciples, they were beginning to desert Him. They were inclined to doubt; they were cold and languishing—they did not believe about Him what they ought to believe; and they did not love in Him that which they ought to love. They did not believe about Him what they ought to believe; for He was God, and they only spoke of Him as a man, lowering their faith to the common and popular notions, treating Jesus Christ as a prophet, admitting that He had been mighty in deeds and in words, but giving Him nothing more, and only recognizing in Him what obstinate and carnal Jews had also recognized, "concerning Jesus of Nazareth, which was a prophet." You see their unbelief. They were cold and languishing in their love; for that is the reason why they were going out of Jerusalem, not daring to declare themselves His disciples, forsaking His side and His interests, no longer hoping in Him, and no longer expecting from Him that redemption of Israel on which they had reckoned: "We trusted that it had been He which should have redeemed Israel." All that, Christians, because they were not persuaded of His Resurrection; for the simple doubt they had as to whether Jesus Christ had risen, or should rise, corrupted their faith, and cooled their zeal. What, then, does Jesus Christ do? He convinces them by a sensible proof that He hath indeed risen; and in that appearance to them, He enlightens their minds, and warms their hearts. He enlightens their minds, unfolding to them what Moses and the prophets had written about Him, and making them revere that Christ and Messiah Whom He sets before them as a God of glory, until at length He completely opens their eyes, discovering to them that it is He Himself Who is speaking to them, and obliging them to confess that He is their God and Lord. And He makes their hearts burn, little by little inspiring them, by means of His words, with feelings of love for His Person; wherefore they said one to the other, "Did not our hearts burn within us, while He talked with us by the way, and while He opened to us the Scriptures?" You see, my dear hearers, the subject of the instruction which I

am going to deliver: you see what those two
disciples were in respect to the Son of God, and
what I know not how many cowardly Christians
are to-day, faithless, filled with love of the world,
and of whom it may be said that they have to
some extent renounced Jesus Christ, although
outwardly they profess to be His disciples. They
bear that title and that name; but they have
scarcely got faith, and are hardly touched with
any feeling of love for that God-man. They only
believe slightly, and hardly love at all, because
true Christian love cannot have any other foundation than faith. I wish, then, to attempt in
this sermon to strengthen that foundation, and to
correct these two disorders, the first of which is
our want of faith; and the second, our want of
feeling. I maintain that Jesus Christ risen ought
to establish perfectly in our minds faith in His
Divinity, and in our heart's love for His sacred
Humanity. Let me explain myself. What is Jesus
Christ? A Being composed of two natures, the
one Divine, and the other Human. The Divinity
demands our faith, and the Humanity our love.
For, saith S. John, it is faith in the Divinity of
Jesus Christ which sanctifies us, and it is the
Humanity of Jesus Christ which hath saved us.
But, to have that Divine faith and that holy love,
we have only to attach ourselves to the mystery of
the Resurrection. In that mystery we learn to
know and to love Jesus Christ; to know Him as
God, and to love Him as God-man and Saviour.

(i.) The Resurrection of Jesus Christ, a powerful

motive to constrain us to believe in His Divinity; that is the first part.

(ii.) The Resurrection of Jesus Christ indispensably engages us to love His sacred Humanity; that is the second part.

(The first part of this sermon is the same as the first part of the preceding sermon, so we pass on at once to the second part.)

It is not hard for me to understand how the state of glory should inspire fear, cause respect or wonder. But, Christians, it seems to me a paradox to say that so striking and glorious a mystery as that of the Resurrection of the Son of God, a mystery which was the triumph of His humanity, which exempted Him from all weaknesses, separated Him from us, and placed Him in a state in which He no longer continued that familiar intercourse with men which had been established between Him and us by His Incarnation—it seems, I say, difficult for me to believe this, and yet it is one of the fundamental articles of our religion, that this mystery ought to arouse all the tenderness of our love for that God-man. For, however we may look at that great mystery to-day, whether we consider its end, examine its circumstances, or regard the effect produced by it in the sacred Humanity of the Saviour, I maintain, and it is true, that it is one of the mysteries wherein His charity is displayed in the most striking manner; and it is a fact that all the other mysteries of His suffering and mortal life, those mysteries of mercy and of kindness, have found in this their accomplishment and fulfilment. How so? Try, I beg you, to understand the train of my thought. As far as it is true that in rising again Jesus Christ entered into His glory, so far is it true that for our sake He has taken possession of that glory, and that He is risen again for our sake; that is what I call the end of the mystery. Because also in the very triumph of His Resurrection He willed to retain the most convincing marks and the most visible tokens of His love to men—namely, the scars of the wounds which He received in His passion; there is the most remarkable circumstance, or one of the most remarkable circumstances of this mystery. Lastly, because in rising glorious, He raised His humanity to a state of perfection, we cannot restrain our love for Him; we love Him, but with what kind of love? With a pure, a spiritual, and an all-divine love; there is the effect, or I would rather say, the very substance of that mystery, considered in relation to ourselves. Give your attention, Christians, to these three truths.

It is for us and for our sake that Jesus Christ rose again. We cannot have the least doubt of this, since the Holy Spirit expressly says so: " He was delivered for our offences, and was raised again for our justification." In fact, according to the way in which the Scripture speaks on the subject, He only raised Himself in order to raise us with Himself, and to raise Himself in us. He only raised Himself, said S. Augustine, to raise our hope in His Person, and to raise again in our hearts that love for Him which sin had extinguished. In a word, according to S. Paul, " He was raised again for our justification." So that grand expression of the Gospel: "God so loved the world, that He gave His only begotten Son," applies as well to the mystery of the Resurrection as to that of the Incarnation; for, at the moment when Jesus Christ came out of the tomb, it was true to say that the eternal Father once more gave to the world His only begotten Son; and that is the thought of the Apostle in that text of the Epistle to the Hebrews which I have already quoted: "And again when He bringeth in the First-begotten into the world." But with what intention did the Father then present Him? Do not let us be afraid of adopting a forced conclusion: that truth of theology is quite well founded and indisputable. The Father presented Him the second time as a Saviour, a Shepherd, a Teacher, a Master. As a Saviour, since it is certain that Jesus Christ by His Resurrection set the seal on all that He had done, and on all that He had suffered for the salvation of men; and that, if He had not risen, that great work of the salvation of men would have been not only incomplete, but undone; and it might have been said,* "Is then the offence of the cross without effect?" "Has Christ died in vain?" As a Shepherd, since the first care of that God-man, at the moment of His Resurrection, was to gather His flock which infidelity had scattered, "for it is written," said He, "I will smite the shepherd, and the sheep of the flock shall be scattered abroad. But after I am risen again, I will go before you into Galilee."

---

* "Ergo evacuatum est scandalum crucis?" "Ergo gratis Christus mortuus est?" Gal. v. 11; ii. 21.

And why? to call you back to that holy fold which I have formed, and into which I gather My predestinated and My elect. As Master and Teacher, since all the time which He spent upon earth after His Resurrection was employed by Him, as we learn from S. Luke, in instructing His disciples, explaining to them the mysteries which concerned Himself, unfolding to them the Scriptures, and teaching them all about the truths of religion: healthful instructions which form to-day, in Christianity, the basis of those Divine traditions which we receive as so many rules of our faith. That is why the adorable Saviour put off for forty whole days the glory of His Ascension, not being able yet to go up into heaven, because His love, said S. Augustine, kept Him on the earth. That is why, all-glorious though He was, He did not cease to converse with His Apostles, appearing to them, visiting them, consoling them, reproving them in a friendly manner, journeying with them, forgetting nothing which would draw them to Him and gain their confidence. That is why in some of His appearances He called them His brethren, a title which He had never given them before His death: "Go tell My brethren that they go into Galilee, and there they shall see Me;" not contenting Himself, as hitherto, with treating them as friends, but honouring them with the name of brethren, as if His Resurrection state had drawn yet closer the bond of union He had contracted with us in becoming man. But with what feelings ought all that to inspire us, Christians? With an eager zeal and a tender love for that God-man. He was raised for us as He died for us: that is the principle on which S. Paul rests that wonderful conclusion, when He tells us that we ought therefore no longer to live for ourselves, or to die for ourselves: "For whether we live, we live unto the Lord: and whether we die, we die unto the Lord: whether we live, therefore, or die, we are the Lord's." "For," adds the Apostle, "to this end Christ both died, and rose, and revived, that He might be Lord both of the dead and the living." He wished by His death and by His Resurrection to acquire a sovereign dominion over the dead and over the living: a dominion not of fear and slavery, but of love and liberty, since it is especially over our hearts He wishes to reign. Indeed, continues S. Ambrose, explaining this passage, how can we acknowledge love but by love? and how acknowledge so perfect a love but by a boundless love in return? This God made flesh did not hesitate to give Himself up entirely for our sake; why, then, should we hold back anything from His service? He sacrificed to us His glorious life, as well as His suffering life: why should we not sacrifice to Him our successes, as well as our adversities, holding ourselves united to Him equally in both cases? He desires neither glory nor triumph, except for us; why shall we ever desire or seek for anything except for Him?

That is not all. The Saviour of the world has so risen that, even in the state of His Resurrection, He still bears the marks of His love for men, I would say, the scars of the wounds which He received at His death. Although His wounds scarcely agree, as it seems, with the happy immortality upon which He hath entered; He takes a pleasure in keeping them; and why? Ah! my brethren, replies S. Augustine, for many reasons which His charity suggested, and with which our piety ought to be touched. He keeps those wounds to assure us that even during His glory He does not wish to forget us; He keeps them to fulfil what He has said to each of us through His prophet, "Behold, I have graven thee upon the palms of My hands," and that with letters which will never wear away: for these wounds of which you see the traces, are so many lively tokens, which will represent thee to Me eternally, and which will speak without ceasing for thee. "Can a woman forget her sucking child, that she should not have compassion on the son of her womb? Yea, they may forget, yet will I not forget thee. Behold, I have graven thee upon the palms of My hands." He retains His wounds to appease the justice of His Father, and to fulfil before Him, according to the thought of the beloved Disciple, the office of Mediator and Advocate: "we have an advocate with the Father." For it is now that we may say to that divine Saviour, "My times are in Thy hand." It is not necessary that Thou shouldest speak to plead my cause; Thou hast only to present Thy hands pierced for me, there is then no grace which I do not obtain, and I hold my salvation assured. He retains those wounds to bind me never to forget His holy passion; so that we may always keep in sight His sufferings, and so that we may make it not only a business and a duty, but even a pleasure to think of them incessantly with feelings of the most lively gratitude, saying with the royal prophet, " If I do not remember Thee, let my tongue cleave to the roof of my mouth : yea, if I prefer not Jerusalem in my mirth ;" and if I do not learn from that to curb my passions, to bridle the guilty excess of my pleasures, and to separate me from the world and from myself. For nothing, saith S. Chrysostom, is better calculated to produce in me these happy results, than meditation on a God, who bears the traces of the cross, even on the throne of His majesty.

Lastly, this Divine Saviour presents to us in His Resurrection the very object that is most worthy of our love, and best calculated to win for Himself all hearts, I mean His glorious, immortal, and impassible Humanity, endued with all the splendour which the Divinity it enshrines sheds upon it, that Divinity which had been so long hidden in secret, but which now begins to break forth and show itself. But in that state, wherein He constitutes the happiness of the saints, hath He not a right to say to us, What is there upon earth you can prefer or even compare to Me ? If, then, you be risen in spirit, as I am in the flesh, do not attach yourselves any longer to those frail and perishing delights, which allure your senses and corrupt your souls, but seek those heavenly and incorruptible delights, of which you already see in My Person so bright an image : " If ye then be risen with Christ . . . . set your affection on things above, not on things on the earth."· Let us stop here, Christians, and let us not go any further in a subject which might lead me too far, if I were to undertake to fathom it and to explain it in all its bearings. Let us be contented to return to ourselves, and to draw from the three considerations that I have set before you the lesson they naturally convey. For doth a charity, so constant as was that of Jesus Christ for us, a charity which He hath shown, not only up to His death, but even beyond the limits of death, touch us as it ought, and as He Himself promised it would? Can we say to-day with the two disciples in the Gospel that our heart is burning with zeal: "Did not our heart burn within us?" Do we at least bring home to ourselves the indispensable obligation which binds us to consecrate ourselves sincerely and completely to Jesus Christ? Do we believe, as we ought to believe heartily, that all our wealth consists in this perfect devotion; and that on that, if I may so speak, depends our whole destiny under God? That is to say, do we love Jesus Christ with a love which bears any proportion to His love for us? If we love Him so, let us take courage, because our names will be written in the Book of Life. If we love Him less, let us tremble, because faith teaches us that he who loveth not the Lord Jesus is accursed. Yes, my brethren, said S. Paul, I regard you all as accursed, if you be indifferent to that God Man, and unconcerned about His interests. In vain might you work in the world the greatest miracles, in vain might you speak the language of angels, in vain might you have all the gifts of heaven; if you have not charity for Jesus Christ, you are not in grace with God, and consequently in God's sight you are only objects of abomination: why? Because, according to the words of Jesus Christ, God only loveth men in so far as they love His Son: "For the Father Himself loveth you, because ye have loved Me." I say more, should I even love God, without love for Jesus Christ, I should be nothing, and I should deserve nothing: God would not hold Himself honoured by my love, because He wishes to be loved by me only in Jesus Christ, as He wills not to save me except by Jesus Christ. This is the reason why S. Paul, speaking of the charity of God, ascribes to it always this peculiar circumstance that it is shut up in Jesus Christ, "by the grace of God in Christ Jesus." For, as S. Thomas reasons, it is for God to prescribe to me how He wills me to love Him; and it is for me to love Him according to the form He hath prescribed to me. But He hath expressly declared to me that He wills that I should love Him in the Person of the Saviour; it is then in the Person of that Saviour that I must henceforth seek for God, love God, hope in God. Outside that Saviour there is no longer any God for me, no more grace, no more mercy, no more salvation for me, because there is, saith the Scripture, none other Name under Heaven by which we may attain to a life of happiness.

But, reflect for a moment, my dear listener, and consider, but consider attentively, whether living as you live, in the engagements of the world, in the intrigues of the world, in the midst of the snares and temptations of the world, you have for Jesus Christ that attachment of mind and heart which is required by the religion you profess. Examine carefully if, in the bustle and tumult of human affairs, you preserve towards Jesus Christ all the gratitude which is due to him as your Redeemer; if you be zealous for the glory of His Name, if the interests of His Church be dear to you, if you follow His precepts, imitate His example, keep His law: for these are the tokens of a true and genuine love. Moreover, it matters not that it be not a love which makes itself felt; that this true and genuine love doth not work in you the same effects as in certain souls specially chosen and favoured by God: it would be a mistake to take that as a test either of the obligation, or even of the perfection of that divine charity which ought to unite us to Jesus Christ: it is one of the most subtle delusions, of which the enemy of our salvation makes use, to cause the weak to despair, and to harden the careless. I say that you ought to love Jesus Christ, but I do not say that you ought to feel that love, for it may exist, although you do not feel it. It ought to be in the reason, and not in the feelings; it ought to be in the practice and in the deed, not in the pleasure nor in the sweetness of the affection: it may even sometimes be more perfect, when without being perceptible and sweet, it is noble and effectual, embracing all, and engrossed by nothing; overcoming nature by pure grace, and in the midst of dryness and barrenness, sustaining an evenness of fidelity which is never deceptive. And there you see, Christians, on the other hand, how you may console yourselves, when God does not give you those tender and affectionate feelings, for which people sometimes pray; but also you see how you will be condemned, if you have not that reasonable

Christian love which I demand. For that love, divine though it be, will not be kindled in you without some effort on your part. God will draw you towards it, without your exertions, by secret inspirations; but your consent to the inspirations of God, your acts of love towards Him, which can have no merit if they be not free—all this must be the effect of your co-operation with God. Whilst, without doing anything, you are contented to say with so many worldlings: I have not yet got that fervent restless love for Jesus Christ, but it is a gift from heaven for which I am waiting, you will wait in vain, and God will eternally pronounce against you that awful decree, which comes to us in the words of S. Paul, "If any man love not the Lord Jesus Christ, let him be anathema."

Ah, my brethren, let us forestall the effect of that terrible threat. May that Saviour, raised for our justification, not be for us a rock of offence, and the cause of our condemnation. Let us make Him live in us, as S. Paul did, so that we may say, after that Apostle, "I live; yet not I, but Christ liveth in me." And how can that be? By a sincere love, by a lively gratitude, by an unshaken fidelity; by a perfect imitation of the virtues of that God-Man, who is our pattern upon earth, and our glory in a happy eternity.

THE END.

www.ingramcontent.com/pod-product-compliance
Lightning Source LLC
Chambersburg PA
CBHW022118230426
43672CB00008B/1427